David R. Palmer ∾ Pathways to serenity.

D1416742

*Overcoming your addictions
one day at a time*

PATHWAYS TO SERENITY

Overcoming Your Addictions One Day at a Time

Pathways to Serenity

Overcoming Your Addictions

One Day at a Time
Second Edition

©2012 by David Palmer
One Day at a Time
Little Rock, AR 72212

ISBN: 1484032462
ISBN 13: 9781484032466

A CIP catalog record of this book is available from the Library Of Congress.

Proofing and editing: Angie Peters
Cover: Rene Hein

Printed in the United States of America.

MISSION STATEMENT

Our mission is to reduce alcohol and drug abuse by promoting awareness, prevention, and treatment availability in the following ways:

- as a catalyst for fundamental change in public attitudes towards substance abuse

- "putting a face" on the benefits of recovery

- implementing unique teen/young adult, military, and prison outreach initiatives

VISION STATEMENT

We envision a nation whose citizens recognize substance abuse as a major health problem and seek to eradicate the associated heartache of broken families, broken dreams, and broken lives through a message of hope and recovery.

DEDICATION

This book is dedicated to my family and to those who, freed from their addictions, have experienced the blessings and joy of recovery. Their lives have been transformed and on these pages we discover how they did it and how we can do it.

TABLE OF CONTENTS

INTRODUCTION

About Your Addiction…
A Message of Hope and Recovery

This book is mainly about people who have experienced the blessings and joy of recovery from their addictions, how they did it, and how you can do it. My purpose is to give you hope and encouragement. The rest is up to you.

You will find my story, the one I tell at 12-Step meetings, in appendix 1. I hope you will conclude when you read it that, "If this guy can do it, I can, too."

There are also nineteen chapters in the book that will help you better understand the resources available to you. There are chapters, for example, on people we are especially interested in—adolescents, veterans, and prison inmates—and about programs like Alcoholics Anonymous, Al-Anon, and Celebrate Recovery.

I call these chapters "pathways to serenity" in the title of the book and emphasize taking it no more than "one day at a time," a vital key to recovery. The photo on the front cover is meant to reassure those who seek recovery that there can be happiness after you drop the alcohol, drugs, or other addictions. And there will be moments of serenity, but not every moment. That's where the "one day at a time" comes in.

The stories about people and programs are snapshots. People and programs change; some in recovery have slips and may never come back, while others succeed. It is also true that some programs succeed while others fade away. That's life, and readers must take this into account in charting their own recovery. This, then, is a freeze frame of people dealing effectively with their addictions through programs that work. We must remember that they are contending with an adversary—addiction—which chapter 5 of the *Big Book* of Alcoholics Anonymous describes as "cunning, baffling and powerful." Many, regrettably, will not make it.

Of the many courageous people introduced to you in this book, we can only say with some assurance that they were clean and sober when we spoke to them.

Two years ago, my eldest son, David, sent me an e-mail on my eightieth natural birthday and close to the thirtieth birthday of my recovery. He asked me to publish his letter in *One Day at a Time*, my nonprofit newspaper and website, and I quickly agreed.

If you are suffering from an addiction, I hope you will read his letter below, as well as the rest of the book, and will be encouraged to give recovery a chance. If you are already in recovery, I hope you will find in these pages further confirmation that you have made a decision that is changing your life for the better.

Here is David's letter, followed by my reply:

Hi Dad,

I don't know when your cutoff for submissions to your newspaper is, but I have a testimonial/letter to the editor for *One Day at a Time* to propose for your consideration. I hope you like it.

Love, David

———

A SPECIAL LETTER TO THE EDITOR

A Son's Birthday Wish...

My Dad turns eighty next week. At an age when many are content to sit back in quiet retirement, he works out in the gym several hours a day, attends church and Bible study classes weekly, writes articles and book reviews and, if that is not enough, owns and manages a small but growing business committed to helping those who have lost almost everything, including hope.

People will often call or write to thank him for enriching, even saving, their lives or the lives of a loved one. I can think of no greater reward in life than hearing those words. He is passionate in his work and, despite his age, unwavering. But it has not always been so, and his story has been an inspiration to many, but most of all, to me.

Some thirty-plus years ago, I had been anxiously awaiting wired funds from Dad to be put towards a property we were buying together with my brother. When it didn't arrive, I called him and was surprised to hear a woman answer the phone (he and my mom had divorced).

When I asked to speak to my Dad, [the woman] told me, "He can't speak right now." When I expressed my sense of urgency, she hesitated, then offered, "Right now he's very sick and passed out from drinking a bottle of vodka. We're friends from AA. He called us and we're here to help him. I'll tell him you called." And then she hung up.

I remember the long silence, then the sense of helplessness and loss. I thought of my mom, who struggled with the fallout of his alcoholism and their divorce, mired in the depths of her own depression. My parents were lost in an unending cycle of pain, and I felt helpless to do anything. I was scared and feeling "homeless" in the truest sense of the word.

My dad had hit the proverbial "bottom," and we were all there with him, each feeling desperately alone and without hope. And while I didn't feel it at the time, the healing in our family had, with that bottoming, begun.

Dad has shared his journey of recovery in his publication in the past, so I won't repeat [it]. I will only add that he and my mom are now happily remarried—to each other, enjoying their kitten, Luke—and I was able to build a beautiful home on that property of thirty-plus years ago in Hawaii, where they visit me every year.

And after a lifelong struggle for a meaningful career, my dad now has a publication and website called *One Day at a Time* whose mission is "presenting a message of hope and recovery to a nation in need"—a job he truly loves. My dad is, of course, this paper's editor and publisher, David Palmer, and I am very proud to be his son.

Happy birthday, Pops.
I love you, David P.

————

Dear David:

This is the best letter I've ever received from anyone.

I would have given anything not to have caused my family so much pain. I didn't mean to, and I am so grateful for your understanding and forgiveness. I think the night you refer to was April 9, 1979. It was indeed my last drink and my bottom.

God gave me the chance to make amends for some of the damage I caused, and nothing has brought me more joy than being able to help you realize your Hawaii dream and be a part of it. I really love the photo of you and me and Mom on the scuba diving boat in our diving gear, laughing it up. We were beginning to look like a happy family again.

We do enjoy our little kitten, Luke. We found him on Christmas Eve. Mom swept him up in the pelting rain at one of our busiest intersections where he sat, all fifteen ounces of him and soaking wet, as the traffic bore down on him. Ten minutes later, the vet across the street gave him some shots, and Mom brought him home and introduced us. We don't really know where he came from, but he is such a joy, we think God sent him.

You are such a fine and admirable man, and Mom and I pray constantly for your happiness. We are grateful that Emily loves you and that you love her. She is very kind and thoughtful to us, and we couldn't be more pleased that she is in your life.

I have to have cataracts removed in March and so we are thinking that we would schedule our trip to Hawaii for the Thanksgiving/Christmas/New Year's time of year. How does that sound?

I love you, David. Thank you! You're the best!
Dad

Note: To my reply to my son, David, I want to add that our two younger sons, Michael and Chris, and my wife, Joan, were also affected by my alcoholism, and they, too, have been forgiving and loving. I am very grateful and proud of their achievements in life.

———

THE ONE DAY AT A TIME MISSION

When I started the quarterly newspaper, *One Day at a Time,* with a companion website in Little Rock, Arkansas, we noted under the front-page banner our mission of "presenting a message of hope and recovery to a nation in need." It's still our mission.

In the beginning, I had three specific goals in mind:

First, I wanted to expand my own personal knowledge of addiction and recovery in order to help a grandson who was having trouble with drugs and had almost died in an automobile accident. You will find his story, which includes an intriguing spiritual twist, in appendix 1.

Second, I thought the recovery story had been underreported in the media. A lot of information about addiction is out there, but information is not necessarily knowledge. And, besides, where were the thrilling stories of people and families who get over their addictions and lead fantastic lives?

Third, I believed making a difference had to begin at the grassroots level with families, neighborhoods, and communities. National campaigns are fine, but recovery, I believe, is achieved mainly through local programs and relationships.

I find support for this conclusion in a project financed by the Robert Wood Johnson Foundation (RWJF), which in the 1990s gave out roughly $45 million in a series of grants to fifteen communities, including Little Rock.

The Fighting Back project produced a variety of milestones in the substance abuse reduction field—some of which endure today.

Little Rock's successful grant proposal (written by Frankie Sarver, wife of the late Bob Sarver, Arkansas Commissioner of Corrections during the Winthrop Rockefeller administration) stated that "people and communities—whose behaviors are partly defined by fear, denial, hopelessness, and passivity—are dysfunctional in the same ways.

"The disease of substance abuse," she said, "affects an entire city much the same as the disease affects its individual residents. *Denial prevents its identification, and an unwillingness to deal with the problem and blaming others prevent recovery.*"

In her proposal she went on to say:

Today with the problem of substance abuse affecting every segment of the city and affecting every culture, age, and income group, the city cannot continue to deny the problem or place blame on others.

In order for the city of Little Rock to have power against the problem, initiatives must be created which break the denial, reduce the fear, restore faith in the ability to change, and restore faith in the ability of public systems to respond.

And every resident must own and act against the problem.

So what have I learned after eight years of running my company, One Day at a Time? Eight conclusions quickly come to mind:

1. **Reducing substance abuse is a worthy cause.** Substance abuse kills, sickens, disables, destroys marriages and families, and imposes a huge financial burden on our economy. Some call it the number-one health problem in the nation.

2. **Recovery is not just for alcoholics and drug addicts.** There are many kinds of destructive addictions. Addiction is widespread and, by some definitions, universal (i.e., "sin" is an addiction and everybody sins).

3. **Momentum is growing in the fight against substance abuse and other addictions.** Churches and other faith-based institutions are increasingly confronting addictions of all kinds and offering programs of recovery. Universities are doing groundbreaking research. Hospitals and other caregivers are developing new treatments.

4. **People who are informed are better able to deal with addictions.** People who know about the scope and consequences of substance abuse, who discover where to get help, who see how other people recover, and who learn about the availability of both secular and spiritual resources have the best chance of avoiding addictions or recovering from them, and can go on to help others who are fighting the same battle.

5. **Education about addictions should begin early, in the home.** Teenagers whose parents talk to them regularly about the dangers of drugs are much less likely to use drugs than those whose parents don't, yet only one in four teens reports having these conversations.

6. **When substance abuse is reduced, communities benefit.** In healthy communities, workforces become more productive and costs associated with healthcare, crime, accidents, homelessness, and incarceration go down (the RWJF "Fighting Back" project, for example). And with every success, individuals and communities develop more courage and the will to act boldly.

7. **Substance abuse is implicated in major social problems.** In 80 percent or more of prison populations, as well as in the ranks of the homeless, substance abuse is involved. The potential for

reducing the cost in money and human suffering is huge in this one area alone.

8. **Momentum is growing in the fight against substance abuse and other addictions.** Churches and other faith-based institutions are increasingly confronting addictions of all kinds and offering programs of recovery. Universities are doing groundbreaking research. Hospitals and other caregivers are developing new treatments.

Dr. Kitty S. Harris, director of the Center for the Study of Addiction and Recovery and Center for Prevention and Resiliency at Texas Tech University, put it beautifully in a recent article: "Instead of a goal of simply abstinence, we are advocating the goal of a totally transformed life. A life free from addiction and filled with opportunities for full and complete participation in society."

Dr. Harris has defined what I believe recovery is: transformed lives. And that is what I am after with this book.

Here is what she wrote in full:

There is perhaps no better time than the present to be in the field of addiction counseling, treatment and research.

As someone who has worked with individuals struggling with the disease of addiction for almost three decades, I am happy to see the field transitioning to recovery-oriented systems of care.

I know that recovery can and does change the lives of individuals and families impacted by addiction. I also know that recovering people are one of our greatest assets in the battle against the epidemic of addiction facing our country.

As we make this transition, it is helpful to see how far we have come in our understanding of both addiction and recovery and how this understanding has influenced our profession and practice.

The idea of alcoholism as a disease was first introduced in the United States in 1784 by Dr. Benjamin Rush, a signer of the Declaration of Independence. His observations and subsequent writings first introduced the idea of abstinence as the only effective cure for alcoholism.

However, the idea that alcoholism was a disease would not resurface in the American mainstream again until the creation of Alcoholics Anonymous in 1935.

Though Bill Wilson, a cofounder of AA, intentionally refrained from using the word "disease" to describe the alcoholic condition, the primary text of this group includes a prologue written by Dr. William Silkworth in which individuals suffering from alcoholism are described as having a "physical allergy" to alcohol.

It is now a widely accepted notion that alcoholism is a disease; though it was not until the 1956 classification of alcoholism as a disease by the American Medical Association (AMA) and the 1960 publication of E.M Jellinek's *The Disease Concept of Alcoholism* that the "disease concept" coalesced into a scientific paradigm for looking at addiction.

The formation of the disease concept moved the field forward in many areas, including the medicalization of addiction treatment. The trend emphasized the neurobiological underpinnings of addiction and served to counter the belief that addiction is the result of immorality or weak character.

From this early conceptual work, our field was given the bedrock on which we now base much of our profession and practice. We still adhere to the ideas of Dr. Benjamin Rush that abstinence is the most effective cure for alcoholism. The ideas put forth by Alcoholics Anonymous offered us the Minnesota model of addiction treatment which has become the basis of our modern treatment industry.

Furthermore, Dr. Silkworth's "physical allergy" has led to scientific investigations into the metabolic processes related to the consumption of alcohol and drugs and has prompted the brain science of addiction that is offering us better understandings of the production and reuptake of neurotransmitters as they relate to addiction and recovery.

With all of this information readily available, you must be asking many of the same questions that I am. Where are we going now? What will our legacy look like to future generations? How will the profession look back on our decades of addiction counseling, treatment, and research? I hope they will see that our contributions have advanced the field as much as those of our predecessors.

We have offered the rigor of scientific inquiry into evidence-based practice. We understand the importance of individualized treatment and we have advocated tirelessly for underserved and disadvantaged populations. We have invited adolescents and young adults into the realm of recovery and have designed counseling and treatment interventions expressly for them.

We have worked with the criminal justice system to get incarcerated addicts the help they need to decrease recidivism [relapse into previous behavior]. Most importantly, however, we have pushed for the continuum of care and recognized recovery as an equally critical part of this system.

Recovery-oriented systems of care will be our greatest contribution. Our counseling, treatment, and research focus is moving away from a triage model. Instead, we now understand that addiction is a chronic disease necessitating a lifetime of change.

The greatest by-product of our contribution will be the reduction of stigma associated with addiction. Recovery-oriented systems of care integrate families, communities, employers, faith-based organizations, and our governments into the process of treating the addicted person. By involving the entire system, we teach society that recovery is a reality and that it benefits everyone when a recovering addict rejoins his/her community.

I do not know what the future will hold in the decades to come, but I do know that I am proud of the work we have accomplished in the decades that I have been a participant in this field. Our predecessors moved us from addiction as a moral flaw to the disease concept.

We have taken that mantle and moved from the treatment of a disease to systems of care that promote, enable, and advocate for a lifetime of recovery. We have moved out of judgment to healing of an illness, to the restoration of lives. The evolution of recovery is something that we can all be proud of for generations to come.[1]

CHAPTER ONE

Alcoholics Anonymous: Still the Gold Standard for Recovery

My psychiatrist fired me in 1978. He told me he couldn't fix me or my addictions to alcohol and tranquilizers, and said I should call Alcoholics Anonymous that very day.

I was deeply hurt by his lack of feeling and steely demeanor, and was frightened by the prospect of losing my prescription to Valium. But I decided I'd better cooperate and sought his help in finding such a meeting.

He then accused me of wasting his time, and said I should call the AA central office in Denver, get meeting schedules and a temporary sponsor, and go to a meeting that very night. I was living in Boulder, Colorado, at the time.

I was hung over, and this seemed like a tall order. I was tempted to go back to my condominium, pour myself a glass of bourbon, and forget the whole thing, but what was happening to me because of my drinking and my pain and loneliness scared me. I was completely without family or friends, and at age forty-nine I was physically and emotionally breaking down. And I had no spiritual life.

So I called the central office, got a list of meetings, and was given the name of a man to contact to be my sponsor. His name was Don, and when I called him, he was matter of fact, and seemed to understand what I was going through. At the same time, he didn't seem to want to dwell on the details. Quite the contrary. He began to outline a program of recovery that would begin that very evening.

I went to my first AA meeting that night on Pearl Street in Boulder, and shortly after that got a permanent sponsor. Looking back on the next thirty-two years of my sobriety, I can say that my life has been completely transformed. (Read the details of my journey in appendix 1.)

In his best seller, *The Road Less Traveled*, psychiatrist Scott Peck called the creation of Alcoholics Anonymous in 1935 "perhaps the greatest event of the twentieth century." Today, well over one hundred thousand AA groups operate around the world, with an estimated 2 million members. In a city like Little Rock, Arkansas, where I live, four hundred meetings take place each week. AA meetings are free and are sustained by passing the basket at every meeting. Giving is voluntary.

Under its twelve "traditions," AA doesn't promote itself, and public understanding of how it works is often limited. I have benefited enormously from AA. I believe in it, and pray that you will, too. I have included the 12 Steps of AA and chapter 5 of the *Big Book* on "How It Works" in appendix 2.

To give the reader an understanding of the spiritual essence of the program, I have included below an account of my participation in a retreat on St. Simons Island more than two decades ago.

THE ST. SIMONS RETREAT

The late Dr. Conway Hunter used to sponsor an annual, four-day Thanksgiving retreat at St. Simons Island off the Georgia coast for people in recovery from substance addictions, mainly alcohol. In November of 1990, I joined a contingent from Little Rock led by the late Dr. Don Browning and his wife, Joanne, to the retreat. I was about ten years sober, and felt in need of a spiritual jolt.

A Catholic priest known only as Noel said in one of the opening monologues, "As addicts, it is important for us to remember that our first addiction is not to alcohol and chemicals. It is to being apart. To being isolated and alone. Our addiction really is to nonliving."

Noel went on to say that this style of "nonliving" is contrary to what God had in mind with the Creation.

"God created us to be together," Noel said, "to be with each other and with Him. The Scriptures certainly make this clear, and it is what the AA program teaches us. The *Big Book* tells us to share our experience, strength, and hope *with each other."*

This theme of sharing our lives with each other and not going it alone cannot be overemphasized.

Hunter, a Georgia physician, millionaire, and entrepreneur widely known in recovery circles for his treatment facility for impaired physicians, died in 2003. The retreat basically died with him, but the memory of it lingers.

Some of the things that made the retreat special were the warmth of Conway and his wife, Charlotte; the magnificent and somewhat mysterious seaside setting; and a format that demanded participation and promoted a sense of belonging. It was an experience that was nurturing and loving on many levels.

Epworth By The Sea, a Methodist facility where the guests stayed and where daily meetings were held, provided a theologically sturdy base from which to contemplate spiritual matters within the added context of an ageless sea and sky and the centuries-old, giant live oaks lining ancient thoroughfares.

———

SPIRITUAL RENEWAL

Clearly this was a place for spiritual renewal. And that brings us to Thanksgiving night, 1990, and my report.

A hundred yards from the sea, I wrote, the guests gather under a hunter's moon in an early-nineteenth-century tabby house—once a shelter for plantation slaves and now a refuge for those who are finding their freedom in recovery—to talk about gratitude.

Warmed by a blaze in the huge fireplace, the participants speak of the goodness of God and of their growth in recovery. They speak of healed marriages and families, triumph over illnesses, and of the ability to deal with the pain and heartbreak of life with God-given strength and wisdom.

Some have been coming to Epworth By The Sea for many years. For some, the people there are their family on Thanksgiving, and that is the way Dr. Hunter intended it to be. Years ago, he began asking those in AA and others on similar journeys to come home with him to his beloved Georgia coast for Thanksgiving, and it was this pilgrimage that evolved into the retreat.

Gracious living is a part of the Thanksgiving package, and there is lots of sizzle to the spiritual steak. The retreat begins, for example, with a bountiful Thanksgiving dinner, and it also includes high tea served by Charlotte on Saturday at the Hunters' spectacular home on Sea Island within a few blocks of the famous Cloisters.

This year's dinner was at the Jekyll Island Club, a facility of significant charm and sense of history that was once the playground of the nation's wealthiest families. The centerpiece for dinner on this day was a table loaded with such southern staples as smoked ham, turkey, candied yams, and Key lime pie.

Charlotte's high tea, an elegant affair not unlike high tea at the Ritz in London, provides further support for the thesis that God has given us a life to be enjoyed, certainly for those who prefer clotted cream on their scones.

Indeed, it was Noel who said with a broad smile and a brogue as thick as Irish Mist, "The first thing God will ask us when we see Him for the first time is, 'Did you enjoy your life? Did you enjoy the life I gave you?'"

For most, the answer would be, "Not until I began to do things your way."

———

CONTACTED BY GOD

As people—mostly alcoholics in recovery—spoke at meetings over the four days, their stories revealed lives characterized by vast stretches of isolation, alienation, and loneliness—that addiction to nonliving that Noel spoke about—before they chose sobriety and began their spiritual journeys.

That is when we come to know God and begin to achieve serenity.

There is a moment in sobriety "when we are contacted, contacted by God," Noel says, and we begin to achieve a kind of serenity that comes from living the life that God has given us.

The retreat is a potpourri full of insights and rich perspectives furnished by its diverse participants, many of them involved in treatment center work. This year was no different.

There was Max, a psychiatrist whose years of teaching and study have illuminated the field of recovery. It was Max who reported at dinner that forty AA groups in Russia have sprung up in the last two years—complete with "the God concept."

There was Stephanie, who had just completed her thesis which, among other things, proved that God exists. It showed, too, that as addicts accumulate years of sobriety, their concept of God becomes deeper and more internalized.

There was Laurie, the consummate shopper who went for treatment with her bathing suit under one arm and a copy of *Vogue* tucked under the other. Today she is a physician in charge of the patients at a small treatment center.

There was Hal from the State Department, the unofficial "president of AA" who reminded us that we are spiritual beings undergoing human experiences, and who suggested that our egos would be better off with less flattery. "Flattery is OK," he said, "if you don't inhale it."

There were Conway and Charlotte Hunter, charismatic and compassionate, and many others who told their AA and Al-Anon stories with warmth and conviction.

It is appropriate to quote seventeenth-century English poet John Donne as an epilogue to the Thanksgiving retreat. As many will recall, Donne wrote, "No man is an island…any man's death diminishes me, because I am involved in mankind; and therefore never send to know for whom the bell tolls; it tolls for thee."

ANSWERING THE BELL

This brings me to Columbus A. He is one of those who answered the bell, big time.

At about eight o'clock on the morning of April 9, 2011, Columbus called me.

"Happy birthday!" he said with his usual infectious good cheer, as he has done annually for the past twenty years.

Columbus, a recovering alcoholic, was referring to my sobriety date, the date I capitulated and put the plug in the jug thirty-one years ago.

Okay, you say, it's nice that he calls you on your "birthday." What does that have to do with me?

If I was the only one he called, it would still be a big deal to me, but the important thing is that Columbus calls about five thousand recovering people in four states and a foreign country or two on their "birthdays" every year. That's an average of a dozen or more calls a day (higher on New Year's Day, when all those resolutions are in play).

And it's not just a hello and goodbye. Columbus personally buys about thirty-six thousand minutes of time annually on his telephone service.

Columbus and I are friends, and have been for more than thirty-one years. We may not see each other a lot, but we know each other well and have a lot in common.

We first met in late spring of 1979 at a 12-Step meeting at Baptist Hospital in Little Rock. He was a patient in the hospital's alcoholic ward, and I was living at home, going to meetings every day around the city, and trying to do what my sponsor instructed.

Both of us had tried—and failed—to get sober before, but this time, as it turns out, we have made it through more than thirty years and counting. Columbus had his last drink three days before I did, on April 6, 1979.

Over the years, we saw each other at meetings, and both of us served on boards—Columbus at Serenity Park, a treatment facility, and I at Wolfe Street Center, a provider of AA and Al-Anon meeting rooms, where we had the high privilege of serving with and learning from the late Joe McQuany. McQuany, who died in 2007 with nearly fifty years of sobriety, was a world-famous authority on alcoholism and the 12 Steps, author of the *Recovery Dynamics* curriculum and several other books, the founder of Serenity Park and cofounder of Wolfe Street Center. (Read more about McQuany, his life, and his legacy in chapter 5.)

In the days before Wolfe Street was founded, Columbus and I attended McQuany's Wednesday lunches and Monday-night 12-Step meetings. Columbus and I only see each other once or twice a year now, but we share a common deep faith in God and are committed to following a program of recovery calling for us to help others and keep our own side of the street clean.

A week after I got the birthday call from Columbus, I called him back and asked if I could chat with him about his telephone ministry. A few days later, on a gorgeous spring morning, we were drinking coffee at his kitchen table and swapping stories. He also showed me the computer on which he maintains his lists of names and records of his calls.

———

LAUNCHING HIS MINISTRY

Columbus launched his birthday ministry in 1991 with a list of members and birthdates of the "Last Chance" recovery group in Little Rock, a meeting he still attends. As time passed, he added other rosters as well as names he would get from referrals.

He starts making calls at seven every morning, and usually finishes by mid morning.

If Columbus doesn't personally know the person he is calling, he opens with, "I'm a friend of Bill W's [short for the late cofounder of AA, Bill Wilson], and I'm just calling to wish you a happy birthday." He uses a variation of this if a spouse or other family member answers the phone.

Sometimes Columbus hears bad news during these calls; some people he's trying to reach have had a relapse or another health or family problem and are unable or unwilling to talk.

Conversely, it is not uncommon for a few people, confused about their birthdates or simply impatient, to call Columbus—many times with a touch of irritation in their voice—and ask, "Why haven't you called?" Others have been known to take calls on cell phones during important board meetings or social gatherings.

Liz, an eighty-eight-year-old recovering alcoholic in Niagara Falls, has been a favorite of Columbus' over the years, and he had talked to her at some length the previous week about what was going on with her and her program of recovery.

"All was well," Columbus reported.

Another old-timer, ninety-three-year-old Minnie O. from Spartanburg, South Carolina, died this year with fifty-five years of sobriety.

"She was an inspiration," Columbus said, "and always seemed happy to hear from me. She was still attending meetings up until her death."

That was not the case with another call. The previous week, my friend had talked to a woman with five years of sobriety who was having a bit of a struggle. She had begun to question her program.

Columbus' call helped.

"I was looking for a sign," the woman said, "and you're it."

The important need that Columbus fills is providing the people he calls with another connection, another relationship.

———

RELATIONSHIPS AND RECOVERY

To digress for a moment, John Baker, a recovering alcoholic and founder of the Christ-centered Celebrate Recovery program at Rick Warren's Saddleback Church in California (see chapter 3), has said that recovery is based on "relationships."

John Townsend, a clinical psychologist, divinity school graduate, and author, agrees. At Saddleback's Summit meeting in 2006, he expanded on Baker's statement about our deeply felt need for others, saying that, "In recovery, everything begins and ends with relationships. People keep coming back because they connect. They don't know this at first. All they know is that they're screwed up and in pain."

Getting back to Columbus, I asked him who, among the thousands on his call list, had the longest sobriety. Columbus was not sure, but he did recall a man from Dumas, Arkansas, whose sobriety date had been 1947.

"He probably had at least sixty years [of sobriety] when he died," Columbus said. "He was a friend of Joe McQuany's in the early days."

McQuany, who was black, was instrumental in helping integrate Arkansas' all-white 12-Step meetings in the sixties. Columbus, who is also black, recalled with a laugh that someone had suggested early in his recovery that he ask McQuany to be his sponsor, an idea he rejected, thinking, "They're just trying to push me off on another black guy."

Today," Columbus says, "I don't see color anymore."

Columbus, whose mother and father were educators, grew up in a solid home, attended the University of Arkansas at Pine Bluff, and was drafted into the army in 1967, serving two years—most of it in Germany. He recently retired from his supervisory job at Dassault Falcon Jet and, prior to that, he had worked for Reynolds Aluminum, Levi Strauss, and Kraft Paper Company.

———

FADING HEALTH

Columbus first realized he had to do something about his alcohol problem in 1973. "My health was fading and the job was about to go," he says, adding that over the next six years, while he slipped in and out of sobriety, his wife, Virginia, threatened divorce.

What finally did him in were a wrecked car and a DWI (driving while intoxicated) charge in January 1979, followed by Virginia's third trip to a divorce lawyer. It was the beginning of the end. Columbus, who had his first drink when he was nineteen years old (a can of Colt 45 at a baseball game), had his last when he was thirty-four and on his way to Baptist Hospital.

He is justifiably proud of his parents, both schoolteachers; his wife, Virginia, also a schoolteacher; and, his three children, two girls and a boy, who are also schoolteachers. And, get this: Each of his children married schoolteachers as well. His four grandchildren are not working yet, but teaching is on the table for them as an option, too.

None of Columbus' children has had trouble with alcohol or other drugs except for one very minor infraction.

"Once, my daughter came home after having too much to drink and said, 'Oh, Daddy. I guess I'll have to join Bill W.' I told her she'd have to get drunk more than once to qualify," Columbus said with a laugh. His daughter is fine.

Speaking of his kids, Columbus notes with pride that KARK-TV, Channel 4, in Little Rock has given each of his daughters its Humanitarian of the Year award for their volunteer work in the community.

Today, Columbus goes to four or five 12-Step meetings a week. He figures he actually needs only two, but he isn't sure which two, so he goes to twice that many just to be sure.

"Sometimes people ask me how come I go to so many meetings when I have so much sobriety," Columbus said. "I laugh and say, 'You took a bath yesterday, didn't you? Why not take one today?'

It's also a way, Columbus reminds us, to avoid that "stinkin' thinkin'" that develops with neglect of our programs of recovery.

MY VISIT TO AKRON

So what is it about this program of Alcoholics Anonymous that seems to bring out the best of people? Let me continue with a brief report on my first visit to Akron, Ohio, the birthplace of AA.

In the summer of 2007, I was driving north from Little Rock to our family cottage in the Thousand Islands on the U.S./Canada border when I saw a sign on Interstate 76 for Akron, the birthplace of AA.

I had never been there, and on an impulse, I called the Chamber of Commerce from my car to see if I might take a tour of "Dr. Bob's" House (Dr. Robert Smith) at 55 Ardmore Ave. in Akron.

The person I spoke with at the Chamber gave me directions, and within twenty minutes I pulled in front of the house on a tree-shaded, cobblestone street where Dr. Bob and Bill W., two drunks, had launched Alcoholics Anonymous in 1935.

I had, by this time, managed to accumulate a number of years of sobriety, and to be in this city at this place moved me deeply. I entered the home with reverence.

There was the original coffee pot in the kitchen, the cot on the second floor where Bill W. spent many nights as he and Dr. Bob pursued their dream of sobering up drunks—themselves included. And there was the laundry chute where Dr. Bob pitched his empties when his wife, Anne, approached.

Prior to Dr. Bob and Bill getting together, Bob and his wife had joined the Oxford Group, a nondenominational evangelical movement that gave members a chance to talk about their prayer needs. Dr. Bob confessed at a group meeting that he was a silent drinker and couldn't stop. He asked for their prayers. This group provided many of the spiritual underpinnings for AA's creation and growth.

Akron's automobile tire heiress, Henrietta Seiberling, was in that group and was among those committed to pray for Dr. Bob. One day, a friend of

Seiberling's, Bill Wilson, came into town in pursuit of a business venture. Upset when the venture fell through and feeling the need for a drink coming on, Bill asked Henrietta if she knew another drunk he could talk to who might help reduce his cravings. His theory was that only another drunk could understand what he was going through and help him maintain his sobriety. Seiberling got Dr. Bob and Bill together; the two men met for six hours talking about the problems they were going through as alcoholics. That meeting in 1935 was the beginning of Alcoholics Anonymous.

―――

ENCOUNTER WITH GOD

The *Big Book* of Alcoholics Anonymous, now in its fourth edition, was written by Wilson and Smith, and provides the AA program's curriculum.

David Brooks, whose column appears regularly on the op-ed page of the *New York Times,* wrote a column in 2011 about Bill Wilson's encounter with God and the beginning of AA, and portions of it are reprinted below.

"On December 13, 1934," Mr. Brooks wrote, "a failed stockbroker named Bill Wilson was struggling with alcoholism at a New York City detox center. It was his fourth stay at the center and nothing had worked."

Brooks continued:

This time he tried a remedy called the belladonna cure—infusions of an hallucinogenic drug made from a poisonous plant—and he consulted a friend named Ebby Thatcher who told him to give up drinking and give his life over to the service of God.

Wilson was not a believer, but later that night, at the end of his rope, he called out in his hospital room, "If there is a God let him show Himself! I am ready to do anything. Anything!"

As Wilson described it, a white light suffused his room and the presence of God appeared. "It seemed to me in the mind's eye that I was on a mountain and that a wind not of air but of spirit was blowing," he testified later. "And then it burst upon me that I was a free man."

"The movement," Brooks stated in his column, "is the subject of a smart and comprehensive essay by Brendan L. Koerner in the July 2010 issue of *Wired* magazine. The article is noteworthy not only because of the light it sheds on what we've learned about addiction but for what it says about changing behavior more generally."

Brooks continued:

Much of what we do in public policy is to try to get people to behave in their own long-term interests—to finish school, get married, avoid gangs, lose weight, save money. Because the soul is so complicated, much of what we do fails.

The first implication of Koerner's essay is that we should get used to the idea that we will fail most of the time. Alcoholics Anonymous has stood the test of time. There are millions of people who fervently believe that [the] 12-step process saved their lives. Yet the majority, even a vast majority of the people who enroll in the program, do not succeed in it. People are idiosyncratic. There is no single program that successfully transforms most people most of the time.

The second implication is that we should get over the notion that we will someday crack the behavior code—that we will someday find a scientific method that will allow us to predict behavior and design reliable social programs. As Koerner notes, AA has been the subject of thousands of studies. Yet no one has yet satisfactorily explained why some succeed in AA while others don't, or even what percentage of alcoholics who try the steps will eventually become sober as a result.

Each member of an AA group is distinct. Each group is distinct. Each moment is distinct. There is simply no way for social scientists to reduce this kind of complexity into equations and formulae that can be replicated one place after another.

Nonetheless, we don't have to be fatalistic about things. It is possible to design programs that will help some people some of the time. AA embodies some shrewd insights into human psychology.

In a culture that generally celebrates empowerment and self-esteem, AA begins with disempowerment. The goal is to get people to gain control over their lives, but it all begins with an act of surrender and an admission of weakness.

In a culture that thinks of itself as individualistic, AA relies on fellowship. The general idea is that people aren't really captains of their own ship. Successful members become deeply intertwined with one another—learning, sharing, suffering, and mentoring one another. Individual repair is a social effort.

In a world in which gurus try to carefully design and impose their ideas, Wilson surrendered control. He wrote down the famous steps and foundations, but AA allows each local group to form, adapt, and innovate. There is less quality control. Some groups and leaders are great and some are terrible. But it also means that AA is decentralized, innovative, and dynamic.

———

CHANGING WHOLE IDENTITIES

Alcoholics have a specific problem: They drink too much. But instead of addressing that problem with the psychic equivalent of a precision guidance missile, Wilson set out to change people's whole identities. He studied William James' *Varieties of Religious Experience*. He sought to arouse people's spiritual aspirations rather than just appealing to rational cost-benefit analysis. His group would help people achieve broad spiritual awakenings, and abstinence from alcohol would be a byproduct of that larger salvation.

In the business of saving lives, the straight path is rarely the best one. AA illustrates that even in an age of scientific advance, it is still ancient insights into human nature that work best. Wilson built a remarkable organization on a nighttime spiritual epiphany.[2]

Unlike Prohibition, which focused on clamping down on the supply of alcohol and failed, AA focused on drying up the demand for alcohol through visions of a far better life. The modern-day "War on Drugs," a largely government-run program, is a flop, just like Prohibition was in the twenties. And for the same reason. In both cases, the emphasis is on reducing supply rather than demand.

The Global Commission on Drug Policy verified this outcome in a widely published release on June 2, 2011 which said, *"The global war on drugs has failed* with devastating consequences for individuals and societies around the world." Those of us who have had experience with drugs, including alcohol, know that recovery is based mostly on attraction, the promise of a better life.

John D. Rockefeller, a fierce advocate of temperance and prohibition, fought hard for the passage of the Eighteenth Amendment to the Constitution outlawing alcohol in 1920, and he fought just as hard twelve years later for its repeal in 1932.

"On that day in 1932," *Wall Street Journal* columnist Mary Anastasia O'Grady wrote in June 2011, "John D. Rockefeller Jr., a vociferous advocate of temperance, called for the repeal of the Eighteenth Amendment in a letter published in the *New York Times*."

She continued:

Rockefeller had spent hundreds of thousands of dollars lobbying for the constitutional prohibition on alcohol. But his letter did more than admit the error of his investment. Because of his moral authority on the matter, it effectively ended the conservative taboo against admitting that the whole Prohibition experiment had failed.

———

RESTORING PUBLIC RESPECT

Rockefeller had not changed his views on the destructiveness of drink, and he asked for ongoing "support of practical measures for the promotion of genuine temperance." But he insisted that lifting prohibition was essential if America was to "restore public respect for the law."

Rockefeller's reversal came to mind last week when former Federal Reserve Chairman, George Schultz, former Federal Reserve chairman Paul Volker, former NATO Secretary General Javier Solona, three former Latin American presidents from Brazil, Columbia, and Mexico, and the current prime minister of Greece (among others) issued a joint report—as the Global Commission on Drug Policy—describing the drug war as a failure and calling for a paradigm shift in global drug policy.

Like Rockefeller the commission members do not embrace a laissez-fair policy toward drug use. But they recognize, as he did, that the attempt to use force has been disastrous. They recommend alternative approaches to controlling substances and more emphasis on treatment for addicts.

The parallels between the situation Rockefeller faced and today's scandalous war on drugs are dramatic. The wealthy philanthropist had begun his campaign against alcohol with great expectations. "When the Eighteenth Amendment was passed, I earnestly hoped—with a host of advocates of temperance—that this would be generally supported by public opinion, and," he wrote, "that tee-totaling would eventually take hold."

That this has not been the result but rather that drinking generally has increased; that the speakeasy has replaced the saloon, not only unit for unit, but probably twofold if not threefold; that a vast army of lawbreakers has been recruited and financed on a colossal scale; that many of our best citizens piqued at what they regarded as an infringement of their private rights have openly and unabashedly disregarded the Eighteenth Amendment; that as an inevitable result respect for all law has greatly lessened; that crime has increased to an unprecedented degree—I have slowly, reluctantly come to believe.

He noted that any benefits from the Eighteenth Amendment were more than outweighed by the evils that had developed and flourished since its adoption, evils which were likely to lead to unspeakably worse conditions than those which prevailed before.

———

GANG VIOLENCE ON THE RISE

So here we are today once again investing capital and effort in reducing the supply of drugs when we would be better off concentrating on the demand.

American jails are taking in record numbers of young minorities and converting them into hardened criminals; gang violence is on the rise. Organized crime is undermining geopolitical interests in places like Mexico, Central America, and Afghanistan. Thousands of innocents, including children, have been killed in the mayhem.

Having produced nothing but hardship for the most vulnerable, disrespect for the rule of law, terror in formerly peaceful cities, and profit opportunities for gangsters, drug warriors now want to militarize the southern U.S. border.

"If history is any guide," says Angelo Codevilla in his essay, "Our Borders, Ourselves" in the May 16, 2011, issue of the *Claremont Review of Books,* "this isn't going to end well." Look at what happened, he warns, in the Peloponnesian War when hostility broke out on the Athenian doorstep: Having lost a friendly border, Athens turned itself inside out trying to secure an unfriendly one.

The border is unfriendly not because of too few fences, drones, or soldiers, but because American drug habits finance the traffickers. "These dollars, and nothing else," writes Mr. Codevilla, "are responsible for the near collapse of law and order south of the border, and for the insufficiently publicized corruption on the northern side.

"We have met the enemy and it is us," the Claremont Institute scholar posits: "Even if our southern border were completely closed off...it would do nothing to change the fact that mind-altering drugs have become morally and politically acceptable to mainstream American society."

Americans can cut their demand, perhaps with education and by stigmatizing use as was done with cigarettes. But until then, victory is unlikely. As Mr. Codevilla notes, "America's assumption that restricting supply can somehow make it safe for us to tolerate widespread drug use has itself proved to be a habit forming narcotic that has reduced our sensitivity to moral rot. Rockefeller could not have said it better."[3]

It is interesting to note that barely three years after the repeal of the Eighteenth Amendment, Bill Wilson and Dr. Bob Smith founded Alcoholics Anonymous. It was a program of attraction that did what Prohibition could not do: It sobered up millions, and with more than one hundred thousand meetings worldwide, it continues to do so.

Early in the game, Rockefeller offered AA money to pursue its work, but, sensing that no good would come of it, AA turned him down. It remains the policy of AA to operate with money raised through the contributions of individual meeting groups.

Some critics of AA are skeptical of its spiritually based curriculum, but there is ample support for its results. This does not mean there are no problems. One is that AA attracts an increasingly older crowd and there aren't enough meetings for young people who seek recovery through interactions with people of their own age.

———

HARVARD PSYCHIATRIST BACKS AA

Dr. John F. Kelly, an associate professor in psychiatry at Harvard Medical School and associate director of the Center for Addiction Medicine at Massachusetts General Hospital, is clear about his support for 12-Step programs and the growing interest in them among scientists.

Speaking at Texas Tech at an addiction studies conference in 2011, he said, "There has been a significant increase in scientific interest and rigor focused on AA over the past twenty years." He highlighted some areas of particular interest, including fundamental statistics:

- Alcohol, Dr. Kelly noted, is the third-leading cause of death in the U.S., and is the leading risk factor for death among males aged fifteen to fifty-nine. Five thousand people under age twenty-one die as a result of alcohol annually.

- Opiate overdose is the leading cause of accidental death in thirteen states and second overall in the United States.

- In the U.S. in 2008, the latest year available for data, 22.2 million members of the population age twelve or older were addicted to alcohol, drugs, or both. Alcohol alone was close to 15 million.

- The economic burden in the U.S. associated with alcohol and drug misuse approaches $400 billion annually, far exceeding the cost associated with other medical conditions. Cancer, for example, is $107 billion and heart disease is $96 billion. (Joseph A. Califano Jr., head of the National Center on Addiction and Substance Abuse at Columbia University [CASA], puts the number at a $1 trillion.)

- Alcohol dependence is highest in the eighteen-to-twenty-year age group, at 12.5 percent, and the next highest is 10.8 percent in the twenty-one to twenty-four age group. At age sixty-five to sixty-nine, alcohol dependence is below 1 percent.

- In 2009, 16 percent of those in college had used in the past thirty days. Of those not in college, 11.7 percent had used.

Given these numbers, it's no wonder scientists have been casting about for solutions and are giving 12-Step programs a serious look.

"Twelve step programs," Dr Kelly said, "work as well as professional interventions and have the advantage of being plentiful in most communities and available at various times, often when addicts need them the most. They are free, there's no paperwork, and patients can attend as intensively and as long as they desire. Also, meetings are available at high-risk times." (At the cocktail hour, for example, or at daybreak when hangovers raise the ante.)

AA is the single most popular recovery program of all, Dr. Kelly noted in his lecture at Texas Tech. It attracts about 2.4 million a year. Outpatient rehab draws 2 million, inpatient rehab attracts 1.2 million, and outpatient mental health draws in 1 million. The rest get treatment at hospitals, private doctors' offices, emergency rooms, and in prison or jail.

Editor's note: AA and many other 12-Step meetings are sensitive about using whole names, and this is a good time to explain our position.

We rely heavily on testimonials to make the case that recovery is something to be embraced, not feared. Testimonials are a powerful tool—probably a little more so when full names are used.

To varying degrees, anonymity is always a factor, and we do not publish any testimonial without first reviewing it with the author and getting approval to proceed with a full name or first name and initial. We discourage the use of names of other people in testimonials and do not publish unsigned testimonials.

Alcoholics Anonymous (AA) stresses the need for anonymity in its 12 traditions. This has come to mean using first name and initial when members speak about an association with AA—i.e., "My name is Tom S. and I'm a member of Alcoholics Anonymous." Use of the full name is acceptable when there is no reference to AA. Most people have many associations and as citizens are free to put their full name on any document they choose.

Celebrate Recovery, a rapidly expanding, Christ-centered 12-Step program, aggressively promotes recovery to those who seek it, and putting a name on it, some feel, adds power. Still, others may prefer just first name and initial, and that's okay.

As for the secular world, many universities are doing groundbreaking work on studies of the brain that will help in the treatment of addiction. Anonymity is not usually an issue in this area and is addressed on a case-by-case basis.

CHAPTER TWO

Living with a Drug Addict?
You Need Al-Anon

If you are living with an alcoholic or have anything to do with one, chances are you need help, and Al-Anon meetings are a cheap and, for many, a priceless resource. More than twenty-four thousand of these free, 12-Step meetings are available in 133 countries, meaning there is probably one near you.

More than 150 million Americans, roughly half the population, are affected directly or indirectly by the disease of alcoholism and other drug addictions. Research also shows that every alcoholic's behavior affects at least five others in his or her circle of family members, relatives, and associates.

Al-Anon Family Groups describes itself as "a supportive network that provides friends and families of problem drinkers with the opportunity to share their experiences to find strength and hope."

I know that at the suggestion of a meeting, some may recoil with the standard comeback: "He (or she) is the one with the problem; why do *I* have to go to meetings?" But the fact is that you are, in many ways, just as sick as your friend or loved one is, and if you will go to meetings and work the steps, you, too, will benefit. So let's take a look at Al-Anon.

Like AA, Al-Anon has been around for more than seventy-five years. It was cofounded by Lois Wilson, wife of AA cofounder, Bill Wilson. A wonderful book called *The Lois Wilson Story: When Love Is Not Enough* by

William G. Borchert is a great love story, and it explains how Al-Anon got started.

Here's a sample:

Picture, if you will, eight women parked in front of the Clinton Street, Brooklyn, home of Bill and Lois Wilson. Their car motors are running, and they are steamed.

On this night in 1938, their husbands, most of them newly sober, are attending a meeting of Alcoholics Anonymous with Wilson. What ticks the ladies off is that their husbands have replaced drinking with AA meetings, leaving them once again alone and unloved.

At that moment, Lois, with suddenly heightened awareness of her own resentment and anger, realized that spouses, too, have been touched by alcoholism and must seek and find a dramatic change in their own lives if they are to get well and stay well.

THE BIRTH OF AL-ANON

Lois, on that night in Brooklyn, brought the women in for a get-together of their own in the kitchen and out of it emerged Al-Anon Family Groups, the fellowship Lois cofounded with her good friend, Ann Bingham. Like Alcoholics Anonymous, the impact of Al-Anon has been huge. Today, Al-Anon Family Groups are active in practically every city across America, and membership is estimated to be close to a million.

In his book, Borchert tells a moving and powerful love story about two charismatic figures who really did change the world. The fact is, Bill and Lois, both attractive and smart, were absolutely nuts about each other. In the early days, they would hit the road in motorcycle and sidecar, and the first thing you know, they'd be off in the canebrake making out.

It was not all play, however. Bill was a stockbroker, and on their road trips, he would visit companies and gather firsthand information about how they operated and how they were doing. Indeed, he is credited with being a pioneer in the field of securities analysis, a vital component of investing.

As Bill's drinking increased, Borchert's book records, Lois would frequently lose her temper when he would embarrass her at parties or at home in front of friends and family.

"I got mad at him, terribly mad," Lois said. "I'd throw all kinds of things at him, but it really didn't make a difference. That talk is wasted on a drunk. He wanted me to help him stop his drinking. You couldn't be mad at him then. You just had to forgive him."

In 1939, four years after Bill quit drinking and founded AA with Dr. Bob, the Wilsons lost their Clinton Street home where Lois had been born and where she had lived with her husband during his battle with alcoholism and later during his final recovery.

They had no money and very little coming in, and for almost two years lived out of suitcases, moving fifty-one times, living mainly with generous AA friends and in a room above an old AA clubhouse on 24th Street in New York City.

Finally, in 1941, as the result of royalties he received from the book he wrote called *Alcoholics Anonymous*, also known as the *Big Book*, they moved into a home in Bedford Hills, New York, overlooking the Hudson River. Lois named it "Stepping Stones."

For the next thirty years, Bill and Lois lived out their days traveling in the service of their twin ministries.

In 1971, Borchert writes, Bill Wilson, stricken with emphysema, died at the age of seventy-six, and the world finally discovered who founded the fellowship of Alcoholics Anonymous when the *New York Times* published his full name on its front page.

At first, Lois was almost crippled with grief, but she eventually rallied and carried on her work for the next seventeen years. But she never got over Bill's death. When the end came for her, as she lay dying, she asked for a pad and pencil, and scribbled the words, "Tell them…I want to see my Bill."

Lois Burnham Wilson, at ninety-seven years old, joined her beloved Bill later that evening of October 5, 1988. She was buried next to her husband in the small family cemetery in East Dorset, Vermont. Her name is chiseled on the simple, white marble gravestone, but true to the organization's principles of anonymity, there is no mention of Al-Anon. Bill's gravestone, equally discreet, makes no mention of Alcoholics Anonymous.

———

MEET MARY P.

Mary P. was a vastly different sort of Al-Anon member than Lois, more of a rough-and-tumble type. But she, too, has had a powerful impact on both men and women trapped in sick relationships with alcoholics.

Mary founded a "black belt" Al-Anon group in Rose City, Arkansas, just across the river from Little Rock, and later in her life she toured the world speaking to Al-Anon groups. But let's pick up her story on a winter night in 1976, about a year before she began her recovery. On this night, Mary decided she would kill her alcoholic husband, her second, when he came home from work.

Frustrated by her inability to control his drinking, Mary finally said to herself, "It's not the drinking, it's him. He's the problem, and I need to get rid of him." Attracted to the image of herself as a widow, she had rejected the divorce option in her plan and went straight to murder.

As for the means, she eliminated both an ice pick in the neck and running over him in the family car. Instead, she chose drowning her husband in the bathtub when he came home drunk. Her goal was to make it look like an accident.

With her mind made up, the first night he showed up drunk, she hit him. When he fell, he hit his head on the coffee table and the impact knocked him out. She filled the bathtub, took off his clothes, and pushed him in. Like a sinking ship, he slipped beneath the surface of the water.

Then Mary thought to herself, "What am I doing? This is premeditated murder!" She pulled him up by the hair, but then quickly convinced herself that no one would catch on...and so she shoved him back under.

As Mary tells this story to predominantly female audiences whose members have had similar inclinations with errant spouses, the laughter begins to build and increase as she describes pulling this drunk man out of the water, letting him slide in again, and then finally pulling him back out, restarting his breathing with CPR, and dragging him, still unconscious, to the bedroom.

She then tells of fluffing up the pillows, propping him up in the bed, and grabbing her hair dryer. ("His hair tends to curl, and he likes it straight like Conway Twitty," Mary explains.) When she left her husband sitting bolt upright in the bed, every hair in place, she closed the door, went to her room...and cried.

Over the next three days, the patient, suffering from acute alcohol poisoning, would call out, but Mary stayed away. On the third day, her husband emerged. About a year later, in January 1977, Mary turned to Al-Anon and her husband began attending Alcoholics Anonymous meetings.

Since then, Mary has probably told the bathtub story over a hundred times to audiences around the world—beginning with her Rose City home group, which was housed for many years in the stone building that her grandfather built in 1933 at 803 Water Street.

———

MAKING A POINT

The bathtub story makes the point that Mary's husband was clearly one very sick alcoholic, but it also reveals that she was sick, too—partly because she was surrounded by the effects of alcoholism as a child, and also because she married two (her first husband was also an alcoholic). Neither Mary nor her husband really knew what sickness each had. That came later. The story also offers vicarious pleasure to those who have gone through the torment of living with an alcoholic and are glad to see one getting roughed up.

Over the past thirty-five years, Mary has become widely recognized in Al-Anon circles, much like the late Joe McQuany, the recovering alcoholic who received global recognition in the field of alcoholism.

So what, exactly, is Al-Anon? To quote the definition on the organization's website:

Al-Anon is a fellowship of wives, husbands, children, parents, other relatives, and friends of problem drinkers.

Members of [Al-Anon] groups share their experience, strength, and hope with each other in order to solve their common problems—fear, insecurity, lack of understanding of themselves and the alcoholic, and damaged personal lives resulting from alcoholism, a family illness.

By attending Al-Anon meetings and applying the twelve steps of recovery adapted from Alcoholics Anonymous (AA) to their personal lives, many have found the help they need to deal with the effects of living with or having lived with the alcoholism of another.

As Mary immersed herself in Al-Anon, she began to contemplate her dysfunctional childhood that at least partly explained the anger and violent streak that manifested themselves.

———

RAMPANT ALCOHOLISM

Alcoholism was rampant on Mary's mother's side of the family, but she was partly shielded from abuse by her father, a career Army officer. She doted on him and became "daddy's girl," and his death when she was twelve years old devastated her. "I lost my faith in God and declared war on my mother," she says, describing her mom as a woman who didn't drink, "but probably should have."

In 1960, Mary graduated from North Little Rock High School with honors and made her escape. She married an Air Force aircraft mechanic and moved with him on his assignment to Newfoundland.

While she drank a lot in the early days, Mary says her real drug of choice was adrenalin, an addiction that resulted in infidelities, rage, and other destructive behaviors. After she had manipulated her husband's reassignment from Newfoundland to Little Rock Air Force base instead of Wichita, Kansas, they ultimately divorced.

After that, Mary devoted part of her free time to the 1960s hippie movement, parting her long hair in the middle and hanging out with a bad crowd. She also added the phrase, "Always keep somebody around you who is doing worse than you are" to her list of perspectives on life.

Mary also began dating her current husband, a welder from Pumpkin Bend (known to locals as "Punkin' Bend"), Arkansas, and after a four-year courtship they were married in Jacksonville, Arkansas. In 1969 they settled down in Rose City, Mary's hometown not far from Jacksonville, two years later.

For the next seven years, her husband's alcoholism progressed, and he would drink and leave and be gone for days. Meanwhile, Mary's growing resentment was starting to boil over.

"When he drank, I got violent," Mary says, and she punished him. "He became my child. When he misbehaved, I physically whipped him. I knocked his teeth loose and broke his bones," she says.

Not long before the bathtub incident, Mary was "playing hide and seek" with her husband. He was hiding at Club 70 in North Little Rock, and she was looking for him. When she found him sitting at a table with a woman, Mary punched her husband and the woman in the face, turned the table over, and attacked the bouncer who was attempting to intervene.

When the police arrived, they arrested her and took her to jail.

Mary says there is a reason "Al-Anons" tend to lash out with anger. "When drunks drink, they actually do get some relief from their pain," Mary says. "Al-Anons don't get that kind of relief, and they don't know what to do with that pain."

Now seventy-two with an unlined, sweet face framed by closely cropped white hair, Mary is celebrating thirty-five years of recovery and looks nothing like the "wild woman" she was—and she says she feels nothing like her either.

———

BOOKED SOLID

Mary sponsors Al-Anon women all over the world and is in great demand as a speaker. She also presents workshops for couples struggling with relationships.

Quick to say that she is not a big deal, Mary says, "Al-Anon is a way of life for me, but I don't pretend to be an authority on it. I'm an authority on me. Like the book says, 'It's principles before personalities.'"

Tapes and CDs of Mary's speaking engagements are in great demand, and in her eight-disc collection called *Doin' the Twelve Steps,* she describes her own recovery with both insight and humor.

The first step for both AA and Al-Anon is, "We admitted we were powerless over alcohol—that our lives had become unmanageable" and, like most, Mary had problems admitting both powerlessness and unmanageability.

Once she got beyond these obstacles with her sponsor, she began working the steps and regularly attending meetings. She also began eliminating some destructive words in her vocabulary. Not four-letter words, but phrases like, "What if?"—which is living in the future; "Yes, but"—which really says, "I hear you, but I ain't gonna do it"; and "I know"—which says, "You can't teach me."

Mary has had the same sponsor for thirty-five years, and they are as close as two people can be. Mary hated asking the woman to be her sponsor, but she had what Mary wanted: "She was always smiling and sincere, and she wasn't afraid of me."

———

A RACIST

The sponsor was also black, and Mary hated blacks.

"I was raised a racist, and I told her up front I didn't like—I used the 'n' word—and she said, 'Me neither.' Turned out her definition of the word had something to do with behavior but nothing to do with color."

Thanks to her sponsor, Mary says, "I have come to accept all people, regardless of color or other differences."

Mary, who had used intimidation as a defense, had met her match and ultimately came to realize that she felt she had to be in control, sometimes using intimidation, because she was "scared to death."

In the initial stages of recovery, she remained angry most of the time, which prompted her sponsor to pose the question, "If you admit you are powerless, why are you upset over all the things that make you angry?"

Mary's sponsor also discouraged her from doing too much thinking.

"You can't think yourself into right thinking," she said. "Your thinking is broken."

Instead, her sponsor said, she should seek "understanding, which leads to knowledge, which leads to wisdom. And wisdom comes from God."

As with most Al-Anons, Mary had trouble with denial and tells a story to illustrate the point:

A priest and a rabbi and an Al-Anon find themselves in hell, and when asked by Lucifer why they are there, the rabbi says he got hooked on pork and couldn't stop eating the forbidden food. The priest says he got involved with a young woman and violated his vow of celibacy.

The Al-Anon says, "I don't know what you are talking about. It's not hot, and I'm not here."

The bottom line, Mary says, is, "We have to surrender. We are powerless over everything. You don't have to like something to accept it."

———

AN INTERVENTION

Al-Anons love the concept of interventions. By way of example, about fifteen years ago, I was approached by a distraught and codependent wife, an acquaintance named Ruth, who explained to me at the top of her lungs that she had had her fill of an alcoholic husband (Jim) and was not going to take "no" for an answer in her request that I "do something about him."

Furthermore, she had definite ideas about how I should go about it. I had my reservations. My program of recovery advocated "attraction" rather than "promotion," and her ideas seemed far too aggressive.

In the end, Ruth prevailed. I adopted her argument that, "You can't just stand there and watch a church burn. Put out the fire. What can you lose?"

So it was that two aging 12-Steppers, artfully concealed in the shrubbery, found themselves on a stakeout one summer evening in one of Little Rock's better neighborhoods. My companion was the late Wythe W., who had also bought into Ruth's sales pitch.

Ruth's plan was for us to invade the home, confront Jim, and sell him on sobriety before he passed out—and, if possible, take him to a 12-Step meeting. She would leave the house at about 6 p.m., signaling to us—her accomplices crouched in the bushes—that the coast was clear.

Ruth's husband, Jim, had a predictable end-of-the-day routine: He would come home, grab a bottle and a glass, drop in the easy chair, turn on the stereo, get wasted, and then go to bed. The usual. You could almost set your clock by it.

So, sure enough, at the appointed hour, Ruth left the house, smiled at us with an affirming nod, hopped in the car, and drove off.

So far, so good.

We walked across the street, Groucho-like, and peeked through the screen door. From somewhere inside, a dog immediately began barking. It seemed like a bad sign possibly indicating cosmic disapproval of our scheme, but we pushed open the door a crack and found that the dog was friendly and ready to sell out his master to two perfect strangers.

We began to climb the stairs in the direction of the loud music, and I ventured a quavering "Hello?" to announce our arrival. No response.

At the top of the stairs, we rounded the corner and confronted Jim, who was sprawled in his chair holding a drink and staring at us uncomprehendingly.

Equally stunned, we dropped our folksy script and rushed into a pitch about the rewards of sobriety and the need for quick action. We closed with an invitation: "How about going to a meeting with us?"

Dazed by the startling events unfolding in his study, Jim surprised us (and no doubt himself, too) by accepting the invitation. Off we went to a meeting, where Jim behaved himself very well and appeared to be soaking up wisdom while Wythe and I smiled and winked at each other over our coup.

"Well, Jim, what did you think of the meeting?" I asked on the way home in the car, expecting an outpouring of gratitude.

Instead, he answered, "God, I've got such a headache! Don't those drunks ever quit talking? How's that supposed to cure you of anything? Just drop me off in front of my house. Please!"

Crushed, we dropped him off and drove away into the night.

In the following days, Ruth thanked Wythe and me for trying, and while it appeared Jim hadn't changed, we took comfort in the fact that we had tried and that, after all, he might eventually come around.

Then a strange thing happened. I began to see Jim at 12-Step meetings, and he and Ruth seemed to be putting it all back together.

A couple of years ago, my wife and I were in Eureka Springs attending a weekend conference for people in recovery, and Ruth and Jim were there, just as happy as could be. They came up to us, Jim put his arm on my shoulder, and with a warm smile, he said, "You saved my life. Thanks."

Could there be any sweeter sound than that?

I began to think about what we had done, and I thought to myself, "Okay, so our methods were a little clumsy, but it worked."

I think it worked because we had a limited objective, although we didn't realize it at the time. We wanted simply to get him to a meeting and then let God do the rest. We also made it clear to him that we were not there to judge him, but to share our experience, strength, and hope.

One or two alcoholics talking to another is very much in the tradition of Alcoholics Anonymous, and is a good option to consider. If you have a problem with someone you are close to who has a substance abuse problem, you should also consider turning to a treatment center or outpatient facility. They have been there hundreds of times and offer solid professional advice. I know of a number of successful interventions.

Actually Ruth, Jim's wife, became so conversant with the principles of Al-Anon that she began to contribute an Al-Anon column to my local recovery-focused newspaper, *One Day at a Time*. Here are two of her published columns.

———

CHOOSE FREEDOM NOT FEAR
BY RUTH MITCHELL

My Higher Power (MHP) likes to keep me busy with challenges. I have learned through the program that it's not so healthy to create my own chaos, because the challenges MHP provides are quite enough, thank you very much.

I have heard over and over again, "God won't give you more than you can handle"…blah, blah, blah. Are these people nuts? Have these people seen my credit card bill? Have they walked in my shoes and lived with my attention deficit problems? Have they met my spouse of thirty years, and have they met me? Do they know I get up sometimes three times a night to let my elderly dog out the door?

Just before the holidays this year, we had a huge drama event at our house. It took me completely by surprise, and sent me into despair. I was calling AAs and Al-Anons all over the state so that I could get guidance and hear God through them.

One advisor told me to continue being myself, another told me to get to Al-Anon and still another told me I was accepting unacceptable behavior. One Al-Anon even had the gall to tell me to ask myself what was my part in it.

Wonderful support group I have. No, I'm serious they are! But finally, one morning, MHP actually spoke directly to me. The message was this—it doesn't matter who you are, you can't run away from yourself, and you can't hide from your higher power, no matter how hard you may try by drinking, drugging, making stupid choices, looking for geographic cures, OR, Al-ANONS take note, allowing another human to replace your higher power no matter how temporarily, or obsessively, you indulge in this fallacy.

This "Aha!" moment sent compassion flooding through me, compassion coming directly from my higher power, and for the first time in my life I felt a glimmer of what unconditional love might be like. I was able to forgive myself and the party who had thrown me into such a snit. The program was working for me, and God was doing for me what I could not do for myself.

We hear about unconditional love a lot. And, to this moment, as I write this, I'm not sure humans are capable of unconditional love, but I know God is. It was a mini miracle for me to feel the compassion that might instead have been well-justified anger, self-pity, or even poisonous self-destructive behavior.

I am coming through this trauma, with renewed awareness, new commitment to be FREE, not FEAR-Filled. ("Wordies" take note, in the word "Fear" the vowels are encapsulated by the F and R. In "Free" the vowels are outside the F and R. I know, I know—too much Scrabble.)

I wish I could share my experience, strength and hope and tell you Serenity comes easy after all these years, that love is a noun, not a verb, and that if you adopt a spiritual life, you will no longer experience setbacks, but that is not my *experience*.

But here's my *hope*. If you have been fortunate enough to pick up this publication, you have questions about someone else's addictions because you are being held hostage by them. Please don't despair. Go to an Al-Anon meeting for starters. Listen and learn. There will be people who you may not know, "but they will love you in a very special way."

More than likely, you will run into people you do know. Your first reaction may be, OMG, they know my secret! But the truth is, they have lived your secret. They will become a support group that will save your life, rejuvenate your spirit, and be there for you when the alcoholic, recovering or not, may be unable to assist you with your challenges. The support of Al-Anons will become your *strength*.

There is an adage, you can't squeeze blood out of a turnip, and a country-western song that wails the message not to "look for love in all the wrong places." If you are trying to do this metaphorically, then come to Al-Anon, where God can help you. May this year be the year you decide to choose FREE not FEAR!

———

NOTHING HAPPENS IN GOD'S WORLD BY MISTAKE BY RUTH MITCHELL

After almost two decades in the program, my husband and I joke a lot about the dysfunction of our relationship. Like how we don't listen to each other, which is often the case. Setting all our disagreements aside, we will celebrate our thirtieth anniversary at the end of March. This is truly a miracle, considering our lives were disrupted by the insidious creeping in of the progressive disease of alcoholism.

But something that came out of my husband's mouth a few years back has changed my life. It's a quote from the *Big Book*. He could tell you what page to find it on, I'm sure. But what he said and what I heard has become a tenet for me to live by. It's very simple, really: "Nothing happens in God's world by mistake."

Wow, this simple truth puts a lot of things in perspective and makes sense out of a whole lot of circumstances in my life, because I can't see around corners.

For instance, if I lose my job, I have the opportunity to explore my options and find a better job than the one I had before. If I break my arm, I get the opportunity to come to have a better understanding and compassion for someone with only one arm. If I get my heart broken in love, I have the opportunity to discover something about myself that I might never otherwise know.

And yes, if I marry an alcoholic or addict, I have a great opportunity for finding a way of life that is much more fulfilling than if I had not been so challenged.

Okay, it's a little easier, no it's a lot easier, to see now with hindsight, but having the 12 Steps, the strength of the group, and the sponsorship that I have both given and received; these have been gifts that far outweigh the enormous pain I endured when I was the prisoner of my circumstances as I watched a loved one slowly drink himself to death. An even greater gift has been to gain this understanding that absolutely "nothing happens in God's world by mistake."

I am no theologian, and I don't know why bad things happen to good people. I don't know why there is suffering, violence, and pestilence in the world, but I do know if I live a faith-based life with the confidence that "God could and would if He were sought," then I don't have to live in fear. Yes, I am truly powerless over much, but by relying on my all-powerful higher power, I can live each day knowing that I will benefit in some way from each experience I encounter.

From the moment we are born, the fact is that we are dying. I believe we have the opportunity to experience both heaven and hell right here in this brief time we are on earth. If we can accept the power that is there for the asking, if we can let go of the idea our will is to be sought at all costs, then we can choose heaven. If we are confused and think we are the one in charge, then we truly will experience frustration and roadblocks at every turn.

The paradox of my life was that I sought freedom at all costs, and yet it wasn't until I accepted that God was in charge of my destiny that I truly experienced freedom. When I let go of the alcoholic and placed him mentally in God's hands, then he was able to get sober and I was able to focus on making my life better.

We have so many choices, but living within the life-sucking parameters of alcoholism, we lose sight of this. We have a choice; which will you choose? Will you choose to believe that God will take care of you, or will you choose to think you must shoulder all the weight of the world?

I can guarantee you, you do not have the strength to hold the world up; it will crush you. Your future hangs in the balance of this decision, but just to let you know: I have come to believe that nothing happens in God's world by mistake, and if a stubborn, independent person such as me can grasp this concept, you can too.

Now that you know what Al-Anon is all about, take the pop quiz (appendix 4) and see if it's about you.

CHAPTER THREE

Christ-Centered Programs on the Rise

The time has come, and from all over the world the faithful arrive. They fill the cavernous worship center at California's Saddleback Church, and, murmuring with anticipation, they wait.

Then, with hands held high, the percussionist, barely visible behind his drum kit, clicks his sticks, and the "World's Most Dangerous Recovery Band," through condo-sized speakers, fills the air with sound.

Three thousand wildly cheering believers, most of them recovering addicts, many of them tattooed and some with pierced ears, noses, and tongues, jump to their feet. Not your usual Sunday church crowd, perhaps, but no less devout.

It's a glorious morning, and this is the opening salvo of the annual Christ-centered Celebrate Recovery (CR) Summit meeting at pastor Rick Warren's twenty-thousand-member church in the heart of Orange County, California.

Founded more than twenty years ago at Saddleback by Warren and staff member John Baker, Celebrate Recovery has become an international program well worth the attention of those suffering from addictions.

During their three days at the Summit meeting, visitors learn a lot and they will have fun: They will dine at the Celebrate Recovery Barbeque, with its "Recovery Burgers," "60-Day Chips," "12-Step Chicken," "Serenity Sausage," "Willpower Pickles," and the ever-popular "Keep-Coming-Back Onions."

They will share box lunches and gallons of coffee at umbrella-shaded tables or stretched out on the grass. And later, they will attend an evening concert featuring New Zealand's electrifying Parachute Band.

This glimpse of Celebrate Recovery reveals a fervent and hip addition to what Christians have become used to over the years with the Salvation Army, Union Rescue Mission, and more conventional church fare.

The Celebrate Recovery ministry is similar to Alcoholics Anonymous and Al-Anon 12-Step programs in its approach to recovery. CR also has 12 Steps (appendix 3), which are almost the same as AA's but, unlike AA, its spiritual focus is specifically on Jesus Christ rather than "God" or a "higher power." AA also focuses exclusively on alcoholism, whereas CR deals with a variety of "addictions, hurts, and hang-ups."

Seventeen thousand churches worldwide now support CR programs. In contrast, AA has more than one hundred thousand meeting locations around the world, many of them in rooms provided by churches.

Visitors to Saddleback come to further their own recovery and to learn how to better encourage others back home to do the same. To the extent they succeed, they believe, individuals, families, communities, and eventually the world will benefit.

As it is evolving, Celebrate Recovery ministries are also dealing with huge social issues like prison recidivism and the homeless, and adherents are joining forces with other ministries to address these problems.

———

THE PURPOSE-DRIVEN LIFE

In his book, *The Purpose Driven Life*, a 25-million-copy best seller urging people to follow God's plan for them and to serve others, Warren provided the spiritual underpinnings for the Celebrate Recovery ministry.

In the book, Warren says, "I believe great churches are built on broken people, willing to abandon pride, pretensions, and self-righteous posturing.

When we reach the end of our rope and give up our self-sufficiency, that is when God moves into our lives with healing and growth."

It was Baker, a recovering alcoholic, who came up with the Celebrate Recovery plan, sold it to Warren, and watched it flourish. As host of the annual event, Baker spoke at the conference of his own addiction and reaffirmed the goals and intentions of the Summit at Saddleback.

"For a lot of years, I was a functional alcoholic," Baker said.

He was also a fighter pilot, vice president of sales and marketing for two major food manufacturers, and accomplished much in other areas. By the age of thirty, he had reached an impressive list of life goals. So what did it matter that he drank a little too much? Only that it finally caught up with him.

"Finally, alcohol became the problem of my life," he said. "It was time to make a choice—to admit that I was wrong and surrender and begin doing it God's way or continue drinking. I chose the world's way and turned my back completely on God for five years."

Going through a thirteen-month separation from his wife prompted him to start attending AA meetings, he said. "And I also started to get back to the Bible. My wife and kids started attending Saddleback Church, and the kids asked me to go with them. I did, and that Sunday morning I heard Rick Warren's message and heard the music, and I knew I was home."

Baker's wife, Cheryl, who shared the podium with him, confessed candidly and with self-deprecating humor to her own contribution to marriage difficulties.

"I spent all my energy in masking my life," she said. And when confronted, she invoked the "codependents' motto," stating with finality, "I am fine and in control, thank you very much."

———

VALENTINE'S DAY

In the end, Baker took Cheryl to dinner on Valentine's Day of 1991, made his amends, and said he wanted to help and be a part of her life if she would have him. She agreed. Shortly after, they renewed their wedding vows and are now celebrating more than forty-five years of marriage.

Their son, John, is also a recovering alcoholic with over ten years of sobriety. He, too, shared the podium with his mother and father.

It was soon after the reconciliation that Baker began to work on implementing a vision that God had given him about recovery. He began with a thirteen-page, single-spaced letter that he submitted to Warren.

"I didn't know Rick very well when I submitted it, but he called me into his office later and said of my proposal, 'Great, John. Do it.'"

And so began the Celebrate Recovery ministry, which complements and does not replace the regular Sunday service at churches that offer it. It is more comprehensive than AA and the range of addictions it addresses.

With its "get-real" focus, Celebrate Recovery tends to be a much grittier version of a traditional Sunday morning worship service, and it is also carefully structured to make it a safe place for the needy and hurting to come, bare their souls, and recover. Most of those attending the Summit meeting were there either to start a new CR ministry or to learn how to run an existing ministry better, and everyone got an operating manual that included mission statements, organization charts, job descriptions, and other operating details.

While this focus on organization and policy is necessary, Baker says, the ultimate aim is recovery, which is highly personal and based on relationships.

Churches, many of which have embraced Celebrate Recovery, believe it is long overdue and very much what Jesus had in mind. But "getting real," at least in Purpose-Driven Life terms, is not to everyone's taste.

Some Sunday churchgoers and conservative pastors, possibly unwilling to disturb comfortable routines to confront their own dysfunctions, find the recovery message inappropriate.

Under the headline, "A Popular Strategy for Church Growth Splits Congregants," the *Wall Street Journal* ran a front-page story in June 2006 reporting on a split at Iuka Baptist Church in Mississippi over the use of Warren's "purpose-driven" approach.

"MADISON AVENUE" MARKETING

As reported in the story, dissidents took exception to Saddleback's "Madison Avenue" marketing, mission statements, and other business-style strategies.

A later story also included a reference to Rev. Bob DeWaay, author of a book critical of the Saddleback approach, in which he stated that, "The Bible's theme is about redemption and atonement, not finding meaning and solving problems."

A spokesman for Warren responded to DeWaay with a comment that, "Mr. Warren believes the Bible addresses sin and redemption, as well as human problems."

To those who suggest that the Celebrate Recovery message concerning addiction/recovery message is somehow inappropriate, Bob Wood, a Celebrate Recovery founding pastor at Fellowship Bible Church (FBC) in Little Rock more than ten years ago, stated at the outset that, "We're not a hotel for saints, we're a hospital for sinners."

Wood, who has since moved to a larger church in Las Vegas, is a recovering drug and sex addict himself and a Saddleback alumnus. He led FBC's Friday night meetings, which began to attract two hundred to three hundred regular attendees, many of them not regular Sunday churchgoers.

I was a leader of a chemically dependent group in the early days of the program at FBC and have attended the Friday night meetings ever since. Wood was a good friend, and we talked regularly about his ministry. He also led the FBC group that attended the Saddleback Summit meeting.

While Celebrate Recovery may lose the support of some traditional churchgoers, it attracts another large audience—the non-churchgoer. Drawn to the hands-on approach and redemptive message, the "unchurched" are flocking to its doors. At Fellowship, about half of those attending come from outside of the regular churchgoing body. At Saddleback, it's about 70 percent.

One Sunday, Wood took to the pulpit and spoke to the thousands of parishioners who attend Fellowship Bible Church to address the problem of addictions. His appearance before several thousand parishioners at the main Sunday service was not the usual. Historically, pastors have tended to tiptoe around the problem of addictions. Generally speaking, it hasn't been a popular subject simply because congregation members are often in deep denial and want to keep it that way.

"Everyone here has hurt others or been hurt by others. This is a place for restoration," Wood began. "Those in the congregation who think otherwise are mistaken," he continued. "The addiction numbers for churchgoers are the same as the national averages.

Here are additional points from Wood's sermon:

- Many think of addictions in terms of alcohol and drugs, he said, and indeed, they are high profile and devastatingly destructive. But there are others: Methamphetamine use is reaching plague proportions; children under age ten are using deadly inhalants; and prescription drugs for the sophisticated and discriminating user are gaining momentum.

- Eighty-five percent of the inmates of our prisons and jails are in on drug-related charges.

- For every drug or alcohol user, there are ten people in the wake of their storm, many of whom have become sick themselves.

- An estimated 100 million people struggle with the effects of codependency.

- There are 40 million hits a day on pornographic websites. Two-thirds are men and one-third women. As for physical, sexual, and emotional abuse, one in four women has been abused as children and one in seven men.

- There are an estimated 10 million females and 1 million males suffering from bulimia or anorexia, and an estimated 25 million overeaters.

How should we respond to those who are in pain and come to us?

"We don't want someone who will try to fix us or give us pat answers or Bible verses or clichés," Wood said. "We want someone who will be real with us, love us, and accept us. Maybe we want someone who will just sit in the mud with us for a while."

———

GROWING IN GRACE

Not every pastor is attracted to the Celebrate Recovery model. Take Don Blair, for example.

Blair, a recovering alcoholic and believer in the principles of AA, is an evangelical Christian who serves as "minister of recovery" at St. Andrew's church in Little Rock and is taking his message to the streets.

Like an apostle, Blair is a "fisher of men" who corrals panhandlers, prisoners, people in treatment, and anyone else he thinks might have a problem with drugs and alcohol, and brings them to church.

No one is immune from his attention—and that includes diners at the next table in a restaurant to whom he may introduce himself on a hunch.

Those who need help come to Blair's Wednesday night Growing in Grace (GIG) meeting he launched with his wife, Donna, also a recovering alcoholic, more than eight years ago. The meeting, which is basically a church service separate from the regular Sunday service, has a mixture of music furnished by a praise band, biblical teaching, biblically based 12-Step discussion meetings, some serious praying, and a meal.

"Almost every Wednesday night during an altar call, at least one person comes to Christ," Blair says, "and hundreds more rededicate their lives to Christ."

The altar call usually arouses an intense emotional and physical response, and this also occurred when Don and Donna were "baptized in the Holy Spirit in the spring of 2002."

Blair believes these concepts, among others, "put a stronger emphasis on deliverance and salvation than some other Christian churches," but he hastens to add that a diversity of programs offers a healthy menu of choices to those seeking recovery.

Many other churches are also addressing the problem of substance abuse forthrightly. The Assembly of God's Teen Challenge program goes back to the 1950s, just to name one (more about Teen Challenge in the next section), and there are many others deserving of respect.

Still, there are other churches that hang back and content themselves with referring parishioners to outside counselors or perhaps with making room for Alcoholics Anonymous meetings. One of the problems, Blair says, is that recovery doesn't sell very well when preached from the pulpit.

"Unfortunately," he says, "a lot of the people sitting out there don't believe—or else deny—they have an addiction problem, and they don't want to hear about it."

TEEN CHALLENGE

Jonathan L., at the time of our first interview a couple of years ago, was in his fifth month at Teen Challenge in Hot Springs, a "Christian growth program" for troubled men, most of them recovering drug addicts. At a robust twenty-five, Jonathan, no stranger to the more conventional drug and alcohol treatment centers, said he had never been happier.

Founded fifty years ago in gang-ridden Brooklyn, New York, by a Pentecostal minister, twenty-six-year-old David Wilkerson, Teen Challenge is one of the oldest, largest, and most successful programs of its kind in the world. It was launched to respond to murderous gang activities and soon expanded to help those addicted to drugs and alcohol and tranquilizers.

At last count, there were 178 Teen Challenge programs in the United States and another 150 in other countries around the world. There are three in Arkansas: one in Hot Springs Village for men, one in Morrow for boys, and a third in Russellville for women.

Most of the centers offer twelve- to eighteen-month residential programs designed to help individuals learn how to live drug-free lives. The programs are discipline oriented and offer a balance of Bible classes, work assignment, and recreation.

Most of them, supported by donations, are free or very low cost.

It's hard to imagine Jonathan, a healthy-looking specimen, with the barrel of a .357 Magnum in his mouth ready to pull the trigger, but it was that suicidal impulse that brought him to his knees and eventually into the rustic facility adjoining Hot Springs Village.

In that first interview, Jonathan, who grew up in Russellville, described his childhood and early teens as ideal. His parents, he said, were rock-solid, "godly people." His father, Randy, his "hero," owned a car dealership and his mother, Beverly, whom he "adored," was a housewife. Jonathan and his older brother, Lance, were close, he says, and got along well.

Jonathan earned good grades in school and was heavily involved in outside activities, he says, especially sports. "I was really into athletics—football, baseball, soccer, dirt bikes, you name it. I even wanted to get into motocross racing and make a career of it."

He played, he says, with almost manic intensity and suffered a variety of broken bones and more than one concussion. This was consistent, he believes, with his childhood hyperactivity, for which he took both Ritalin and Adderall, powerful and sometimes addictive drugs with potentially dangerous side effects.

JONATHAN'S DESCENT

It was probably when he was sidelined with an injury at about seventeen that his descent into his personal hell began with abusing alcohol and soon included opiates and other prescription drugs, cocaine, meth, ecstasy, and marijuana. By age twenty, he was living in his own apartment and had a series of girlfriends, most as sick as he was. One of them got pregnant but had a miscarriage.

During that time, Jonathan says, "I couldn't get out of bed without being high. And sometimes I would fall asleep on the toilet and sit there for eight or ten hours."

He supported himself in part with restaurant jobs, but every penny went to drugs, and he became a dealer of drugs, sometimes involving major shipments, to support his growing habit.

During these few years, Jonathan spent time in the Fayetteville county jail on DWI charges and made several attempts at recovery in Arkansas treatment centers, but they were not successful. Sometimes he would get off of drugs briefly, but the drugs would be replaced by other addictive behaviors, including anorexia and other eating disorders and "sick and disgusting" sexual fantasies.

It was then, he said, that he began looking at that Magnum in the shoebox. What saved him was that two young men came alongside and gave him a pamphlet on Teen Challenge. When he read it, he says, he knew it was for him.

"I didn't think I could ever get over my past," Jonathan said, "but this seemed to offer me the chance to be delivered from everything."

At 2 p.m. on June 10, 2008, he clearly recalls, Jonathan flicked away his last cigarette and walked through the gates of Teen Challenge. He hasn't had a drug of any kind since, and that includes an antidepressant he was taking.

Tim Culbreth, the executive director of the Hot Springs Village men's facility, which houses roughly fifty men, is an ordained Assemblies of God minister who has been on the job there for more than thirty years. Married with two grown children and a grandson, he is a graduate of the University of Maryland.

His parents were missionaries, and Culbreth, who has firm convictions and a warm and ready smile, considers what he is doing a calling. He and his staff of fifteen work long hours and many are on call around the clock.

Culbreth's domain is off rural Arkansas Highway 7 just east of Hot Springs Village. The plain wooden sign at the entrance reads "Teen Challenge."On the right-hand side of Walnut Valley Road stands a new Teen Challenge thrift barn and some of the offices. On the left is the facility where the men are housed.

A long, low building stretches along the left side of the road and another like it on a hill on the right. About a quarter of a mile ahead is a log chapel with a cross and huge piles of uncut logs surrounding it.

Culbreth calls the forty-acre facility a "campus" and the residents "students." The students are men—eighteen years old and up—who have taken a beating in life. For many, this is the end of the line. Nothing else has worked.

Those accepted into the program come from the streets, detoxification facilities, hospitals, and jails. Some are referred by pastors and counselors or are court-ordered into treatment by judges. They are for the most part difficult cases, and 95 percent have had problems with substance abuse.

———

NO SEX OFFENDERS

Culbreth, consistent with Teen Challenge policy, does not accept sex offenders or those convicted of other violent crimes. Those who are accepted stay at the facility in a highly structured and disciplined environment for a year to fourteen months. And they are not charged a dime.

Culbreth says, "They are here because they are severely dysfunctional, they can't hold a job, they have a poor record with relationships of all kinds, and most have been crippled by alcohol and drugs. This is usually not the first program they have tried. Many of them are really at the end of their rope."

The Teen Challenge message of recovery, Culbreth says, "is the development of a personal relationship with Christ."

Abstinence from alcohol and other drugs is a must, but the Teen Challenge Bible study focusing on Jesus Christ replaces the traditional AA 12-Step Program focusing specifically on drug abuse, which is also used by the Christ-centered Celebrate Recovery program.

The major recovery "themes" at Teen Challenge, Culbreth says, "are salvation, self esteem, an ongoing relationship with God, and the establishment of family and community relationships."

Conditions at the facility are Spartan. Four men occupy each dorm room, and they look crowded, but the students don't spend much time in them except to sleep. The dorm is kept cool partly because of the use of ultraviolet lights designed to kill germs associated with tuberculosis, sexually transmitted disease, and other afflictions common to the resident population.

The men are up at 6 a.m. They do their daily devotionals and go to breakfast an hour later. Chapel is at 8 and group studies are at 9. Lunch is at noon followed by work details until 4:30 p.m. and supper at 5. After supper, there is study hall and chapel, with some free time before lights out at 10 p.m.

Talking in the dorm halls is not allowed, nor are visits to other dorm rooms. Some TV is allowed—mainly sports and news—and a few visits by family members are permitted. After six months, students in good standing qualify to take two leaves—one for five days and a later one for ten days.

DISCIPLINE FOR RULE BREAKERS

When students break the rules, they are disciplined with extra homework assignments or additional chores, such as splitting the huge logs at the far end of the site. In some cases, a student is dismissed.

Since the students are not locked in, they may consider running away, but Culbreth makes it "very inconvenient" by locking up their wallets and luggage. If they are there by court order and they run, he calls the cops.

The fact is, running away or causing problems in the community is rare, while good citizenship is common. In 2003, the Hot Springs Chamber of Commerce gave Teen Challenge its Organization of the Year award.

"Our neighbors love us," Culbreth says.

Students work with the Senior Olympics, volunteer to help at sporting events, work on projects with local churches, and go into high-risk neighborhoods under a variety of programs. They also help residents in Hot Springs Village tend lawns, a service for which there is a three-month waiting list.

The annual budget at Teen Challenge, which operates under the direction of an executive committee and an independent board of directors, is close to $1 million. Contributions from churches, families, and individuals, as well as an annual fundraising banquet and some direct mail and other promotional programs, are the major sources of financial support.

Teen Challenge also gets a lot of support from its grateful graduates, Culbreth says.

Jonathan was a good student, and at this writing had been sent to a more advanced program at Cape Girardeau, Missouri, from which he has also graduated. Wherever he goes, Jonathan says, he is sustained by a favorite Scripture passage from John 15:7: "If you remain in me and my words remain in you, ask whatever you wish, and it will be given to you."

RENEWAL RANCH SPIRITUAL BOOT CAMP

The phrase "spiritual boot camp" has found new expression in the Renewal Ranch, a free, Christ-centered program for men seeking to recover from chemical dependency and other addictions on a ninety-four-acre farm west of Conway, Arkansas.

Renewal Ranch was founded by James Loy, with the support of a number of local church pastors. Residents participate in a six-month program that provides counseling, Bible study, and opportunities to serve others through community work projects.

They also receive the education, vocational training, and life skills training they need to become productive, contributing members of their families and society through partnerships with local employers, colleges, technical schools, and other community organizations.

At the conclusion of the six-month program, men may choose to remain at the ranch for up to eighteen months to continue their education, obtain employment, or begin a savings plan.

When the men arrive, they are given a two-page "Renewal Ranch Policy" to read and sign. Its rules include: No alcohol or drugs, no fighting, no weapons, no skipping classes, eight-hour work days, and no cell phones or phone calls.

Also on the list are limited contact with family or friends; no back talk to the authorities; and no gambling or stealing. Smoking is limited to designated areas; proper dress and appropriate attitude are expected at all times.

The Ranch has a four-thousand-square-foot bunkhouse, where the men live, eat, and work. Most have tried multiple treatment programs without success, some have been in prison, and all have struggled with a variety of relationships.

Loy, whose appetite for cocaine and other drugs put him in half a dozen treatment facilities and cost him over two hundred thousand dollars with no lasting benefit, knows where these men are coming from. He was just like them until, he says, he found Jesus Christ at a place called John 3:16, a free facility for addicts in Batesville, Arkansas.

Loy stayed six months at John 3:16 and left with his desire for drugs gone. His new desire was to build something like it in Conway, where he had lived and graduated from the University of Central Arkansas.

"Because Jesus paid the price at the cross," Loy says, the men are fed, housed, and ministered to at no charge during their recovery. Not only does Renewal Ranch offer free service, but it does not seek government support of any kind, including grants.

SALVATION ARMY AND UNION RESCUE MISSION: A RICH CHRISTIAN TRADITION

Actually, there is a rich Christian tradition of treating alcoholics and other drug abusers. Both the Salvation Army and the Union Rescue Mission have been pioneers, and both remain active today.

Founded in the late nineteenth century by William Booth, the Salvation Army is perhaps best known for its Adult Rehabilitation Centers (ARC), which began as simply homeless shelters in London in 1881 and now comprises the largest resident substance abuse rehabilitation program in the United States.

The Salvation Army provides housing, meals, and medical care, and the participants engage in work therapy, spiritual guidance, and skilled counseling in clean and wholesome surroundings. More than 120 Salvation Army adult rehabilitation centers are in operation in the United States.

The Union Rescue Mission (URM) was founded in 1891 by Lyman Stewart, president and founder of Union Oil Co. Originally known as the Pacific Gospel Union, members took to the streets in "gospel wagons" to offer food, clothing, and salvation to the less fortunate.

URM's one-year, residential, Christian Life Discipleship Program is the first phase to help broken men build positive new lives. The organization addresses homelessness in both men and women with a program based on "a solid biblical foundation" and also offers "addiction and recovery" classes.

CHAPTER FOUR

Mental Health Treatment: Often a Key to Recovery

Eighty percent of substance abuse problems like alcohol, pot, and prescription drugs are complicated by mental health problems such as depression, anxiety, bipolar disorders, and the like. In these "co-occurring" cases, both the addiction and mental health problems must be treated.

Most psychiatric hospitals have been doing this as a matter of course, usually with staff psychiatrists, but many substance abuse treatment programs have had to add that capability to their staff or make arrangements for it.

Going to free 12-Step meetings like AA, Al-Anon, and Celebrate Recovery are effective ways to deal with an addiction problem, but often medical help is also needed. It was in my case, although I didn't realize it at first. Turns out I had a depression/anxiety problem I was attempting to treat with alcohol.

The fact was, when I quit drinking, I didn't quit using the prescription drug Valium. I did cut way back on it, to about 5 milligrams a day, but I couldn't completely let go. It was like a dry martini in powder form. Or like smoking pot. Under the circumstances, I admitted to myself, it was an obstacle to my recovery.

I knew I couldn't keep doing it, but my attempts at stopping weren't working. So I called psychiatrist Dr. Harley Harber, who is himself a recovering alcoholic and follower of the 12 Steps.

On my first visit, Harley greeted me in his office at The BridgeWay hospital in North Little Rock, Arkansas, with a broad, welcoming smile and invited me to take a seat on an overstuffed sofa in front of a picture window framing the late spring morning.

I was there, I told him, because my sobriety as a recovering alcoholic over the previous six years was giving me little pleasure. And the reason, which I had been hiding from myself and others, I now wanted to deal with.

Yellow lined pad in hand, Harley listened and I talked while he jotted down a few notes. He smiled reassuringly and said not to worry. I would get off the Valium gradually over the next couple of weeks to avoid severe withdrawal symptoms. He said we'd work through it together.

We did, and it worked. Sure, I had some discomfort. Like jumping three feet in the air when somebody shut the door and watching myself momentarily age like Dorian Gray, but I soon recovered and moved on.

In substance abuse circles, in the Little Rock area especially, Harley's name is well known and even revered by some. He has successfully treated a whole lot of folks, and they have gotten well because they felt safe with him and could go through the often-painful process of sobering up with him by their side.

Karen S., a recovering alcoholic who had also struggled with an eating disorder in the past, said, "I get tears in my eyes thinking about all he has given me. I have a life today, so much more than I thought possible."

———

ON THE COUCH AGAIN

About twenty years after I called Harley to set up that first visit, I called to ask if I could spend an hour or so with him in his office talking about trends in substance abuse treatment today and what role psychiatry has to play. So we set a time, and I ended up on Harley's couch again—this time with my own notebook in hand.

Harley, who was by now the medical director for Addiction Services and on the general psychiatric staff at The BridgeWay psychiatric hospital, got his BA degree from the University of Arkansas and his MD from the University of Arkansas for Medical Sciences, where he also took his three-year residency in psychiatry.

He was the only physician in Arkansas to hold certification by the American Society of Addiction Medicine and board status in psychiatry and addiction psychiatry. In the mid seventies, Harley had worked on the Haight Ashbury project in San Francisco, and in later years attended Gestalt therapy training sessions both here and abroad.

Haight Ashbury, a district of San Francisco named for the intersection of Haight and Ashbury streets, became known as the center of the 1960s hippie movement. The late Hunter S. Thompson, an author and icon in the hippie generation and a frequent spokesman, called the area "Hashbury." (Hash is basically a more powerful form of marijuana.)

Gestalt therapy, on the other hand, is about helping people get rid of denials, facing the truth about themselves, and making healthy changes in their lives—not unlike a 12-Step program.

As described more clinically in Raymond J. Corsini and Danny Wedding's book, *Current Psychotherapies*, Gestalt therapy, founded in the 1940s, posits the following:

Most people operate in an unstated context of conventional thought that obscures or avoids knowledge of how the world is.

Self deception is the basis of inauthenticity. Living that is not based on the truth of oneself in the world leads to feelings of dread, guilt and anxiety.

Gestalt therapy provides a way of being authentic and meaningfully responsible for oneself. By becoming aware, one becomes able to choose and/ or organize one's own existence in a meaningful manner.

———

CURRENT STATE OF SUBSTANCE ABUSE

My conversation with Harley about the state of substance abuse treatment today was far reaching. Here are some bullet points from my notes:

- Increasing numbers of medical discoveries will help us treat the physiological aspects of addictions (brain disease itself), *but they do not address our character defects and lack of spirituality. That is up to God and us.*

- A deep and wide chasm exists between what we do and what we believe. The 12 Steps and recovery bring the differences into closer alignment.

- Impaired physicians and airline pilots have the best recovery rates of any groups—85 to 90 percent for physicians and 90 to 95 percent for pilots. That's because there are huge financial and professional incentives (they get to keep their jobs if they recover), and they are given adequate time for long-term treatment as well as significant professional support and post-treatment monitoring.

- Twelve-Step programs are excellent predictors of long-term sobriety. If you can stay clean and sober for a year, the chance of a "slip" drops dramatically. In the short term—less than a year—only one in ten 12-Step newcomers is there and still sober one year later.

- Even if you go to a meeting every day, it isn't enough in the initial stages of recovery. Remember, the founders of Alcoholics Anonymous (Bill Wilson and Dr. Bob Smith) spent a lot of time together. An hour a day is just a beginning.

- You have to get rid of the substance abuse problem before you can treat the whole person.

- There's currently not enough money to fund nationwide treatment programs that will produce recovery rates comparable to pilots and physicians.

"Today, treatment can give you a place where you feel safe and can help you get clean and sober while you are going through the Steps and other aspects of recovery," Harley said. "I just wish it could be longer term."

Shortly after we met that day, Harley left The BridgeWay to resume full-time private practice in addiction medicine. Word has it that he is fully retired now.

RON T'S STORY

For many, hospitalization may be the best way to go. An old friend of mine, Ron T., got better at The BridgeWay. Ron, now an airline pilot with many years of flying and sobriety, provides a vivid account of how his recovery worked:

"The circumstances that led to my last rehab are very similar to those of previous attempts," Ron begins. "I was broke, in bad health, and facing some legal charges. My attorney reached out to me in a personal way. It was clear to him that my troubles were all related to my addiction, and he offered to get all legal proceedings delayed until after rehab. I, in turn, reached out to an old friend who was in AA and related to him the attorney's opinion. He agreed that rehab was the best option.

"I remember spending my last five dollars on beer. It was a six pack of ice-cold Miller. When my friend arrived to take me to rehab, I was quite a sight. I came stumbling out of my cheap hotel room with my beer in one hand and a plastic garbage bag in the other. The bag contained all of my worldly possessions. I don't remember much about our conversation, but I do remember how good that beer tasted. Perhaps I knew it would be my last drink.

"My friend Lew did not seem to be shocked by my appearance. He smiled and said 'Hey, R. T., hop in.' I really don't remember the details, but somehow with the combined efforts of Lew, my attorney, and my family,

I entered rehab for the last time that very day. I was completely broke, but my family had some health insurance on me that I was not aware of.

"The BridgeWay is a beautiful complex on several acres just outside of Little Rock, my hometown. They have a nice dining room with a salad bar. The food is very good as rehabs go. I am an expert on rehab food. This was my ninth. They have a gym, a racquetball court, and a hiking trail. The staff is outstanding. They have real doctors and a twenty-four-hour nursing staff to monitor the patients.

"I knew my detox would be ugly. The doctors said they would help me the best way they could without giving me any narcotics. I was coming off of Dilaudid, a narcotic painkiller, and alcohol. They used Clonidine and Librium to help me stay comfortable during the detoxification process. It was certainly not painless, but I did survive.

"Clonidine is normally used as a blood pressure medicine. It was used in treating opiate withdrawal because of its effect on certain nerve cells in the brain. It tricks the brain into thinking it is being fed an opiate. This is grossly simplified, but this is how I remember it. The dosage must be fairly high to work its trickery. A side effect is that it lowers your blood pressure, which is what it was initially designed for.

"My blood pressure did get really low. I remember different people walking me around the hospital. They said they were trying to get my blood pressure back up. I also remember being really, really cold and sweating profusely at the same time. I don't recall sleeping, but I don't remember being completely awake either. This lasted for several days. I am grateful for the memory loss caused by the detox drugs. Judging from what I was told when I finally came to, it was very ugly.

"I have been through much more painful drug withdrawal. I had been through eight other rehabs. Some were easier; some were worse. I had been through withdrawal in jail without any assistance at all; the cold turkey method.

"I kicked morphine once in my mom's house using vodka. I stayed intoxicated on alcohol every waking moment for four days. This is not easy. It is difficult to drink vodka when you are deathly ill from morphine withdrawal. I vomited up more vodka than I drank. I would not recommend the vodka detox method. After it was over, I was off the morphine, but I had to be hospitalized because of complications with the alcohol.

————

A GREAT STAFF

"The BridgeWay's staff was great. They were not just one alcoholic helping another. They were highly trained professionals. Some of them were recovering addicts and alcoholics, but they were all extraordinary. They knew not to put up with my crap. They knew not to make me too comfortable. They knew I had been through this process many times, and they knew I had always failed to remain sober.

"The group therapy was similar to previous rehabs, but somehow they were able to reach me in a new way. Perhaps I was just more willing to participate in the process. I was growing weary of my plight. I had been drinking for twenty-four years, daily for fifteen. I had been injecting narcotics for fifteen years, daily for ten. I was tired. I was physically unable to continue my life. At thirty-nine, my life was pretty much over.

"There were also the other matters. I had no job, no money, no car, and serious legal problems. I was homeless and my family was furious. They had changed the locks on my mom's house so that I couldn't steal from her any more. I had been here before. I had gone to treatment before for these same reasons. I had always relapsed.

"In AA, they always say, 'Keep coming back.' In families, they don't. I had worn out my welcome with my family and all of my friends. Being a junkie is an extremely physical job. It's not for wimps. You have to get up early, stay up late, and be a junkie all day long. It is hard work and plenty of it. I was tired. I was also very old for a junkie. I also drank more alcohol than most junkies that I knew. I was tired.

"I have, for many years, pondered the question, 'What was different this time?' All I can say now, after more than twenty years of sobriety, is, 'I was tired.' Was my fatigue a gift? Are human bodies designed to absorb only a certain amount of abuse? I don't know. I do know that my experience at The BridgeWay was qualitatively different. I also know that most junkies do not get tired of being junkies until they have ended their short, miserable lives.

"I have come to believe that a power that I don't understand gave me the fatigue necessary to listen. What I heard was simply the obvious truth about my circumstances. I had been blocked from this by my addiction. It seems so simple now, but this truth was far beyond my grasp at the time and had been for many years.

GROUP THERAPY

"On day five at The BridgeWay, they guided me gently into group therapy. The group thought I was flaky and seemed to distrust me. I was flaky. My thoughts and moods changed rapidly. My words did not make sentences. It was as if my mind was not connected to my mouth. When I would try to communicate a thought, it would be gone before I could complete it out loud.

"This was quite frustrating. I began to get angry. Actually, I had been angry for twenty years, but now I knew I was angry. The group became more distant. I became more resentful.

"This cycle would have continued, but two things happened, I think. My words began to make complete sentences. The sentences were not quite complete paragraphs yet, but I was communicating. The second thing was that the group lightened up on me a little. I think the counselors had intervened and asked them to give me a break.

"Kim, a nice looking, blonde lady in her forties, befriended me. She was married with four kids. She would talk about her family frequently. In group, it came out that my father had died a few years back, and that the rest of the family had become estranged from me because of my addiction.

"Kim began to treat me as if I was part of her family. When they would come to visit, I would be included. She invited me to eat with them and to go on walks around the grounds with them. This melted some of the ice that had made me so cold for so long.

"The counselors thought I might have some grief problems associated with my father's death. They asked me to write a letter to him. I had done this before in another rehab center, so I was skeptical.

"That night, I began writing the letter. I am not sure exactly what my feelings were, but I wept for at least an hour. The effect was so profound that I slept peacefully for the first time in many years. I had not really slept at all since detox, so I knew something was going on.

"Gladys, the chief counselor, asked me to read the letter to the group. As I began to read it, the tears began to flow down my cheeks. In embarrassment, I looked up to see how the other addicts and alcoholics were responding. I thought for sure that they would be looking down on me for my weakness. What I saw was a room full of some really hard-core, cynical alcoholics weeping without any shame at all.

"This experience changed the course of my treatment. I felt like part of a group for the first time in years. I will never forget them.

"There were the railroad employees who had flunked drug tests and were sentenced to The BridgeWay by their boss: Dan, who seemed genuinely interested in sobering up, and Joe, who just wanted to do his time and get back to work.

"There was the old lady, Hailey, who had begun to drink after her husband died. There was a young man named Ben who had been the golden boy of his family but was busted for selling drugs at his college.

"A very large country boy named John from the Ouachita Mountains of West Arkansas was there with the rest of them, crying like a baby. Kim was sobbing the loudest, and placed her hand on my trembling arm as I tried to hold the letter steady as I read.

"When I finished reading the letter, everyone came up and hugged me, including the counselors—who had one by one entered the room as the situation unfolded. I was no longer alone. I was with a group of people struggling with the same problem.

"'We' is a powerful word, and it is used many times in the Alcoholics Anonymous Big Book. The concept of one alcoholic helping another is part of the magic that entered my life that day."

―――――

QUALITY LIVING CENTER

Dino Davis is an old friend who has been involved with recovery for more than twenty years. He's a certified counselor, and ten years ago, I tried to help him buy a building in a nice part of town for use as transition housing for recovering addicts.

At the time, Dino also showed me some wretched housing with owners who were exploiting men coming out of prison and treating them like indentured servants without even a pretense of helping them get well. He said he could do a lot better.

Eventually the purchase fell through, but a short time later, Dino finally did get some property for this transition housing. He began taking in some residents and, a few years later, got his license for it and invited me to pay him a visit.

Standing on the brink of the intersection of Roosevelt and Asher, a very rough Little Rock neighborhood, Dino surveyed with pride the treatment facility he had created on two acres of land to serve recovering addicts. It's rough, but that can be a good thing.

Dino and his partner, Curtis Keith, fashioned the adobe-style Quality Living Center (QLC) out of an older building on the site, a motorcycle dealership/car restoration shop. There was also a house that the owner, Ronald Colding, had donated.

The Center was licensed by the state in 2006 and opened in 2007 as a chem-free transitional facility. Accommodating both men and women, the Center began with twenty men on board. QLC offers treatment for substance abuse and mental health problems with a range of residential, outpatient, and transitional living recovery programs, and can house sixty men and women. (Davis and Keith have plans to expand that number to ninety.)

The partners also plan to buy two more contiguous acres before they are finished.

"Our dream," Davis says, "is to turn this into a combination recovery campus and vocational school."

The low-cost (in the $2,500 range), ninety-day residential recovery program is based on the 12 Steps of Alcoholics Anonymous and also involves life skills training, referral, and job placement assistance, relapse prevention, and court liaison services.

Davis, who has worked in the recovery field for most of his 20 yeas of sobriety, began his search for a place of his own nearly ten years ago with Keith, who runs the business side of the operation.

In May of 2011, ten men and five women were in the treatment phase and twenty were in chem-free living. There were also five participating in outpatient programs.

During a tour of the facility, Davis pointed out to me the homey features of the living quarters. We sat in for a minute at a life skills meeting, he acknowledged greetings from a couple of patients and a staff member, he signed a document that was thrust in his face, and we ordered lunch in the kitchen.

"We're like an extended family," he said with a smile. "Our residents are able to practice their sobriety in a safe, secure setting. And when they rejoin society, they will be clean and sober and able to cope better."

QLC also seeks out collaborations with other community organizations. The Centers for Youth and Families, for example, makes available its pool and exercise room to QLC's residents who are taken there in the facility's van.

On Wednesday nights, the van takes residents to the Christ-centered Growing in Grace (GIG) recovery program at St. Andrew's church. It also goes to the Wolfe Street Center for AA meetings and other locations for Narcotics Anonymous (NA) and Cocaine Anonymous (CA).

A SALUTE TO RECOVERY

Four years ago, QLC launched an annual event called "Salute to Recovery" and sent out an invitation to people in recovery or were otherwise active in recovery circles. Held at the Westside YMCA, it was intended to raise awareness of addiction and recovery.

There were several speakers (I among them), and Davis' singing group, Integrity, performed while people got up from their tables and danced with energy and enthusiasm.

Two more banquets were held at the Y before Davis and Keith moved the fourth annual QLC Salute to Recovery banquet to a larger, more attractive room at Little Rock's Doubletree Hotel. One of Little Rock's most respected citizens, Dr. Fitzgerald Hill, president of Arkansas Baptist College, was the main speaker.

Like QLC, Arkansas Baptist College is in a bad part of town, but Dr. Hill is making significant changes with his high standards and entrepreneurial approach. A man of strong Christian faith, Dr. Hill joined Arkansas Baptist College five years ago, and his impact has been enormous.

On a warm May evening, more than two hundred friends, supporters, and QLC graduates flocked to the banquet. Some of them gave brief and moving testimonials about their recovery.

Sharon S., a graduate who was among those who told her story, also wrote a poem, "My Journey," for the Salute to Recovery program. The poem begins:

I'm on a journey, back from Hell.

Drugs led me down a road I thought I knew so well.

It took me places I never thought I'd be.

Now I'm struggling, fighting, and determined to be free.

Sharon's poem ends with the verse:

My life today has great meaning, and this I'm able to share with you.

With each new day I'm able to think things through.

Life is a journey. It starts and ends with you.

Make a decision now. With God's help there's no limit to what you can do.

When Dr. Hill spoke, he prefaced his remarks by noting that he was no stranger to the subject of addiction. "My brother was an alcoholic and my grandfather was a bootlegger," he said.

Dr. Hill graduated from Ouachita Baptist College in 1987 and earned his master's degree from Northwestern State University, where he also served as graduate assistant football coach and later as a graduate assistant coach at the University of Arkansas.

He also served in the Operation Desert Shield and Desert Storm conflicts and was awarded the Bronze Star and Commendation Medal for his service. After the war, he joined the coaching staff at the University of Arkansas for twelve years before being named head coach of the San Jose Spartans.

For his audience largely of people in recovery, Dr. Hill offered words of comfort and wisdom, including these three quotes:

- "Every day I wake up and say, 'It's not about me.'"

- "To grow, you have to get out of your comfort zone."

- "Inch by inch, life is a cinch."

When the Salute to Recovery evening ended, the buzz among those drifting down to the lobby was upbeat, and the Quality Living Center brand name rose another notch.

———

THE OASIS RENEWAL CENTER

The Oasis Renewal Center, an upscale treatment facility on forty-eight wooded acres in west Little Rock, is also a new treatment facility that accepts applications from up to twenty-four guests—men and women age eighteen and over—for its thirty-day program and follow up.

With its log cabin cottages, main lodge, private dining facilities, and scenic walking trails threading through three pristine lakes, it looks more like a rustic resort than a treatment facility.

And that's fine with Carole Baxter, executive director of Recovery Centers of Arkansas (RCA), which purchased the site from The Arc Arkansas a year ago for $1.6 million.

Priced at $15,000 for a month of treatment (with follow-up care) when it opened last year, Oasis is designed to appeal especially to a young, fairly well-to-do clientele, but it is still well below the cost of a Hazelden or a Betty Ford treatment center and the pricier retreats in Arizona and California.

RCA has roots going back to the 1950s and a rich history with the central Arkansas recovery community. This is the company's fourth facility. Its first, Riverbend, on the banks of the Arkansas River in North Little Rock, has served thousands of individuals seeking recovery.

There are also two "transition" facilities under the RCA umbrella—Williamsburg and Steeplechase Apartments, which serve the needs of patients who have been through treatment but are not quite ready to be on their own.

Williamsburg, which offers an outpatient program and "chem-free" living services, is located in a commercial area of Little Rock within walking distance of shopping centers, bus stops, and many businesses. Steeplechase provides private, chemical-free apartments to those individuals who have successfully completed treatment.

Baxter is well qualified to handle the task at hand. She has worked both as a direct service provider and as an administrator in the behavioral health treatment field for the past thirty-six years. And she is optimistic about the future of recovery.

"People with addictive disorders," she says, "now have the realistic expectation of living a full and productive life in recovery. And family members now have access to so much more information about how to provide healthy support for a loved one with alcohol or other drug problems."

Oasis, which has a staff of nine headed by clinical director, Marci Rhodes, emphasizes 12-Step concepts in its recovery model enhanced by a strong emphasis on family involvement, life skills training, and other resources focusing on recovery.

Where there are "co-occurring" mental health issues such as depression and anxiety, Oasis will provide the necessary psychiatric care except for the severe cases that require more intensive care.

Similarly, where substance abusers have secondary addictions such as eating disorders, counselors will address them along with the primary addiction or, in severe cases, will refer them to treatment facilities specializing in these addictions.

A major criterion for admission to Oasis is that the individual be medically and psychiatrically stable. If detoxification is needed, Oasis will assist in arranging these services at a local hospital.

Oasis can also help with interventions by families and employers aimed at getting help for the family member or employee who is struggling. Family members are strongly encouraged to participate in the member's recovery, and Oasis has programs during and after treatment to make that happen.

Treatment services include both individual sessions with a licensed behavioral health professional and process group sessions daily. The groups provide an opportunity for peer interaction in working the first five steps of the 12-Step Program and the individual sessions provide an opportunity for work privately in more depth.

In the first five steps, as those familiar with AA know, the subject acknowledges his or her powerlessness over alcohol, indicates a willingness to surrender to a higher power, prepares a detailed moral inventory, and admits to God and others the exact nature of these wrongs.

TREATMENT ONLINE

Oasis offers a variety of speaker meetings, assignments, and skill-building exercises, and also taps in to an interactive, computer-based system providing behavioral training to individuals in its recovery program.

Developed at Yale by psychiatry professor Dr. Warren Bickel, who did further work on it with Dr. Lisa Marsh at the University of Arkansas for Medical Sciences (UAMS), the computer system includes over seventy programs, including effective problem solving, drug refusal skills, identifying and managing triggers for risky drug use, and managing thoughts about using.

Also included on the list are programs on decision-making skills, increasing self-confidence in decision-making, healthy alternatives to drug use, time management, sharing feelings, attentive listening, drug use and communication skills, giving and receiving compliments, and giving and receiving criticism.

————

MY FRIEND ROGER

I want to end this chapter with a conversation I had with another psychiatrist, Roger Amick, about recovery. Roger and I attended meetings together beginning more than twenty-five years ago.

On a hot July day a couple of summers ago, Roger and I sat in the air-conditioned sunroom of his attractive Little Rock home drinking ice water lightly flavored with cranberry juice and talking about recovery.

Roger was the new medical director for dual diagnosis (both mental health and addiction problems) at The BridgeWay. As I recall, he was Harley's successor.

Roger and I first met in the late eighties at the Cosmopolitan Club 12-Step meetings at St. John's Seminary in Little Rock. At that time, Roger had been through treatment at Serenity Park for various drug abuses, and was living at a halfway house.

I, in turn, had migrated a decade earlier from Boulder, Colorado, where I had publicly run up the white flag at a storefront 12-Step meeting. Both of us were enthusiastic about getting sober and beginning a new life.

Roger is a 12-Stepper to the core, and that plays a significant role in his psychiatric practice. So does his experience at Serenity Park, where Joe McQuany's program "reflected his deep and proper understanding of recovery," Roger said.

Roger sees his role with patients primarily as a teacher and motivator rather than a dispenser of pills. Most of the patients he sees with mental problems— like anxiety and depression—also have substance abuse problems, so when he is sure that they have been properly detoxified, he first talks to them about the nature of their problem. In the case of alcoholics, for example, he explains the disease concept adopted by the American Medical Association.

He also draws upon the 12 Steps for treatment of mental health issues, particularly in the case of depression.

"Steps 4 through 7," he says, "are very helpful in dealing with depression and anxiety. If patients are still depressed after going through these steps, I'll take a look at other options."

DETOXING PATIENTS

Before beginning treatment, some patients must be detoxified so they will not have seizures or delirium tremens, and Roger will prescribe Ativan, Librium, and other drugs to bring them down safely, but that's where most of the drugs stop.

Just as an aside on the drug issue, Roger is keeping an open mind when it comes to the new wave of drugs that act on brain receptors to blunt cravings, ease withdrawal symptoms, and dull the euphoric effects of alcohol.

"They may buy you some time while you are trying to get sober, and that could be a good thing, but they won't remove your character defects," Roger says. "We still have to work on those."

The fact that Roger, as someone in recovery, brings to the table a personal awareness of what addictions are all about should not obscure the fact that he has an impressive medical resume.

He was born and raised in Huntington, West Virginia, where he earned his BBA degree from Marshall University. Roger graduated from George Washington University Medical School with his MD degree in 1974, serving his surgery internship along with his anesthesiology residency there. After that, he finished a critical care fellowship at the University of Florida.

In 1986, he started a private practice in psychiatry in Dallas, and three years later moved to Little Rock, where, in 1991, he was awarded a neuropsychiatry fellowship at the Fort Roots Division of UAMS and established a private practice.

True to form, Roger, boils down his practice into words anyone can understand.

"The top four reasons patients come to me for help," he says, "have to do with their job, their spouse, the law, and the fact that they are just plain sick and tired."

In his medical director position at The BridgeWay, Roger spends a good deal of his time working with patients—most of them inpatients— on a treatment plan for their recovery. Insurance companies are balking at longer term, thirty-day residential care, and properly administered outpatient care seems to work just as well, if not better, Roger says. He has also boiled down treatment options into four categories: outpatient, residential, psychotherapy, and abstinence from drugs and alcohol (with or without a 12-Step program).

Keeping it simple is Roger's way. And that's the way the old-timers who were so important to his recovery and mine used to see it.

CHAPTER FIVE

Recovery:
The Importance of Relationships

Alcoholics and other addicts tend to be loners. I certainly was. In the end, it was just me and the bottle. And so when I was forced to go to AA, I was, on one level, relieved to learn that that there were 12 Steps involved. I figured I could print them up, take them back to the splendid isolation of my condo, and memorize them. Bingo: Problem solved.

I tried this in my first ninety days in AA, had a slip that involved a two-week blackout, and woke up more desperate than ever.

I had missed the point.

It's about working the steps, not just memorizing them, and it's about the people at the meetings and others seeking a higher level of maturity.

———

JOHN TOWNSEND ON RELATIONSHIPS

Beaten and broken, newcomers to a 12-Step meeting—like Celebrate Recovery, for example—are often heard to theorize that they have come to their disagreeable end simply because they made a lot of bad choices. And they see their recovery in terms of making better choices.

They have *a* point. Better choices will help. But it's not *the* point.

Dr. John Townsend, clinical psychologist, divinity school graduate, and author, speaking at the Saddleback Celebrate Recovery Summit meeting, said, "You can't 'choose' your way out of your problem—like having sixteen drinks instead of eighteen drinks."

The fact is, Townsend says, recovery is not something you do by yourself. It's all about relationships—both divine and human. While the 12 Steps are important, he says, you can get them anywhere.

As time goes by, the newcomers give up trying to be stronger and more disciplined on their own, and they come to Celebrate Recovery because they "connect. They come because they find light, and they live in darkness."

Addicts, of course, don't usually do relationships well. Ask any recovering addict what it was like when he hit bottom and chances are he will say, among other things, that at the end he was alone.

The news that it is all about relationships is especially dispiriting for the guys, Townsend notes, who are more at home with tasks and projects. So it takes a little getting used to. It takes getting out of your "comfort zone" to open up with perfect strangers.

I found the most recent hands-on expression of this idea—forming relationships as a key to recovery—at Saddleback church's Celebrate Recovery Summit Meeting mentioned in chapter 3.

Prior to adjourning an early session, CR founder John Baker gave three thousand disciples a "relationship-building" assignment.

"Go out and find four or five people you don't know," he instructed, "guys with guys and women with women. Introduce yourself, and share with them what led you to the Summit, what you hope to learn, how you got into recovery and submit a specific prayer request."

"Whoa! Comfort zone violation!" I said to myself as visions of kicking back with a cup of coffee and a newspaper evaporated. Nevertheless, I found four guys seated at a table on the flagstone patio, asked if I could join them, and they warmly welcomed me. Thirty minutes later, after sharing our fears, disappointments, weaknesses, and hopes, we were on a first-name basis and exchanging phone numbers and e-mail addresses.

Four new friends in recovery. Not bad. And an interesting mix, as it turned out. Rick, who had kicked a nasty drug habit years ago, had built up his construction business and retired, but he wanted to improve the quality of his sobriety.

Kurt was a pastor who struggled with depression and was frustrated and angry in his dealings with his church leadership, whose members were slow to support his programs—including Celebrate Recovery.

Jeff was a psychotherapist who was similarly upset with his church leaders, and Adrien, a younger man and a carpenter, was seeking a growing faith in God.

A BRACING ENCOUNTER

In our thirty minutes together, these men and I had shared intimate details of our lives, and we had prayed together. It wasn't exactly a high-wire act, but it was bracing, nevertheless, and it felt good.

However, on the way home from the Summit, I had what might be called a "self-sufficiency" slip, which found me jumping back into my old "I can do it myself" and "to heck with relationships" thinking.

I was with a group of eleven other people from Fellowship Bible Church in Little Rock and Benton, Arkansas, and we arrived at the Orange County airport at about 8 a.m. to begin our trip home. There had been a bomb scare, and a huge crowd had gathered outside of the terminal. Nothing was moving, and long delays seemed a certainty.

After about an hour, there was some movement back into the terminal, and as a former frequent business traveler, I began to calculate how best to get myself to the gate. I spotted a faster-moving bunch of people and joined them, leaving my group for what appeared to be greener pastures.

Alert to every opportunity to advance, I made great progress. Now, as I look back on my heedless race to the interior of a terminal where explosives had been openly discussed only minutes before, I think about it as a "Yosemite Sam" moment. You know—the one where Sam, lit match in hand, finds himself in a shack filled with powder kegs.

I arrived at the ticket counter with time to spare, only to find that the flight had been cancelled. I was told to get in another line, well behind my group (whose relaxed members, working on their relationships, no doubt, were chatting amiably). Noting my plight, they came to my rescue, providing me with an 800 number to call and a cell phone.

Next, they rented a van, and we embarked for Newport Beach for brunch, shopping, and sightseeing. When we returned to the terminal in high spirits—tanned, fed, and rested—for our 3:30 flight, the crowds had dispersed, and we sailed through.

I came in for some richly deserved kidding for reverting to my inwardly focused, task-oriented mode, but I won't forget the lesson. It is, indeed, all about relationships.

THE NEW YORK MARATHON

A steady rain was falling when I crossed the finish line of the fourteenth annual New York City Marathon on the afternoon of October 23, 1983. My time was four hours, seventeen minutes, and thirty-five seconds.

"Why," you may ask, "was a man of your age [I was fifty-four at the time and in my fifth year of sobriety] want to run 26.2 miles on a cold, rainy day in New York when you could be having eggs Benedict at Longchamps and going to the theater?"

The quick answer was that the New York City Marathon is special. This is Stallone's "Rocky" territory—a day when the average Joes like me—

not just the Kenyans—can finish the grueling race and become heroes if they're willing to train for it.

For a while, those of us who ran it were the Yankees in the World Series, the Giants in the Super Bowl, and the Rangers in the Stanley Cup playoffs. There are just not any fans like New York fans, and we were pumped.

But there was another reason I ran. I had been sober for four years by this time, and part of my program of recovery from the beginning had been to get out of myself, be with other people, and become more physically as well as spiritually fit. Running seemed to be a good way to at least make a beginning.

To some, my training schedule looked a little obsessive. Hadn't I just traded one addiction for another? Perhaps, but is that necessarily a bad thing? In my opinion, if it meant neglecting my responsibilities to my job and family, yes. Otherwise, no.

Also, I had lettered in track in college, and it was natural for me to begin running again. So I ran in my neighborhood and at the track, and as I developed my strength I began running in local 5K and 10K races to make it interesting. In 1982, I ran the White Rock marathon in Dallas.

Let me describe a little more of the 1983 New York City Marathon experience to give you a sense of how it feels.

When I started down the slope of the Verrazano Bridge from Staten Island, where the marathon begins, into Brooklyn, the sounds of the crowds cheering swelled, and I felt as if I were entering an arena—just like Rocky.

The New York City Marathon is an event, and it confers upon participants' momentary celebrity status. As we ran along Brooklyn's Fourth Avenue, children darted out to slap palms with us in little high fives, older spectators offered us water and other beverages, and whole families erupted out of windows to cheer us on in a variety of dialects.

Our trip took us through New York's five boroughs, beginning with Staten Island and then through Brooklyn, as I said, and on into Queens, the Bronx (which included Harlem), and then down through Central Park into Manhattan.

PASSING THE PLAZA

Near the end of the run, as I emerged from Central Park and turned up Fifty-Ninth Street, I looked over at the Plaza, that monument to romance, and I remembered the days of wine and roses.

During the late 1950s and 1960s, I had worked for several advertising agencies in Manhattan—part of the time near the Plaza, where I became overly familiar with the two-martini lunch at the Oak Room and other fashionable watering holes.

I stumbled past my old friend and on into the gray wet afternoon toward Columbus Circle, momentarily buoyed by the encounter. I could almost hear Mel Torme, above the screaming of my quads and lower back, singing "Autumn in New York."

There is camaraderie about a marathon, the kinship of a shared experience, which in the final six miles became almost surreal. Like John Cheever's "Swimmer," seasons seemed to change, runners seemed to age, and a penetrating wintry dampness overtook us as we struggled to keep it together physically and emotionally.

When I crossed the finish line, I heard a race official say sincerely, if not exactly accurately, "Great race. Nice going. Good pace."

On the way to the shelter offered by a fleet of parked, heated buses, I looked across at a young girl walking next to me. She was bundled up, as I was, against the cold in her aluminum foil "space blanket," and she clutched a single red rose, her prize for finishing. We both smiled. We had been in there pitching together for hours during the good times and the bad, and we may not have known one another, but we were close.

Once in the bus, I sat there in my Perrier shorts and New York City Marathon T-shirt, a pewter medal around my neck, exchanging knowing grins with my fellow runners. I felt great. Sure, my muscles were beginning to seize up, but soon I would get off the bus (backwards, because of those quads, as it turned out) and meet members of my family near the Tavern on the Green.

We would have that hot cup of tea I had been dreaming of. And maybe eggs Benedict.

CHAPTER SIX

The Wit and Wisdom of Joe McQuany

Joe McQuany, a Little Rock native, dedicated most of his adult life to helping alcoholics get sober before his death in 2007. An alcoholic himself, he was an active sponsor, ran a men's treatment center for many years, and added a women's treatment center days before his death.

Name a state; he has spoken there. Name a foreign capital; he has spoken there. Paris, Rome, London—you name it.

Books? He is the author of two—*The Steps We Took* and *Carry This Message*—and is one of three who wrote the widely circulated *Recovery Dynamics* counselors' manual used by treatment centers both in the U.S. and abroad.

As mentioned earlier, he was a founder, with two others, of the Wolfe Street Center for AA and Al-Anon meetings and was also a founder of the Kelly Foundation, which provides education and treatment programs for individuals and professionals.

Joe also was a leader in integrating AA meetings in Arkansas back in the early sixties. At his funeral I joined with others—black and white—in mourning his passing at the packed Pulaski Heights Methodist Church in Little Rock.

Joe helped me in my recovery beginning in 1979 and continuing for many years. Most recovering alcoholics in Little Rock know him best for his hour-long Monday night 12-Step meetings at the Wolfe Street Center—where newcomers and veterans sat in rapt attention while he patiently explained with chalk and blackboard how they could get well. These meetings have continued under Larry Gaines, his close associate.

Joe had a serious yet simple message, and he was also very funny— mostly when describing his own shortcomings. He frequently used the family car as a metaphor and often referred to his wife of more than fifty years, Loubelle, a woman of considerable grace and charm and a significant influence on his life.

———

WORDS FROM JOE

For those who heard Joe, the following excerpts from his lectures will be a trip down memory lane, and for others, it will provide a refreshing sample of his wit and wisdom and their relevance to recovery:

- First throw out the ballast. Then go up.
  "Everyone thinks change is based on what you're going to get, but change has a lot to do with what you're willing to get rid of—like a hot air balloon that goes up when you throw the sand out of it. A lot of people don't want to throw the sand out; they want to keep the sand and still go up."

- Practice—not theory—makes perfect.
  "There has been a lot of discussion about these steps, but they are simple, basic tools of change. They are based on one of the oldest laws of human nature; whatever you practice, you become good at. Whether it's baseball, piano, or typing, you learn that skill because you work at it. You can't go to typing class, learn the *theory* of typing, and become a good typist."

- The search for truth can be hard sometimes.
  "Another part of our insanity is our blindness to reality. There is a story of a guy who had two horses. It worried him that he couldn't tell them apart. So finally, he cropped one's tail, and he said that worked for a while, but the tail grew back. Then he thought he would mark one horse's hooves with chalk, and that worked for a while, until the horse walked through some water. Finally, his son got a letter from him saying, 'Well, son, I've finally figured out how to tell those two horses apart. I've discovered that the white one is four inches taller than the black one.'"

- In a maze, the mouse has the advantage.
  "When we are searching for a way out, we are like a mouse in a maze. You can put a mouse in a maze, and when he comes up against a wall, he will search for alternatives until he finally works his way through the maze and gets out. If you ever put him in there again, he will remember the way and go right through. That's how we do it, too. Our believing might be wrong, but if we believe wrong and decide wrong and run into bad situations, all we have to do is come back and change what we believe and try again until we are finally successful. One advantage the mouse has, though, is that once he makes a mistake, he won't make it again."

- Two different things—decision and action.
  "Three frogs were sitting on a log and one of them made a decision to jump into the pond. How many frogs were left on the log? Someone will almost always shout, 'Two!' My friend will say, 'Nope, there were still three. He just made a *decision* to jump. He didn't *do* anything yet.'"

- What makes happiness?
  "I believe the happiest an individual is going to be is when he is in this pattern of living, relying on God and on other people. This is the design of life—to rely on others, as well as ourselves."

- Freedom or bondage—it's up to us.

  "When we don't do the daily things we need to do to live and be free, when we don't face things and deal with them, when we don't admit our faults, when we sweep things under the rug, we give up our freedom. We are then in bondage, and this is manifested by, expressed by, all kinds of problems: alcoholism, drug dependency, codependency, and so on."

- Sometimes the truth hurts.

  "Sometimes getting self-awareness is painful. We've heard it said that the truth will make you free, but at first it will most likely make you miserable."

- Trading in good ideas.

  "We've learned that our lives are like a business; we have a certain stock-in-trade and our lives are based on what we have on hand to trade in. If we are trading with better ideas, they're going to bring better returns into our business of living. As they bring in better returns, then we'll buy into these ideas even more and make them part of our personality."

- Self vs. God.

  "I look at the battles that go on in life, and I look at the resentments and fears, guilt, and remorse, and how these things block us from God and shackle us to the self. Then I look at love, tolerance, patience, courage, and wisdom. These qualities have come from God and they are always within us. In our outer and inner conflicts, we can see the powers of self-contending with the powers of God."

- Praying for potatoes.

  "Somebody told me once that when you pray for potatoes, the next thing you do is go get a spade and start digging."

- Ignorance isn't bliss.

  "We do have self will—we can do what we want to do—or we can choose to live by these principles expressed in the 12 Steps. I think the reason more people choose to live miserable lives, indulging self will, is not because they are evil or bad or sinful or anything like that. I think they are just ignorant; they just don't know."

- Our powerlessness.

  "The truth is that many of the problems we have in life we can't fix. We are powerless over a whole lot of things…sometimes we have to say, 'I can't fix it.'"

- Letting go.

  "To illustrate the necessity of giving up, I often ask people the question, 'What is the first thing you have to do if you want a new car?' Usually, they say something like 'Go to the bank,' or 'Go pick one out.' I say, 'No it isn't. The first thing you have to do is give up on the old one.'"

THEODOSIA COOPER

One of Joe's powerful allies in the effort to integrate AA meetings in the 1960s was Theodosia Cooper. Together they traveled the state with their message of recovery, and four decades later, she was on hand at the groundbreaking for his Serenity Home for Women project.

Theodosia Cooper has an undeniable presence. When she walks into a room in her three-inch heels, heads turn, and people who don't know her whisper to each other, "Who's that?"

Theodosia is a "somebody," and when she arrived at the groundbreaking she caused the usual stir.

As Theodosia, then eighty, looked down from the outdoor podium at Joe, seventy-six, who was seated in the front row, it was a tender moment and full of meaning for those who knew the background.

Forty-four years ago, Theodosia was the psychiatric social worker who helped Joe get sober at Little Rock's state hospital. And together they helped change the course of treatment for alcoholics in the state, especially for blacks.

On one level, they made an odd couple. Theodosia, a minister's wife, had never taken a drink in her life, and Joe had been completely enslaved by alcohol. Furthermore they were miles apart in temperament—Joe, quiet and thoughtful; Theodosia, smart and sassy.

What they had in common was a strong faith in God and an intense desire to serve. And they were magnetic personalities.

THEODOSIA GOES TO YALE

After attending a symposium on alcoholism at Yale University the summer of 1961, Theodosia reported for duty at the Arkansas State Hospital in Little Rock, where Joe, a recovering alcoholic, was one of her cases.

What struck Theodosia about Joe was that "he was educated, and he wasn't angry or defensive like the other black men in the hospital."

It came as no surprise to her, she said, that Joe would become an internationally known author and teacher of the 12-Step program of Alcoholics Anonymous.

"He was a little too humble at first," she said, "but he really knew how to work with people."

Theodosia worked side by side with Joe in his efforts to overcome segregation at the State Hospital and in AA meeting rooms, and helped him launch Serenity Park, where she also served as a member of the board of directors.

Today, Little Rock alone has hundreds of AA meetings and is widely known for its "Little Rock approach plan" of recovery.

Theodosia's country-girl origins and rise to positions of influence and respect in the community is the stuff about which Broadway plays are written. Think *Hello, Dolly* and *Auntie Mame*.

Sure, she's got charisma. But that's not all. She's got a brain. And a heart. And there's a five-page resume with all the degrees and a long record of service and caring for others to prove it.

Born in Jennie, Arkansas, a tiny southeast Arkansas delta community, in 1925, Theodosia was orphaned at age four and went to live with an aunt and grandmother in neighboring Eudora, where she was raised as an only child, worked in her aunt's beauty shop, faithfully attended church, and went to the local schools, where she excelled.

In her high school years, she was class valedictorian, class president, student council member, president of 4-H, and also basketball queen.

During these years, she discovered her aptitude for leadership and motivation as well as compassion for the less fortunate of her classmates. "I always sat with the kids who seemed to be hurting," she says.

As for the boys, she says matter of factly, "I was a flirt. I could get anybody I wanted." Case closed.

———

SHOW BIZ BECKONS

During these days, Theodosia experimented briefly with local show biz, playing and singing with a group of girls whose specialty was imitating the pop singers of the time, both black and white—celebrities like the Mills Brothers, the Ink Spots, and the Andrews sisters.

After her high school graduation, she went to the University of Arkansas at Pine Bluff for her freshman year and then transferred to Arkansas Baptist College in Little Rock, where she graduated with a BSE degree. During this time, she also met and married Jobe Vaughn Cooper, a Baptist minister.

She began her career as a science teacher at Eudora High School, and in succeeding years, her bent toward helping the disadvantaged led her to special education jobs in Jacksonville and Little Rock. When she wasn't teaching, she took on social work research assignments in the field in St. Louis for the Catholic Board of the Children's Guardian and the Methodist Settlement House.

These assignments took her to some dark places where prostitution, child abuse, and drug abuse flourished, and this is where Cooper's concern for the downtrodden and disadvantaged had begun to focus on alcoholism.

During her working years, she took courses at a variety of colleges and universities—the University of Arkansas for special education for the deaf, Eastern Michigan College for special education for handicapped children, and the University of Oklahoma for special studies on poverty and program planning for the disadvantaged.

Then came the summer school for alcohol studies at Yale. It was attended by the leading scientists and educators in the field, along with lecturer Bill Wilson. Theodosia, who had come to believe that alcoholism was a disability and a social ill of major significance, ate up the course work and became a profound believer in the transforming powers of the 12-Step program.

She returned to Little Rock with a heightened concern for the suffering alcoholics in her home state and the resolve to do something about it. When she arrived at the State Hospital, she found that many of its operations were segregated. For one thing, she was dismayed to find that there was a separate ward for white alcoholics, but that black alcoholics and mental patients were thrown together.

INTEGRATING AA

Theodosia put pressure on legislators and other officials to reorganize the State Hospital so that all patients, including blacks, would get better treatment. She and Joe also set about promoting the integration of AA meetings and helping blacks start AA meetings of their own.

In this, she got some help from three white men—Charles Clark, who sponsored Joe for thirty-two years before he died in 1993, Bill White, and Neil Verdock—who began a subtle collaboration aimed at turning the meeting for blacks at the State Hospital into the state's first desegregated meeting.

It wasn't that difficult. The three men—simply, and without fanfare— began attending the meeting for blacks. Bingo. Desegregation.

Not everything went that smoothly, however. A group of blacks in Dumas wanted to start a meeting with the help of Clark in the local Masonic hall, and in their efforts to assist, Theodosia and Joe, traveling in separate cars, were threatened with arrest by state troopers.

Polite but determined, the two pilgrims eventually prevailed.

It took courage.

"I can talk, and I'm not afraid of anybody," Theodosia says today, and in her full regalia—including those three-inch heels—she still has the advantage, even at a very active eighty years, of being very attractive.

The two founded the first black meeting at Wesley Chapel across from Philander Smith College in Little Rock, and in the mid sixties, Joe started attending some of the city's white meetings.

After all these years, Theodosia, who learned the 12 Steps at Joe's quiet insistence, remains a devoted supporter of AA, which she says, "is as close to church work as you can get."

Does she go to meetings? Nope, she says, "They won't let me talk."

As a non-alcoholic, it would have been inappropriate for her to talk during the meeting. Also, while it could have been arranged by declaring an "open meeting," some probably just didn't want to get her started.

Theodosia, who retired in 1987 as administrator for the Division of Rehabilitation Services/Department of Human Services, may have slowed a step or two, but her zeal for service remains undiminished. She serves on many boards and helps on many causes.

JOE THE SPRINTER

Here's something his fans may not know about Joe: He once ran against world-class sprinter and Olympic (Berlin 1936) gold medalist Jesse Owens. It was back in the late 1940s, and a local promoter in Louisville, Kentucky, had arranged it. To make it interesting, the promoter also entered a horse in the race.

History records that Owens beat Joe and the horse, but it was a game effort by Joe, who was no slouch as an athlete. Besides running track, he played football, and when he left Louisville Municipal College, his number was retired.

These little-known facts about Joe come from his younger sister, retired Little Rock schoolteacher and principal Doris Norman, who spent some time on a bright spring morning in late February reminiscing about her brother.

Doris, widowed in 1989 and retired from her job as assistant principal at Joe T. Robinson High School since 1994, lives in a little yellow house with maroon trim at the corner of Izard and Seventeenth streets in Little Rock. Back in the 1950s, the house was a way station for Joe on his path to recovery. More about that in a minute.

Surrounded by pictures of her family and former students, along with papers associated with various projects and some sheet music, Doris says that she has a full life. She plays the piano, does volunteer work for St Paul's United Methodist Church and her sorority (she is a Philander Smith College graduate), and recently took up quilting. She is also a vigorous user of e-mail and communicates with many of her old students, family, and other friends.

She and her Methodist minister husband, Varnell, moved into their new home in 1951, the year they were married, and they raised their three children—Varnell Jr., Mark, and Cassandra—there.

In 1958, Joe, acutely alcoholic and on the run, was out of friends and most of his relatives when he remembered he had a sister in Little Rock who might take him in. He packed a pathetic suitcase and headed south.

When he arrived at Doris' house, she recalls, "He said he was having back trouble and asked if he could stay with us. We said 'yes,' and for the next year he cooked for us and babysat our children."

———

LOUBELLE WILKINS

During his stay, Doris, organist at her husband's church, had an inquiry about Joe from fellow churchgoer Loubelle Wilkins. Loubelle and Joe were introduced, sparks flew, and three months later they were married.

Following the marriage, Joe continued to drink, and on more than one occasion he came to Doris and asked her to chain him to his old bed so he couldn't go to the liquor store. Finally, in 1962, he capitulated.

"Doris," Joe said, "I am sick. I have a disease, and I am going to do something about it." Then he left, with Doris watching him out the window.

"I saw him walking down Seventeenth Street," she said, "and I thought to myself, 'He is going to the State Hospital.' And that's where he ended up."

Loubelle, as well as Theodosia and Doris, all played key roles in his recovery and help us understand why his Serenity Home for Women was so important to him.

———

ADDICTION IN WOMEN

As he surveyed the landscape of society and saw the rise of substance abuse in women, the decline of families and the mistreatment of children, Joe McQuany knew he was right about the need for a women's treatment center at Serenity Park.

"The disease of addiction is growing at an alarming rate in the female population and continues to be overlooked by society," Joe said. "Women have always been the nucleus of the family and community, and the disease of addiction adversely affects the lives of the family and especially those of the children. Children are being raised in the middle of the disease process."

Martha A. Morrison MD, writing on women alcoholics in the back of McQuany's 395-page *Recovery Dynamics Manual*, says, "The increase in the number of women suffering from chemical abuse continues to occur… between 4 to 7 million of the 10 to 20 million problem drinkers and alcoholics in America today are women."

The National Institute on Alcohol Abuse and Alcoholism (NIAAA) in its publication, *Alcohol: a Woman's Health Issue*, provides support for Joe's claim that alcoholism is more damaging to women than to men and that women hide their alcoholism better.

Even in small amounts, alcohol affects women differently than men. In some ways, heavy drinking is much riskier for women than it is for men, according to the NIAAA.

Dr. David J. Hansen, in his paper entitled "Drinking: Men and Women Are Unequal," adds some specifics. He says not even men and women of the same height and weight experience the same effects from consuming identical amounts of alcohol.

Women are affected by alcohol more rapidly because they tend to have a higher proportion of body fat than men. As fat cannot absorb alcohol, the alcohol is concentrated at higher levels in the blood. Women also have less of a gastric, or stomach, enzyme (dehydrogenase) that metabolizes or breaks down alcohol before it enters the bloodstream. Because of this, women absorb up to nearly 30 percent more alcohol into their bloodstream than men of the same height and weight who drink the same amount of alcohol.

Women are also usually shorter and lighter than men, further concentrating the alcohol in their blood. Therefore, when women of average size consume one alcoholic drink, it has almost the same effect as two for the average-size man. If women eat little or skip food entirely, that compounds the effects of drinking alcohol. Hormone changes during the menstrual cycle can also affect alcohol metabolism adversely, increasing the impact of alcohol.

The bottom line is that a woman who hopes to "hold her own" in drinking against a man is putting herself at great risk.

Although men and women are unequal when it comes to being affected by alcohol, that's not true of alcoholic beverages themselves. Standard drinks of beer, wine, or distilled spirits all contain equivalent amounts of alcohol…they're all the same to the Breathalyzer, a device for estimating blood alcohol content (BAC).

Social Drinkers, those who enjoy an occasional drink should, even so, know their limit.

If you're not sure what that is, go to the Drink Wheel website, which will give a projected BAC based on your gender, weight, and quantity of alcohol consumed. For example, if you are a 120-pound woman who consumes two dry martinis in an hour, the Drink Wheel indicates that you will have a BAC of .09, enough to convict you of a DUI in every state.

Here are six suggestions for social drinkers to reduce the risk of overdoing it and hurting yourself or someone else.

- Eat while you drink. Food—especially that with high protein, such as meat, cheese, and peanuts—will help slow the absorption of alcohol into your body.

- Sip, don't gulp, your drinks.

- Don't participate in "chugging" contests or other drinking games.

- Accept a drink only when you really want one.

- Keep active; don't just sit around and drink.

- Beware of unfamiliar drinks.

———

HEAVY DRINKING

An estimated 5.3 million women in the United States drink in a way that threatens their health, safety, and general well-being, according to the NIAAA. A strong case can be made that heavy drinking is more risky for women than men:

- Heavy drinking increases a woman's risk of becoming a victim of violence and sexual assault.

- Drinking over the long term is more likely to damage a woman's health than a man's, even if the woman has been drinking less alcohol or for a shorter length of time than the man.

The health effects of alcohol abuse and alcoholism are serious. Some specific health problems include:

- *Alcoholic liver disease:* Women are more likely than men to develop alcoholic hepatitis (liver inflammation) and to die from cirrhosis.

- *Brain disease:* Most alcoholics have some loss of mental function, reduced brain size, and changes in the function of brain cells. Research suggests that women are more vulnerable than men to alcohol-induced brain damage.

- *Cancer:* Many studies report that heavy drinking increases the risk of breast cancer. Alcohol also is linked to cancers of the digestive track and of the head and neck (the risk is especially high in smokers who also drink susceptible to alcohol-related heart disease, even though women heavily).

- *Heart disease:* Chronic, heavy drinking is a leading cause of cardiovascular disease. Among heavy drinkers, women are more susceptible to alcohol-related heart disease, even though women drink less alcohol over a lifetime than men.

GRAND OPENING

Not one to take the sad fact of women's vulnerability lying down, Joe could take comfort at the grand opening of his new center. On that brisk November day just after Thanksgiving in 2007, the women began to come out of the cold and into the welcoming, sunlit, yellow lobby of his brand new Serenity Home for Women. They sought recovery and a new life, and soon twenty of them would be living in the semi-private rooms.

In the days prior to their arrival, Serenity Park board member and chief fundraiser Dianne McGeorge, beaming with anticipation, had put the finishing touches on the lobby décor by arranging the flowers and straightening the paintings.

Acting as host was the chief financial officer of Serenity Park, Billy DeLuca, part of the management team for many years and a close friend of Joe's. It was a relationship that significantly deepened in the last five years of Joe's life.

Deluca, speaking to the hushed crowd, said that Joe, in his wheelchair, had made his "office" under the beech tree on the park grounds while the project unfolded and had maintained from the outset that "God's grace is sufficient. Billy, it's gonna be OK."

On his last day at Serenity Park, before he left for the hospital where he died, McQuany, joined by Deluca, went for a last look at Serenity Home for Women. "Joe," Deluca said, "stopped his wheelchair at the door and told me to go in while he waited outside. That was humility."

Joe's last project just before he died was the Serenity Home for Women, and it pleased him greatly. It was part of the tapestry of a life characterized by service to others and to God. As he famously said, "I believe the happiest an individual is going to be is when he is in this pattern of living, relying on God and on other people."

CHAPTER SEVEN

Please, Parents:
Talk to Your Children More!

"My neighbor's son died the other day. He was a beautiful kid only twenty-one years into this world. Police and ambulance sirens blared as they raced up our street in an effort to revive him, but the sirens served only as an alarm that a life had been extinguished much too soon."

Steve Straessle, principal at Catholic High School for Boys in Little Rock, wrote these moving words about a young student's death several years ago, and we ask ourselves, "How on earth are we to respond as parents to tragedies like these?"

The simple answer is that parents must talk to their kids more and be more aware of what they are doing. It will cut the odds against them in half. I'll provide more specifics later on, but let us first contemplate Straessle's account of the tragedy of this young man.

The boy's parents are constantly soggy-eyed now, and they busy themselves in the yard in the hope that physical exhaustion will somehow exorcise the pain in their souls.

The boy's father was mowing the yard when I pulled up next to him. I was backing out of my driveway, and the car was filled to the brim with my five kids and their mother. I almost felt guilty as he peered in the back window and caught a glimpse of the activity and promise belted into the seats.

I told him how sorry I was for his loss. My wife quietly began sobbing when she saw my neighbor's face. My neighbor said simply, "He was a good boy; he just had a problem."

My neighbor's son was killed by ingesting drugs that should never have been in his body. There's no use in detailing the slow path of the boy's addiction or in describing the pharmaceutical noose he had wrapped around his neck. The boy's father had responded to the tragedy of a lifetime with great candor and great simplicity. That candor disturbed me.

I've spent the last thirteen years of my life trying to tap into the teenage mind. I feel like a miner constantly picking away at gray matter and rejoicing when I find pieces that hold unspeakable value, dusting off those pieces that might hold promise, and chucking those pieces that have had all the precious minerals torn and wasted by unseen hands.

I speak often with my counterpart at Little Rock Central High School, Nancy Rousseau. We compare notes, trade stories, and try to inspire each other to carry on in the face of adversity.

———

WE WORRY

We represent two extraordinary and storied learning institutions. We're both keenly aware of the unique histories of our schools and the extraordinary parades of personalities who have frequented our buildings. We are often in awe of the accomplishments of our alumni. We are often humbled by the desires of our students. And, we both worry.

We both worry because we're convinced there must be a way to address the root of problems that tend to wrap themselves like boa constrictors and begin a slow, tight squeeze around our children. How can we help parents and their kids? How can we rattle cages without sounding like alarmists? How can we prevent another untimely, soul-bending visit to a funeral home?

Unfortunately, we know what we're up against. You see, drugs and alcohol are waiting for your children. Like predators, drugs and alcohol wait until your son or daughter feels depressed. They wait for your son to get angry and your daughter to desire popularity. They wait for the perfect scenario to spring upon your young ones and offer them a moment of feeling good, of belonging, of leaving reality for a few moments.

The mother of all weapons in fighting drugs and alcohol is just that...a mother and a father. A teacher, a counselor, or a principal. A trusted friend.

The resiliency of the drug culture with younger kids is baffling. The pervasive use of alcohol by teens is mystifying. Nancy and I worry because we have yet to find the words to appropriately articulate just what seems to happen again and again to many of our city's youth.

We have yet to find the perfect parent (and God knows we're far from it ourselves) but we have learned a thing or two from some exceptional individuals who have taught us to embark upon creating a culture of respect for one's body as opposed to a culture of destruction of one's persona.

We've both seen death in our time as educators. We've seen beautiful girls carried to graves by handsome young men. We've seen star athletes leave the playing field for the last time. We've seen the popular kids, the outsiders, the inner city kids, the suburban kids, the academics, and the apathetic brought low by all too early visits with tragedy. We've both seen how life extinguished can affect an entire student body.

———

EMOTIONAL DEATH

And then, we think again. Sometimes even more profound than death in the physical sense is death in the emotional sense. We've seen boys and girls who ingest substances in the hope of altering their personalities or their mental states or their social status. And we wonder where it's all going.

We've asked each other aloud, "Do their parents know what's going on? Do they have a clue as to what we see and hear? Surely they must not; otherwise, they would have moved heaven and earth to protect their most prized endeavor, their offspring."

Most of the teenagers we come across are wonderful and well adjusted. However, some are suffering from self-inflicted flaws that are manifested by alcohol and drug use. No school's student body is above reproach. We have seen the smallest private school, the diverse urban school, and the most rural public school affected by drug use within its ranks, and what is most disturbing is the inability of parents, the inability of schools, the inability of the community to address the snowball as it heads downhill.

We don't have all the answers in dealing with this deep cultural flaw that is inflicted upon our kids time and again. However, we do have some hints that will undoubtedly help.

Drug and alcohol use are symptoms of a larger social problem, a problem that is glorified by those who claim that knowledge, entertainment, and belonging can only be derived from the bottom of a bottle or the tip of a joint.

Self-image is so important to high school kids. Belonging is more than a psychological cliché for some of them; it is a mantra that permeates everything they do. Speak to your children about the confidence that comes from doing right.

Let them know that souls are damaged by dropping to the lowest common denominator. And most of all, tell them you are most proud of them when they make a stand in a crowd. Because that's true belonging. Belonging to one's self.

Speak with city leaders about your desire for a community effort to come to terms with teenage drinking and drug use. Fight the impulse to wink at destructive behavior and the impulse to shrug it off with "kids will be kids." And remember, where your child is concerned, nothing is unforgivable.

———

HE WAS A GOOD BOY

I can hear the Weed Eater churning up dirt and grass at my neighbor's house. The boy's father is edging his yard and is drenched in a combination of sweat and tears. He takes off his safety goggles and flips the switch on the Weed Eater. He leans on the machine for support. And then, my neighbor begins shaking his head back and forth, back and forth so slowly. His lips are moving and while I can't hear him, I can actually see what he's saying. He's saying over and over again in a mantra that arches to heaven's breast, "He was a good boy...he was a good boy...he was a good boy."

Near the end of his book, *How to Raise a Drug-Free Kid: The Straight Dope for Parents*, Joseph A. Califano Jr. quotes a father who also lost a son:

Like so many parents, we didn't heed the warning signs. We found an empty beer bottle in the backyard, we smelled pot on his clothes, we found an unidentifiable pill in the laundry room; we chalked these things up to normal teen behavior, but we were wrong.

One day, I found his backpack sitting on the bedroom floor, the contents spilling out. Inside was the tie we had given him for Christmas. Only it was cut in half, and he had been using it as a tourniquet. Also in his bag were several bags of heroin and some syringes.

Tragically, Jim Bildner, the letter's author, lost his son to a heroin overdose.

Califano is a grandfather, a lawyer, and a one-time Secretary of Health, Education and Welfare in the Carter cabinet who began campaigning against smoking thirty years ago. He now serves as chairman emeritus of the National Center on Addiction and Substance Abuse at Columbia University (CASA), which he founded in 1992.

Shortly after that, he convened a CASA conference on "How to Stop Wasting the Best and the Brightest: Substance Abuse at America's Colleges and Universities." Among other things revealed at the conference was that about one out of three students in the nation's four thousand colleges abuses alcohol, the most popular drug among teens. Chapter 8 in this book deals with alcoholism in our colleges.

The principal antidote to drug abuse in our children is early communication. We've heard it before, but it must be said again: Parents have to communicate with their children earlier and more often.

Here are eight more tips from Califano's book:

1. Be there: Get involved in your children's lives and activities.
2. Set a good example: Actions are more persuasive than words.
3. Set rules and expect your children to follow them.
4. Monitor your children's whereabouts.
5. Maintain family rituals, such as eating dinner together.
6. Incorporate religious and spiritual practices into family life.
7. Get Dad engaged—and keep him engaged.
8. Engage the larger family of your children's friends, teachers, classmates,   neighbors, and the community.

Califano also provides a glossary in the back of his book to help parents understand which drugs are which and how they work. Here's a sample:

Marijuana: particularly damaging for the developing minds of adolescents. Marijuana can impair critical cognitive function related to attention, memory and learning.

Inhalants (popular with young teens and pre teens): Chronic use of inhalants can cause serious damage to the brain, heart, lungs, liver, and kidneys. In rare cases, abuse of inhalants can be fatal.

Ecstasy: Research has shown that ecstasy can cause long-term damage in the parts of the brain that are involved in mood, thinking, verbal memory and judgment.

Opioids: Taking a large dose of opioids at one time can cause severe respiratory depression and death.

When parents begin communicating, there is likely to be some push back from the kids regarding the parents' qualifications for judging others and other diversions. If you're stuck on any of the following, turn to the book.

- "You and dad drink wine/beer/a martini with dinner. Why can't I?"

- "What's the difference between your drinking beer and my smoking pot?"

- "So long as I don't drink and drive, what's wrong with having a few beers at a party? All the other kids do."

- "Prescription drugs are safe. What's so bad about using them at a party?"

- "How could marijuana be bad for you if it's just a natural herb?"

- "Lots of kids on the football/basketball/soccer team/honor roll drink and smoke pot, and they're fine."

- "Most kids who smoke cigarettes don't smoke pot, and most kids who smoke pot don't turn into drug addicts. I can handle it. Don't be uptight."

MORE INFORMATION

Another source of information for parents is a report, "Treatment of Adolescents with Substance Abuse Disorders," published by a government agency called the Substance Abuse and Mental Health Services Administration (SAMHSA). Its 125 pages are full of valuable research and commentary.

"The onset of substance abuse is occurring at younger ages," SAMHSA says, "resulting in more adolescents entering treatment for substance abuse disorders with greater developmental deficits and perhaps much greater neurological deficits than have been observed in the past."

Here is a sample of the points this publication makes:

1. **Adolescent users differ from adults and should receive different treatment.**
   Adolescents tend to have smaller body sizes and lower tolerances, putting them at greater risk for alcohol-related problems. They often use drugs and alcohol for different reasons than adults and don't see the negative consequences of their addictions as clearly.

2. **Programs of recovery should involve the adolescent's family.**
   The family has a possible role in the origins of the problem, and going forward has the ability to change the youth's environment to suit his [or her] recovery. Also, family members usually have problems of their own that may profitably be addressed.

3. **Assessment should be continuous**.
   A program for the adolescent's recovery must begin with an assessment of where he or she is today, along with a plan of action. As time passes, new assessments should be made based on the adolescent's progress and changes in his [or her] environment.

4. **The core components of most adolescent treatment programs are the same or close to it.**
   The main components of a typical residential treatment program include an opening orientation session; a daily schedule of activities (i.e., school, chores, homework, recreation); group sessions involving peers; learning how to resolve conflicts; negotiating agreements between clients and staff called "contracts;" attending an on-site school; and vocational training.

5. **Substance abuse robs children of experiences which help them become mature adults.**
   Substance abuse often insulates adolescents from gaining the experiences that are part of growing up, such as dating, marrying,

bearing and raising children, establishing a career, and building rewarding personal relationships.

6. **Adolescent girls often have different treatment needs.**
In their earliest years, female substance abusers tend, more than boys, to have experienced severe parental rejection and sexual and physical abuse. This kind of family dysfunction requires special care.

7. **A majority of substance abusing adolescents also need treatment for psychiatric disorders.**
Substance abuse and psychiatric disorders frequently go together (with the label "co-existing" or "dual diagnosis.") The most common are attention deficit/hyperactivity disorders, unipolar and bipolar depression, and anxiety disorders such as post-traumatic stress syndrome.

8. **Adolescents who come into contact with the juvenile justice system are likely to have severe problems in a number of areas.**
Substance abuse and the problems that accompany them—illegal activity, homelessness, shame surrounding sexual identity, and coexisting mental disorders—among those who have run up against the juvenile justice system require special handling.

9. **The risk of substance abuse in adolescents rises with a poor family environment.**
Lack of parenting skills, high levels of family conflict, and poor bonding between parents and children increases the chance in adolescents for substance abuse.

10. **Bad grades in elementary school can signal trouble ahead.**
Don't let bad grades go by. Find out what's wrong.

———

THE COURT SYSTEM

If your teenager has been using drugs for a while, the odds are that he or she has had a brush with the legal system.

With this in mind, meet Jack Campbell, Arkansas' Saline County juvenile probation officer. It was midnight on a hot July night a couple of years ago, and when the phone rang, he picked it up, knowing he would probably be going out. Sure enough, there had been a disturbance involving two boys—ages thirteen and fifteen—who are on the list of sixty-four juveniles Campbell was currently riding herd on. The two were chronic troublemakers.

This go-around, they were drunk and disorderly, and when a policewoman attempted to intervene, they assaulted her. She subdued them with pepper spray and took them to the police department, which is where Campbell met them.

The next day, Campbell said it looked like they would have to serve jail time at the Department of Youth Services (DYS) juvenile detention facility in Alexander, Arkansas, considering the charges: assault, intoxication, disorderly conduct, curfew violation, and resisting arrest. But Campbell was exploring other options—like one of several "ranches" around the state that are partially funded by the state as well as private sources. The decision would ultimately be up to the Saline County juvenile court system under Judge Gary Arnold.

Campbell, an ex-Benton policeman, is tough. He carries a gun and handcuffs, and while he is certainly pleasant, he is plainspoken and direct. He has zero tolerance for lying and violent behavior. During the past year, seven boys tried to get physical with him, and he quickly subdued them— without violence.

Campbell also has a heart for juveniles because his own son, J. C. Campbell, was, at age twelve, violent and suicidal. Afflicted with attention deficit hyperactive disorder (ADHD), oppositional defiance disorder (ODD), and depression, J. C. had always been difficult, but when he attacked his mother, Campbell knew something had to be done.

J. C. ended up in the Recover Teen program at Baptist Hospital in Little Rock two years ago, where he was assessed and put under the medical care of psychiatrist Dr. Gary Tharp and therapist Kamie Meeks. A combination of behavioral therapy and carefully regulated medication produced a stunning difference in J. C., Campbell said.

———

A "NOTICEABLE CHANGE"

"Three months after he came home," Campbell said, "there was a noticeable change in his behavior and he steadily improved.

"He is fifteen now, stands six foot three, is on the honor roll at school, and a corporal in the ROTC," Campbell says. "At home, he does the chores assigned to him and then some, and I feel very comfortable leaving him in charge of his ten-year-old brother. It's amazing."

Campbell and his wife are very much involved in the process of J. C.'s recovery, which he feels is vitally important in every family. They always make sure to know where he is and what he is doing, and they closely monitor his use of the antidepressant and other drugs prescribed to him.

"I never was a 'pill man,'" Campbell said, "but I believe now that, properly used, there is definitely a place for prescription medicine in recovery."

Coinciding with J. C.'s recovery was Campbell's decision to work with troubled teens full time by transitioning from his previous position as a Benton cop to his current post as juvenile parole officer. Campbell is one of four juvenile probation officers in the Saline County juvenile probation office, and together they handle over two hundred cases.

It's not just boys that get into trouble. At the same time he was dealing with the pepper-sprayed boys, Campbell was working on a case involving a thirteen-year-old runaway—a meth-addicted girl. She had fled the home of her father and stepmother, whose marriage was coming apart, to her real mom in Texas. Her biological mother was "a raging alcoholic" who systematically beat her daughter, says Campbell. When the girl said she wanted to come back to Benton, her father went to Texas in the dead of night and brought her home.

Campbell wants to help make the situation work, and has discussed it with the Benton parents, who say they want to make the marriage succeed. But the girl, who has been in short-term treatment, needs something longer, and Campbell is considering his options.

Then there's the case of the nineteen-year-old young woman who had been busted and stood before Campbell in his office, her natural beauty distorted by drugs. Asked what drugs she used, Campbell simply said, "She was addicted to everything."

Her father, Campbell said, was a hardened meth addict and her mother was an alcoholic. She was a habitual offender and had been in and out of treatment numerous times with no tangible results. She had also lied to Campbell—something he can't abide.

Campbell pulled out his handcuffs and told her to extend her arms, saying that she had "run out of chances." He hoped he could jolt her into confronting her problems—and into doing something about them.

It worked. She caved in, went through thirty-nine days of treatment at Decision Point in northwest Arkansas, and, says Campbell, "she has completely changed." She remains on probation and faithfully reports to Campbell. She also has two jobs. And whereas she was "cute" before, Campbell says, she is "beautiful" now.

Just to summarize the whereabouts of Campbell's sixty-four kids, three are at DYS in Alexander, one is in court-mandated boot camp at Camp Robinson in North Little Rock, ten are in treatment, and the rest are walking around—including one confined to his home with an ankle bracelet.

When asked whether we as a nation are getting any better at helping kids grow up and be responsible, Campbell said that parents, in his opinion, "are afraid to supervise their kids."

———

JUDGE GUNN

The Huntsville, Arkansas, high school gymnasium is alive with the sounds of four hundred gabbing teenagers when, at 1 p.m., the bailiff shouts, "Please rise!"

The gym is suddenly quiet, save for the scraping of folding chairs as the students get to their feet, and Washington County Circuit Judge Mary Ann Gunn strides purposefully down the aisle in flowing black robes to take her seat facing the students. Judge Gunn's drug court is now in session, and the high school student audience on this late September afternoon is about to get an up-close look at the administration of justice and the availability of grace and salvation.

This is not play-acting. It's the real thing, a point made clear by the arrival of five prisoners in manacles and horizontal stripes—mainly green for men and orange for women. Hobbled by leg irons, they shuffle down the aisle to take their places in the row of seats on Judge Gunn's left.

There is some weeping in the front rows, where many family members of the prisoners are seated, and, in the rows of students behind them, a few jaws have dropped and eyes have widened.

John is the first case on the docket, but before discussing the details, a word about what drug courts are.

A drug court—the first was implemented in 1989 in Miami—is a special court given the responsibility to handle cases involving drug-addicted offenders, offering them an alternative to jail time and fines if they agree to participate in an extensive supervision and treatment program.

In Judge Gunn's drug court, participants undergo nine months of treatment and counseling, attend 12-Step meetings, submit to frequent tests for drugs, report to the judge's office regularly, get a job if they don't already have one, and complete their high school education if that is an issue.

Successful completion of Judge Gunn's "pre-adjudication" program results in dismissal of the charges, reduced or set-aside sentences, lesser penalties, or a combination of these. Most importantly, first-term offenders earn a clean record and gain the necessary tools to rebuild their lives.

In a "post-adjudication" court, which is more common, the defendants have already been convicted, and they are offered removal of their conviction from the record upon successful completion of their treatment program. But this can take time, and, for its critics, it is not as satisfactory as a simple "no trial and no conviction."

In this context, Judge Gunn says her pre-adjudication format offers a better incentive to prisoners.

A HYBRID COURT

Circuit Judge Gary Arnold has been operating a "hybrid" adjudication drug court for over a year in Benton with what appear to be good results. Defendants in his court have already pled guilty and been sentenced, but the plea and sentence have not been entered and are destroyed upon successful completion of the program. Judge Arnold reports that of the forty who faced prison time and have gone through it, only five failed to complete it and ended up in jail.

Because the problem of drugs and crime is much too broad for any single agency to tackle alone, drug courts—both pre- and post-adjudication—rely upon the daily communication and cooperation of judges, court personnel, probation officers, and treatment providers. It is less adversarial than traditional court proceedings.

For example, Judge Gunn had an 11 a.m. staffing session with prosecutors, defense lawyers, and others in her office at Fayetteville's old courthouse building to discuss each of the cases scheduled to come up at Huntsville High School's court session that afternoon. Prosecutor Lisa Dennis and defense lawyers Mike Hodson, John Everett, and Bo Morton together reviewed each case on the docket assembled by case coordinator Peggy Burks and, with Judge Gunn leading the way, arrived at strategies likely to bring the best result for all concerned.

Drug courts vary somewhat from one jurisdiction to another in terms of structure, scope, and target populations, but they all share three primary goals: first, to reduce recidivism, second, to reduce substance abuse among participants, and third, to rehabilitate participants.

Judge Gunn's program gets results, she says: "Eighty-four percent of those who start our program complete it, and of that number, ninety-four percent are still clean and sober a year later."

With her particular concern about alcohol and other drug abuse in children, Judge Gunn spends a lot of her free time visiting schools to carry her message of recovery. At Huntsville, before convening her court, she walks around the gymnasium polling the students in the audience about their use and awareness of drugs.

"How many of you," she asks, "use alcohol or have been with someone who uses alcohol?"

———

ALCOHOL: MOST WIDELY USED DRUG

Of the drugs the judge asks about, alcohol gets about eighty percent affirmatives, marijuana somewhat fewer, and methamphetamine (meth) about 30 percent. When queried about how soon they became addicted to meth, most of the users in her program said they were hooked, "the first time."

After a few more questions and comment, she returns her seat at the long table in the front of the room and goes to work. She summons John, a prisoner who stands before her visibly apprehensive and chastened.

He has been charged with two counts of possession of controlled substances—marijuana and meth. He also has a history of using codeine, Valium, alcohol, and cocaine, and was charged with a DWI in Colorado in 1994.

"What's it going to take to get you clean and sober?" Judge Gunn asks John.

Pointing to about a dozen family members in the front rows, John replies, "the help of my family," and Judge Gunn motions them to come up. Family members gather around John, some hugging and kissing him and some weeping.

Judge Gunn is impressed. It is the type of demonstration she had hoped to see, and she comments to John that he is "so lucky" to have the support of these family members. She orders that he be released from jail and sent to the Decision Point residential treatment center in Springdale for thirty days and be evaluated at that time for possible longer treatment in a facility in Colorado.

It is definitely welcome news to John and his family.

Over the next two and a half hours, Judge Gunn reviews about thirty cases—including the prisoners. During this time, she scolds, cajoles, and praises the charged offenders who come before her.

To Paul, who gets a short reprieve, she says, "Your whole life has been nothing but drugs, and you will not make it in this program if you live with someone who does drugs."

To Betsy, who is pregnant and whose husband doesn't do drugs, she issues a stern warning, "If you are terminated in this program, you are looking at thirty years. Do you realize how lucky you are?"

To Laurel, Kelly Lee, Richard, and Douglas, who have completed drug court, she says to each with a smile and a huge hug: "You have fully complied with our program, and I grant state's motion to dismiss charges!"

"DON'T EVEN HICCUP"

To Nathan: "You don't work, and you have missed your AA meetings. I'll take your case under advisement. Don't even hiccup."

To Adrian, who is falling behind in his schooling, she says: "Drug court comes first in your life. You can do school and drug court at the same time."

To Ivan, she says, "If you test positive, I'll throw you in jail."

And to those in the audience who are in residential treatment, she says, "I think you'll find a whole new world out there."

Judge Gunn reports that 284 have graduated from her drug court and 119 are presently enrolled. Thirteen candidates are waiting to come in, and thirty-four are being assessed as to their suitability for the program.

Back in Benton on a fall afternoon, Judge Arnold congratulates five graduates of the yearlong program and directs them to the shredder, which will literally destroy their records. One, Steven, who had faced 225 months in prison for felony drug violations, elected to keep his record as a reminder of his drug-filled past.

"If I may," he said, "this is kind of an odd request, but I'd like to keep this as a reminder of where I've been and where I am today."

In contrast, Marie, a drug user for thirty-four years who was facing a ninety-eight-month sentence, went for the shredder. "I do believe it (the drug court) saved my life," she said.

Eric, a thirty-six-year-old former mortgage banker and cocaine addict, was looking at eighty-four months in prison when he signed on.

So what will happen to these successful graduates as they face life in the coming months and years? Judge Arnold hopes they will stay in touch and give one another encouragement. He is looking into forming an alumni group to facilitate the process.

LOCK THE MEDICINE CABINETS!

One in eight Arkansas adolescents has taken a prescription pain reliever medication illegally. One in twenty has done so in the past thirty days. And nearly 7 percent admit to using an over-the-counter medication to get high, half of them within the past month. Surveys also show that teenagers are more likely to have abused prescription and over-the-counter drugs than street drugs like ecstasy, cocaine, crack, and methamphetamines.

The abuse of these potent drugs can damage evolving young brains, and they are sometimes deadly. From 2003 to 2007, fifteen Arkansas children aged twelve to seventeen died as a result of overdose involving prescription drugs, seven of them from the pain relievers oxycodone and hydrocodone.

So where are these adolescents getting their prescription drugs? Mostly, as it turns out, from their parents' or grandparents' medicine cabinets. It's easy (60 percent of the teens say so), and it doesn't cost them a dime.

In response to the growing problem, Fran Flener, Arkansas' drug director, has launched a statewide campaign, basically on a shoestring, to increase public awareness of the problem. She announced the initiative in Little Rock at the capitol rotunda on March 12, 2011.

The thrust of the campaign is that parents, grandparents, guardians, and trusted adults have a key role to play helping the children in their care avoid the dangers caused by prescription drug abuse. The majority of teens report that their parents, not their peers or the media, have the biggest impact on their decision to stay drug free.

Also, parents, never give your prescription medications to anyone else for any reason. It's illegal and potentially could cause the start of someone else's addiction.

MONITOR, SECURE, AND DISPOSE

With regard to prescription drugs, the keys to success are condensed into three words: "monitor, secure and dispose."

- **Monitor**—Take note of how many pills are in each prescription bottle or packet and keep track of refills. If your teen has been prescribed a drug, control the medication and monitor the dosages and refills.

- **Secure**—Keep all medicines, both prescription and over the counter, in a safe place, such as a locked cabinet. Also, tell relatives, especially grandparents, to lock up or hide their medications. Finally, talk to the parents of your teenager's friends. Encourage them to secure their prescriptions.

- **Dispose**—Discard expired or unused prescription drugs. First, mix the drug with an undesirable substance, such as used coffee grounds, kitty litter, or dirt to discourage use, put it in an empty can or bag, and then place it in the trash. Do not, authorities say, return unused portions of prescriptions to pharmacists. By law, they cannot accept them. Many drugs should not be flushed down or toilet, where they may contaminate the water supply, but the list of thirty that can be flushed (accessible on the Internet) does include powerful drugs like Demerol, OxyContin, Percocet, morphine sulfate, methadone, and Fentora.

WHY TEENS USE

Gaining an understanding of why teenagers want to use prescription drugs is helpful. Here are the top reasons given in a survey by the Substance Abuse and Mental Health Services Administration (SAMHSA):

- To deal with the pressures and stress of school (73%)

- To feel better about themselves (65%)

- To "look cool" (65%)

- To deal with problems at home (55%)

- To feel good (40%)

Kids exposed to a high level of risk factors (such as availability of drugs, family conflict, parental attitude favorable towards drug use, poor performance in school, and depression, for example) are more apt to abuse drugs. By the same token, kids with a high level of "protective factors" (such as positive peers, religious involvement, academic accomplishment, involvement in pro-social activities, and strong family environment) are less apt to abuse.

———

THE GOOD NEWS[4]

- Nationally, non-medical use of prescription drugs experienced a slight decrease from 3.3 percent in 2007 to 2.9 percent in 2008.[5]

- Awareness is growing. Parents are recognizing the risks involved in youth prescription drug abuse much better than in previous years.[6]

- Parents, grandparents, guardians, and trusted adults can make a tremendous impact in helping the children they influence avoid the dangers caused by prescription drug abuse. The majority of teens report that their parents, not their peers or the media, have the biggest impact on their decision to stay drug free.[7]

———

WHAT CAN YOU DO?

- Talk to your children about the dangers of using prescription drugs. Research indicates that kids who learn about the risks of drugs are up to 50 percent less likely to use drugs.[8]

- Have family dinners. Eating dinner together five to seven nights a week as opposed to zero to two nights reduces the chances your children will abuse prescription drugs.[9]

- Set and enforce a curfew, and monitor your teens' late-night activities.

- Lead by example—be a good role model. Don't use illegal drugs. Don't get drunk. Don't smoke.

- Don't assume your teenager or his/her friends have not, do not, or will not use prescription drugs because they are "good kids." Plenty of good kids make bad choices.

- Never give your prescription medications to anyone else, for any reason. It is illegal and potentially could cause the start of someone else's addiction.

- Treat your (and your child's) prescription medications as if they were a loaded gun. Allow no access by anyone other than yourself.

- Learn the signs and symptoms of prescription drug abuse. If your teen shows symptoms of depression or is engaging in prescription drug abuse, seek professional help immediately.

- Volunteer for a community coalition working to prevent drug abuse.

———

CLOSING THOUGHTS

Arkansas and other states face significant challenges in preventing and stopping prescription drug abuse by its young people.

Parents, relatives, guardians, and trusted adults provide the first line of defense in protecting loved ones. Fortunately, there are proactive steps available to them.

Parents can lay the groundwork for prevention by educating their children about alcohol, prescription, and illegal drug use. The mere expressing of drug use is a protective factor.

Also by following the simple steps of "monitor, secure, and dispose," parents and relatives, major and unwitting providers of prescription drugs, can dramatically decrease their use.

CHAPTER EIGHT

Three Special Articles for Parents

Steve Straessle, the principle of Catholic High School for Boys in Little Rock, worked for the legendary Monsignor George Tribou as a teacher and then replaced him as principal following Father Tribou's death at age seventy-seven in 2001.

Straessle has continued in Catholic High's tradition of aiding spiritual growth in his students and providing quality academics, and in his position as both teacher and principal he has seen his share of tragedy, much of it substance abuse-related.

Straessle is also a gifted writer. He has contributed six pieces over the years to *One Day at a Time*, mostly about the tragic loss of young lives and his insights into what parents can do to stop it.

This chapter includes three of his pieces. (A fourth is included in chapter 7 on teenage drug abuse.)

———

NEVER UNDERESTIMATE YOUR ABILITY TO INSPIRE YOUR CHILD

This morning was one of those mornings. You know, one of those mornings where the sunrise is just right, where the crisp air brings lungs alive, and where the overall silence magnifies each creaking branch and each leaf scratching the street.

I spent several careful minutes scraping a thin sheet of frozen dew off of my windshield today. I usually haphazardly scrape a design that Jackson Pollock would be proud of, but this morning I carefully carved away the layer of ice. I meticulously went back and forth across the windshield and soon, everything was clear.

The whole process made me think about teenagers. You know, that less-than-perfect-but-so-full-of-goodness teenager who was sleeping like a child in your home this morning and awoke suddenly looking older.

You've seen him almost every day of his life but suddenly he's changing and looking more like a man. It's as if someone began scraping the layers of childhood from him, carving him into the adult you want him to become. But, he's not finished. You have so much more to teach him. His school has so much more to teach him.

And so, the new year begins. What will it bring in your home? In your teenager's school?

My experience in the classroom over the last eighteen years has taught me quite a bit about teenagers and about their parents. And the most important thing is simply this: *never underestimate your ability to inspire your own child.* You set the example. You lay down the foundation. You set the parameters. You prioritize, maximize, and glamorize.

Your kids are watching you. They are picking up on your habits, and they are taking note of how you approach life. They're soaking it in. Your kids learn from you, their first teacher and the most important one. Most times, they will hold in disdain that which you cannot stand. They will lift up that which you glorify. They will feel the first flicker of fire in the belly when you challenge them to strive for a goal. It's not a perfect system but it's built-in, it's inherent to the family structure. The important aspect of the system is to make sure it's not wasted.

Your child's high school builds upon what you have started. It's a good partnership because good schools will mirror what good parents want for their kids. Good schools will feed the mind and nurture growth. Good schools will not say "yes" every time. Instead, good schools will say, "Be willing to work, and we'll help you get there."

But, when the dark days come (and they do for all of us), don't be discouraged. Rare is the boy who will tell his father, "Dad, thanks for punishing me today. I know that I was wrong and your guidance has helped me see the error of my ways."

Rare is the girl who will tell her mother, "Mom, thanks so much for challenging me to do better. Thanks for accepting nothing less than my level best. Thanks for not changing your mind when I threw a fit and screamed hateful things at you. I'm better because you stuck to those parameters."

Chances are, you won't experience that kind of *instant* gratification. Instead, if you dare to inspire your child by using a strong standard, a strong example, and a strong soul, you will experience the *immortal* gratification of seeing your children grow into the men and women you always knew they could become. It's a difficult process. So is everything else that is worthwhile.

And that's the reason you support your child's school through volunteerism, patient understanding, and a desire to make the entire school community better. Your child will grow, but he needs to be fertilized with the inspiration that a good parent can provide. Your child will become better, but she needs to understand instinctively that scraping away the layers of childhood is a good thing.

As for parents, well, we need to understand that scraping is the only way to see clearly. It's the only way to see a child become an inspirational adult. Let the new year begin.

———

MISSING THAT GOOD BOY—A MESSAGE FOR OUR CHILDREN

It happened again. Devastatingly again. One of us lost his son. And not just lost him but lost him in a way that didn't have to happen. We're still grieving the loss. We're still wringing our hands and looking to our own kids hoping, wishing, praying that we don't lose them. It didn't have to happen.

The boy was a gentle soul with dark hair and a face that favored his mother's. He was kind, and he was clever. The boy, Patrick Clemmons, had a creative flair that permeated everything about him from the music he loved to the clothes he wore. We loved that about him. We loved that he had a sense of adventure that allowed him to reach into realms that most kids don't even know exist.

Patrick was not a bad apple, a thug whose demise was inevitable. It wasn't like that. He was an Eagle Scout. He was on athletic teams at his school. He was a National Merit Commended Scholar. The last time we saw him, he was mowing the yard for his parents. Patrick was the anti-thug. He was a good kid.

The problem was that Patrick tiptoed along the line of good decisions versus bad decisions until he inevitably crossed it. We say "inevitably" because you can't walk a tight rope forever; eventually you will fall. And fall he did. It started small, his dad said. It started with easy-to-find and alarmingly acceptable marijuana.

We don't know what the attraction was for him. Maybe it was acceptance into a crowd. Maybe it was an escape from some secret pain that even his closest friends didn't know about. Maybe he just had that personality where a little bit was never enough. We don't know. All we know is that when it took, it took him hard, and he was soon moving on from marijuana into stronger drugs. Every time, it was a little more dangerous.

Patrick's parents were aware and on top of his problem. They spared no expense, they pulled no punches, and they did not hide behind social graces. We spoke to his mother at a drug awareness and prevention seminar. His father searched for help from those of us who had been there. They both encouraged their son, told him they just wanted their boy back, and would move the heavens to make it happen. No holds barred. He was their son.

Patrick tried, too. He went to rehab, he involved himself in positive activities, and stayed close to the family. But then the drugs would call to him and, inevitably, he would answer.

After returning from a more than two-month stint in rehabilitation, Patrick found a place where opiates were available, and he was defenseless against the lure. He overdosed. His life left him. And we, as fathers, almost immediately sensed that the world was less because someone's beloved son was lost. And we, as fathers, wept.

It snowed the day before the funeral. A cleansing, whitewashing snow. We watched it in the streetlights and couldn't help but notice that it seemed to sparkle more like glitter than ice crystals. Turning our eyes to the heavens, we allowed the snow to gently brush our faces leaving tiny wet marks like the kiss of a child. It was gentle. It was peaceful. It reminded us of the boy who needn't have been lost.

The church that would host the funeral put out an email asking for help clearing the sidewalks in anticipation of the ceremony. Several fathers trudged to that church to help. Mothers, too. With the sidewalks cleared, we walked home. On the way, we passed by Patrick's house and saw his father outside, clearing his own sidewalk. As we approached, we prayed silently for the right words to say but we knew there was no such thing.

We listened to him. He was devastated. His voice shook, and he could not wrap his mind around the loss. We nodded. We shook his hand. We offered anything he needed. He had to get ready for the funeral and asked if we would help clear his sidewalk. Anything, we said.

Another father showed up with salt and a shovel. We worked silently while Patrick's family moved about inside, slowly dressing and willing themselves to make it through the day. One dad showed up, a neighbor, who had lost his own son to drugs three years before. We quietly spoke of the sorrow.

We shoveled and scraped and pushed the snow to clear the sidewalks and the driveway, and we hoped that the exertion would exorcise the sorrow that was tickling our souls. We, as your fathers, plotted and strategized to make sure it never happened again.

One of us commented that kids have only a finite number of no's in them. He said that every time you use up a no, you get closer to a yes. So tell the kids to avoid the near occasion of sin, he said. Don't just prepare yourself to say no, better to avoid those situations entirely. As our children, you have to understand why we say such things to you.

You should know that we've had to see our friends bury their children, and there is no deeper pain in the world. You should know that the next time you tell us something is not fair, we are going to challenge you. We are going to explain to you that it's not fair for you to dull your senses and deny the world your true potential. We are going to tell you that it's not fair when you make us worry. Unfair? Unfair is parents having to bury their own child.

When you want to do something that might lead you down the wrong path, we're going to tell you "no" and we're going to stick to it. When you ask us "Don't you trust me?" we are going to tell you wholly and unabashedly "no."

But understand that our lack of trust has nothing to do with your integrity. We think you are becoming solid young men and women. Our lack of trust has nothing to do with a lack of integrity; it has to do with a lack of experience.

As adults, we struggle to get out of tough situations. As kids, you don't have the life experiences to realize that tiptoeing a dangerous line inevitably leads to suffering.

When you complain about going to church, to school, or to family activities, we're not going to listen at all. Church gives you the opportunity to recognize a higher power at work in your life. School gives you the opportunity to expand that great mind of yours.

And family, well, family gives you the opportunity to be part of something greater than yourself. Your family loves you without condition, and you need to be part of that group, a group based on genuine love, instead of any other group based on shallow definitions of belonging.

You see, we're your parents, and that means that we want you to excel. Sure, we know you are not perfect, no more so than any of us are or were. But you have to understand that the world is a beautiful place, and it is made more beautiful by you being you. Not a dulled you. Not a you trying to fit in somewhere that is beneath your potential. Not a you that is trying to escape reality instead of meeting it head on.

We finished clearing the sidewalk and walked home to get ready for the funeral. The snow crunching under our feet reminded us of when Patrick was just a boy and went sledding with all the neighborhood kids. And we missed him. Deeply. We missed that creative boy, the Eagle Scout, the athlete, the good mind and kind heart that he was.

And then we, your fathers, let out a sigh, a silent prayer, that would comfort Patrick's family and protect our own.

We missed that good boy.

———

CHANGE COMES TO OUR CHILDREN LIKE THE FEEL AND SCENT OF A JULY RAIN

It comes across the landscape when you least expect it. Bubbling, churning, rolling clouds turn the sky dark and fill the nose with a scent of dampness. The air temperature cools just slightly as that first gust of wind cascades from the heavens and into the sweaty corners of the soul. And then, thunder. So far away at first that it's difficult to figure out if it's an airplane, a huge green truck lifting a heavy dumpster, or if it really is...the sound of rain. Cooling, soaking, gentle rain. In July.

July is the month that temperatures spike and heat headaches abound. It's when tempers flare and menial tasks become Herculean efforts. It's so hot that the air above asphalt waves in desperation and vibrates to the pounding sun's rays. All that you can hope for is a respite. All that you can hope for is a bit of comfort. There's nothing better than July rain.

Have you ever met someone who is like rain in July? Someone who conquers the wasteland of your worry and the landscape of your fears and covers them both in the comfort of hope? You can find that this year. You will find that sometimes, that which you hope for the most will come storming out of the direction you least expected. School can be a difficult experience but does not have to be.

We, as your parents, want you to be happy, but more important; we want you to be happier later on in life. Which means you have to practice right now. We want you to fill your school days learning, reaching, and exploring. We want you to be creative, to think great thoughts, to marvel at all there is to know. We want you to grow. And to figure out some things about yourself. We want you to be confident.

So, if you really want to make the most out of your school year (which would make us incredibly happy and limit the nagging oh so much) then look for some July rain. Look for those experiences that might be off the beaten path but are no less important to the formation of the future you.

If you are a student/athlete, then make sure you are both. Never complain about homework when you have the privilege of wearing the school's colors. You get the glory of athletics but you should also revel in the sanctity of academic accomplishment. Know that most high school athletes end their careers right there. Know that you have had the wonderful opportunity to be part of a team, to think on your feet, and learn about leadership. That's the glory of athletics. But, don't let it minimize the lasting hold of academics. No complaints.

Make an effort to break from the pack and find some folks different from the mold you travel with. Undoubtedly, you (just like your parents) have made many mistakes in finding friends so far. If you are like us, you've found users, spotlight seekers, ne'er-do-wells and jackasses, and you've maybe even been one of the above yourself from time-to-time. But take a little time to look for the kids that don't fit the homogeneity that so haunts high school life. Look for the eccentrics. The quirky kids. The ones who really don't care what fashion label you wear or what car you hope to drive. You will find that the very eccentricities that often isolate people are actually interesting characteristics.

While we're on the subject, be a good friend. Always. Be a good friend and you'll find good friends in return. Don't treat your relationships like clouds that can be blown in whatever direction the winds desire. Find those who will make you better, one way or another. And never sacrifice a true friendship for the lure of popularity. Popularity ends. Friendships don't.

Be respectful to your classmates and the adults who make up your school community. Good manners go a long way in these parts and so does treating folks like you wish to be treated. It's simple.

Attack the academic opportunities that you have. The most common complaint about kids your age is that the lack of motivation is a prevalent curse. It's not that we expect you to be super-charged every day. It's not that we expect you to be tireless or flawless or blameless. It's that we know you even better than you know yourself. We know what potential lies hidden under the mountains of television and video game garbage that are weighing down your soul. We know what potential is waiting to be tapped and released into your brain and overcome your body like a river crashing through a thirsty desert.

We understand that many of you struggle academically and we love it when you refuse to give up the fight. We adore it when you dig deep to eke out C's and a spare B here or there. It means that you understand the complexities of life better than most kids your age. Life is not fair. But life's unfairness is never cause for surrender.

Yes, we admit, we want you to overachieve. We want you to overachieve because we know that is the closest guarantee to success in this life. And really, underachieving is just not what it's cut out to be. It might be cute in small-budget comedies, but real life rarely rewards those who revel in apathy. Just work hard. Make mistakes, learn from them, work hard again. Use that good, creative mind to think.

Lastly, look to your school year for what it is at its base: an opportunity to better yourself through experience and learning. Don't be a bystander. Use what you learn for the improvement of others. Because, one thing we know as an absolute, is that everyone needs a little July rain.

CHAPTER NINE

College Program Tackles Partying, Emphasizes Learning

Fifty thousand college-eligible kids in America today are too strung out on alcohol or other drugs to get in—let alone make the grade. The way things have been, it's probably just as well. If some of these kids want to sober up, college is probably the last place they should go. Over the years, colleges and universities have actually been breeders of substance abuse. Think Animal House.

About half of the college students today binge drink and/or abuse other drugs—and almost a quarter of them meet the medical criteria for being dependent on alcohol and other drugs. That comes to about a million students in four thousand colleges.

It's enough to give a parent pause: *If my child has avoided alcohol and other drugs, do I want to send him or her to a college where he or she can learn to drink?* Or: *If my child has struggled with addiction, should I send him or her into an environment that will make it worse?*

These are good questions.

Fortunately, change is in the air, and there is another option: sending your child to a college that provides for kids who are in recovery or who want to be in recovery. The numbers of these colleges are growing.

For example, one major university—Texas Tech in Lubbock—took the lead seven years ago in developing a program that is now being replicated on other campuses. This program is having an impact and could ultimately help transform some of the four thousand college and university campuses from "party cultures" to "learning cultures."

Party cultures are nothing new. Over the years, administrations at numerous institutions have attempted various "crackdowns"—directed mainly at fraternities and sororities. Some may have succeeded in stanching the flow of alcohol, but few have truly addressed the root cause—addiction.

In 2007, the National Center on Addiction and Substance Abuse (CASA), which has been mentioned in previous chapters, convened a daylong conference in New York City, bringing badly needed attention to drug abuse on college campuses. The title of the conference was "How to Stop Wasting the Best and the Brightest: Substance Abuse at America's Colleges and Universities."

After two morning sessions—one entitled "Getting the High Out of Higher Education," directed at college presidents, trustees, and alumni, and the second called "Parent Power: The Role of Parents"—Lesley Stahl, coeditor of *60 Minutes* and a member of the CBS News staff, took to the podium to talk about "Substance Abuse Among American College Students." Among Stahl's five panel members was twenty-two-year-old Anna Thomas, a vivacious 2008 graduate of Texas Tech University and a person in recovery. She is on staff at the Center for the Study of Addiction and Recovery (CSAR) at Texas Tech.

Intrigued by the reports from the CASA conference, I visited Texas Tech for the first time in 2008, and then again in 2011. The Center serves about eighty students who are in recovery and enrolled in its Collegiate Recovery Community (CRC) program. Most of these students live off the Texas Tech campus, avoiding the typical college dorm life that consistently tolerates drug and alcohol use.

Students participating in the program spend most of their on-campus free time in the recovery-based environment provided by the Center, where they have access to 12-Step meetings, a computer lab, a den area with a big-screen television, and a recreation room complete with ping-pong, pool, and foosball.

Although students use the facilities for a safe haven during breaks, they attend classes with the general college population, seeking various degrees, such as liberal arts, engineering, and business.

Some of the participating students seek a four-year degree in community, family, and addiction services, and others pursue an interdisciplinary minor in addictive disorders and recovery studies, making them eligible to become licensed chemical dependency counselors.

The Center takes applications from those who have at least one year of sobriety, as well as from those already attending Texas Tech who find themselves in trouble and are looking for a place to recover where there is the opportunity to attend 12-Step meetings and to socialize informally with those of like mind who are members of the CRC. The average grade point average for students at the Center usually ranges from 3.4 to 3.6, and students are expected to spend time in community service. Following the 12-Step philosophy, service is crucial to maintaining long-term, quality sobriety.

Endowed scholarship funds designated specifically for students in recovery from drug and/or alcohol addiction and eating disorders are available, and financial assistance, based on GPA and ranging from five hundred to two thousand dollars, is available to all of the participants in the CRC.

Here are some other key facts about the Center and the Collegiate Recovery Community program:[10]

- More than five hundred recovering students had graduated from Texas Tech with the aid of CRC. Fewer than 7 percent of these students had relapsed while participating in the program.

- The CRC had enrolled students from more than twenty states and three foreign countries.

- CRC students maintained a collective GPA of 3.34, which was higher than the university's overall GPA. Many of these students successfully pursued graduate and professional school placements and competed for prestigious internships throughout the country.

- CRC continues to offer course credit and research opportunities in addiction and recovery studies to all students and faculty at Texas Tech.

- CRC continues to host more than twenty recovery support group meetings a week on the university campus. These meetings, open to recovering students, faculty, staff, and members of the local community, include Alcoholics Anonymous, Narcotics Anonymous, and Co-dependents Anonymous. CRC has also helped start support groups for those struggling with gambling and eating disorders.

———

NO ISOLATION

Dr. Kitty S. Harris, director, who was quoted at length in our Introduction, emphasizes that she intends to protect her students, but she doesn't want them isolated in their recovery.

"I want our students to have a true college experience," she says. "I don't want them to feel separate. I don't want them to feel 'apart from.' I don't want them to feel different."

Dr. Harris has been on the faculty at Texas Tech for more than twenty-five years and has had significant clinical experience in adult, adolescent, and family therapy. She has been the recipient of many awards, including being named the counselor of the year by the Texas Association of Alcoholism and Drug Abuse Counselors.

Dr. Harris, with her quiet competence, her heart for adolescents and young adults, and her spiritual focus, is impressive in her dedication. She says:

I love adolescents because they're responsive. They have these horrible chips on their shoulders, and they act like they hate the world, but if you can break through that wall, they're just so vulnerable.

They have so much to give, if you value them. If you work with adolescents and value them, it teaches you unconditional love, the ability to look beyond what the outside looks like. Truthfully, my position at the center is very much a spiritual calling. I really believe that this is what I was supposed to do next.

In late February 2008, I flew to Lubbock, a community of two hundred thousand, for a visit with Dr. Harris, her staff, and her students. I spent the first hour of my visit with Dr. Harris and Associate Director Mandy Baker, then they turned me over to my hostesses for the day, staff members Anna Thomas, the CASA panelist, and Administrative Business Assistant Ann Casiraghi.

Anna led my tour of the basement of the Center, where students gather to play games, pray and meditate, and play music. Other stops included visits with staff members Matt Russell, who is responsible for replicating the Texas Tech model on other campuses, Stephanie Rushing, who is doing groundbreaking work in the field of eating disorders, and Dr. Sara Smock in research, who is focusing on learning more about recovery and what helps people succeed.

Part of succeeding, Dr. Smock says, goes back to the importance of relationships in recovery. "Social support," she says, "is the piece that explains why people are successful."

With regard to eating disorders, Dr. Harris says, "What we have found oftentimes is that the 12-Step model of AA works very well with people who are struggling with eating disorders. The steps help them get into a position where they can recover and learn to feed and nurture their bodies in healthy ways."

TATTOOS AND GOTHIC

The students we passed in the halls or chatting in the foyer near the entrance were cheerful, a little shy, and respectful—some sporting tattoos, piercings, and a little gothic style dress here and there. At a 12-Step meeting with recovering students Logan, Matt, Brooke, and Laura, and staff members Anna Thomas and Jake Wood, I first gave them a brief account of my own recovery, and then we went around the table and they gave theirs. Most said they began experimenting with alcohol and hard drugs when they were little more than children. Near the end, they had given up all hope. They didn't know if they would live to be twenty or twenty-five, let alone attend a major university.

I didn't take notes during our session, but the quotes below from other students that appear in CRC literature give a feel for what they said that day:

- "When I was addicted," Brian said, "pretty much my whole life revolved around getting and using drugs. I didn't have a goal. Now I have ambition, my life has momentum, and I have things to look forward to."

- "Now I have a lot of different goals," Alana said. "I want to be a doctor, a mother. I want to be a good sister, a good daughter, a friend. I have gained more happiness and contentment in everything I do."

- "My life was like a tree that was wilted and dead," Sara said. "Since I've been in recovery, the tree has been nourished, and it's growing. I'm happier and a lot brighter. My life has totally changed."

———

LOSING A SON

Sometimes lost in the discussion of addiction is the impact on loved ones. Annette K., a member of the CRC advisory board, lost her son, Rich, to addiction. She wrote, "I've seen recovery from drugs and alcohol make total changes in people. I believe in the healing this program offers. The Center provides an opportunity for me to interact with students and people in recovery and keeps a part of my son alive. I know that this program's successes would mean everything to him."

Annette's son, Rich, is one of many tragic statistics that include the following:

- Fourteen hundred college students die each year from alcohol-related injuries.

- Seventy thousand alcohol-related sexual assaults occur each year among college students.

- Six hundred thousand college students per year are assaulted by another student who has been drinking.

- Four hundred thousand college students report having unprotected sex while intoxicated.

- One hundred thousand college students report having been too intoxicated to know if they consented to having sex.

Dr. Harris believes that Americans are heavily into feeling good, the quick fix, and immediate gratification. She said:

One idea I've always believed in is that the reason we have a problem with alcohol and drugs is because the substances work.

For the kids at the Center, the substance did meet a need. It was exciting, or it made them feel not so bad, or it made Mom and Dad's divorce not seem so tragic, or it made that last breakup with that girl not so overwhelming.

These kids get into substance abuse, and the sad part is that because they are so young, and they have such poor judgment, they're sucked in and sucked under before they realize it.

The most satisfying part of the Center to me is that we love these students. We help them re-socialize. We re-parent them if they've lacked family support. We try to give them an unconditional, loving environment in which to grow and flourish.

We are able to return these individuals to the community, to the society they hid from during their active dependency and addiction, and allow them to come back to those places where they can become who they are.

———

MY SECOND VISIT

In April 2011, three years after my first visit, I returned to Texas Tech to attend the second annual Collegiate Recovery and Relapse Prevention Conference. I learned that forty-four colleges had signed up since my 2008 visit, and that more than two hundred visitors representing fifty colleges and universities around the nation and others who work in the addiction and recovery field were at the conference.

The visitors came to see how Tech's CRC program works, and they came to hear the speakers, among them Harvard's Dr. John B. Kelly (mentioned in chapter 1).

Dr. Kelly said, "As a whole, colleges are dangerous places for those in recovery," but his research on the effectiveness of Alcoholics Anonymous and other 12-Step programs with adolescents suggests the potential for a resource that has been relatively underutilized.

Staying home and not going to college is an option, but it has a downside too, Dr. Kelly points out. A college education has potential payoffs that would be denied.

Fellow Harvard psychiatrist, Dr. George Eman Vaillant, Dr. Kelly quotes, has said that "college education and hope for a better future trumps wealth and social prestige as a pathway to health and happiness."

Furthermore, Dr. Kelly says, college men live longer than less educated men.

All of the students in Dr. Harris' program are in recovery, and a major part of that involves regular participation in AA and other 12-Step programs, which are particularly effective, Dr. Kelly says, because of the high proportion of young people at meetings.

The 12-Step groups currently meeting at Tech are Alcoholics Anonymous, Narcotics Anonymous, Eating Disorders Anonymous, and Sex and Love Addicts Anonymous.

COMMUNICATION PROBLEMS

The benefits of free and effective 12-Step meetings have been documented, but research shows they are less effective for young people because, on average, the meetings cater to an older crowd.

Eighty-nine percent of those who attend AA and NA meetings are over thirty, and the disparity in age creates communication problems in a setting in which good communication is a key component of recovery.

For example, of the four hundred or so 12-Step meetings in Little Rock, where I live, only one meeting listed caters to teenage and college-age kids—"Barely Legal Young Peoples." Plus, there is one statewide organization called ARKYPAA (Arkansas Konference by Young People participating in AA), which is an outreach for young people seeking recovery.

Despite the promising aspects of 12-Step groups, Dr Kelly reemphasizes his point that age differences create problems.

"Age differences," Dr. Kelly says, "suggest that adolescents, who typically have less severe drug-use profiles, consequences, and psychological concerns, find it difficult to relate to older members and their more severe withdrawal complications and recovery-related psychological challenges surrounding marriage, children and employment."

On the other hand, he says, "When adolescents attended meetings where at least some other young people are also present, the outlook got better. They attend more often, get more involved and have better post-treatment substance abuse outcomes compared to those attending adult only meetings."

Another key finding about adolescents, according to Dr. Kelly, is that "the more meetings they attend, the better."

Kelly's study of one group with a year's sobriety showed that 57.8 percent of those who attended one meeting a week were still sober and 69.1 percent who attended more than one were still sober. Of those who attended no meetings, 39.4 percent were still sober.

When you ask young people what they like best about the meetings, Dr. Kelly says, they cite reasons including: not feeling alone; getting support from others; knowing that recovery is possible; having a place to talk; getting advice from others; being able to tackle the challenge of recovery "one day at a time"; and being able to rely on structure.

"Given [the students'] developmental state and Zeitgeist, college environment confers high relapse risk," Dr. Kelly says. "And, unlike adult relapse, the majority of youth relapse events occur as a result of exposure in social situations where alcohol and other drugs are present." This includes places such as dorms and fraternity houses.

AA and most other 12 Step-meetings work and they're free. Don't let anyone tell you otherwise, Dr. Kelly concludes.

———

SUMMER SCHOOL

Another contributor to raising alcohol and drug awareness is the thirty-seven-year-old MidSOUTH Summer School on Alcohol and Other Drug Abuse Programs at the University of Arkansas at Little Rock (UALR). The program goes on for a week each June and its aims are to further educate counselors, teachers, and others on the issues of substance abuse treatment and prevention. In the process, it has raised student and community awareness of addiction and the possibilities of recovery over nearly four decades.

Every year, exciting speakers come to MidSOUTH to share their experience, strength, and hope. Four years ago, William Cope Moyers was on the program speaking about his memoir, *Broken: My Story of Addiction and Redemption.* Cope, the son of broadcast journalist Bill Moyers who is now on staff at Hazelden addiction treatment center in Center City, Minnesota, begins his memoir with a story in which a disciple asks a rabbi why the Torah says to place holy words *"on"* our hearts instead of *"in"* them. The disciple is told that this is because our hearts are closed; the words must rest on top of our hearts until the heart finally breaks so the words can fall in.

This is an apt description of Moyers' journey, his failed attempts to get clean and sober, and the spiritual awakening that saved his life. Until he learned to "get out of God's way," he says he could not let the truth of the 12 Steps and the wisdom of its followers seep into his cracked and broken heart and finally take hold.

As he put it in a letter to his wife dated October 13, 2005: "Eleven years ago yesterday, I finally understood what recovery was all about. Sitting still, experiencing the pain, anger, fear, sadness, joy, freedom, and peace. Not on my agenda or my timelines. It only happened to me when I stopped trying to make it happen, when I gave up looking for it and allowed recovery to find me."

Some might call Moyers' story courageous, but he doesn't see it that way. "Maybe it's because I lived with such secrets and shame for so long, I feel it is easier to be honest. It's easier to be in the light than in the shadows," he said.

Moyers not only lived in the shadows of crack cocaine and alcohol addictions, he lived in the shadows of his famous father. When William got arrested in his early twenties, the event made national news. And, in 1994, it was Bill Moyers who found his son in an Atlanta crack house after a four-day crack cocaine binge that nearly killed William.

"My father is huge in the book, as many fathers are to sons," said William. His memoir includes letters from Bill Moyers—letters that, he says, are "a testament to a father's love for his son, a father's confusion with his son, and ultimately, a father's satisfaction with his son."

Contrary to his previous practices, William Moyers breaks anonymity in his book by talking about Alcoholics Anonymous. "I had to reveal I'm in AA because to do otherwise would be a lie, and this book is the truth," he explained. "Not talking about my program of recovery would be like a marathon runner not talking about training.

"Although I'm breaking my anonymity, I protect the anonymity and confidentiality of others in the program. This is everybody's story: the still-suffering alcoholic, recovering people and families, and, hopefully, those who don't have a clue about my disease. I wrote this book to help smash the stigma of addiction and carry the message."

A big part of smashing the stigma comes with getting people to accept addiction as a disease like cancer. Six years ago, Moyers was diagnosed with skin cancer, so he can speak intimately about both diseases. "Both diseases are chronic, progressive, and life-threatening," he said. "Nobody deserves to get either one.

"Continuing care is an essential part of treatment, and reoccurrence of the disease is always a possibility. Yet public attitudes toward the victims of these diseases are as different as night and day.... Why is addiction the only disease without a ribbon of hope to wear out in public?"

ERIN'S STORY

It was close to midnight on April 10, 2002, when Erin, an attractive twenty-two year old, left a tavern in West Little Rock, hopped into her bright red Saturn, buckled her seatbelt, and headed west on Arkansas Highway 10. During the evening, Erin had consumed three glasses of wine—not much by her standards, but the night before, she had partied hard on drugs and alcohol. She was an addict and an indifferent student whose main interest was in partying.

Six miles down the highway, Erin lost control of her car, careened into a ditch, rolled the car two or three times, and landed upside down. The car roof was crushed and so was her spine. She was conscious and in a lot of pain, but from the waist down she felt nothing. She was paralyzed. She could have been dead, but the one thing she had done right was fasten her seatbelt.

The first paramedic to reach the scene said, "Don't worry, Erin. We'll get you out." And they did, but it took two hours of cutting, while she drifted in and out of consciousness.

Later, they found that Erin had a blood alcohol content of .216, more than twice the legal limit. She was convicted of driving under the influence and heavily fined. Because of the alcohol in her system, doctors were afraid to add painkillers to the mix when she got to the hospital, which meant she had to suffer excruciating pain without sedation.

It has now been more than nine years since the day of the crash, and Erin is coming up on ten years of continuous sobriety, thanks to regular attendance at 12-Step meetings and a relationship with and help from her sponsor.

Erin is still in a wheelchair, but she has made a life for herself and her family that is truly inspirational. She married, bore three children, graduated from college, and got a great job with a university. In September of 2011, she received a "Best Mom on Wheels" award from the Christopher and Donna Reeve Foundation, and local television station, KTHV, Channel 11, celebrated with a special feature on Erin's family.

Christopher Reeve, many will remember, was an accomplished actor and director who was paralyzed in an equestrian competition in 1995. He created the foundation in 1999 to develop treatments for paralysis associated with spinal cord injuries. Reeve and his wife are both deceased but their mission continues.

Erin's husband, Ryan, wrote the letter below to the foundation nominating his wife for the award:

I would like to enter my wife for the mom on wheels contest. My wife's name is Erin. We have had three children, but one passed away after three days. Hagen is seven and is blind in one eye, and Koen is five.

My wife is a perfect wife who wants to enjoy life and show our children that you can live life to the fullest and accomplish a lot even when you have obstacles to overcome. My wife has graduated college and now works.

She does more than most mothers who aren't injured, and I feel deserves this award for all her hard work and sacrifice. She has never once said she couldn't do something because she couldn't walk. She gives it her best every day, never gives up, and is an inspiration to all who know her.

I love my wife very much and couldn't be more proud of her strength and what she's accomplished since she lost the use of her legs. Even though she can only use half her body, she's twice the mom.

After her accident, Erin went through several months of hospitalization and rehab, continued her schooling, and regularly attended her meetings—where she met Ryan in the fall of 2002, six months after the accident.

She was immediately attracted to the six-foot-two, 220-pound "former bad boy" image. When she asked another girl about him, the girl agreed that he was cute but seemed awfully "rough."

At this stage, neither Erin nor Ryan, both recovering drug addicts, looked like a prospect for the strong and healthy marriage that has emerged. At age sixteen, Erin had taken her first drink, and it was a big one—a half bottle of vodka followed by a half bottle of Jack Daniel's. As time went on, she added a variety of drugs to her list of addictions.

Her job history was spotty. She worked as a receptionist in a hair salon, as a car wash attendant, and in a variety of restaurants—and lost all of those jobs one way or another, mostly because of substance abuse.

Ryan, as she found out later, was living at a chem-free house and was working at a local sub shop when she met him. He had been a heavy drug user, which played a significant role in his prison record. He had spent about three years in Arkansas, Texas, and Mississippi jails and prisons. He was released to Serenity Park, the Little Rock treatment center, and then to the chem-free living facility.

The two began dating and Erin became pregnant. On February 21, 2004, the couple was married at Little Rock's Trapnall Hall, and she rolled down the aisle in her wheelchair accompanied by her father, Tim, also well known in recovery circles.

After the wedding, Erin and Ryan spent a night at the Capitol Hotel, a luxurious downtown hotel, for their honeymoon, then settled down and made plans to raise a family. In May of 2004, Erin gave birth to twins, a boy and a girl, who were born fifteen weeks premature. Tragically, the baby girl died three days later. As Ryan stated in his letter, the boy, Hagen, had several defects, including being blind in one eye. About two years later, Erin gave birth to Koen.

Today, Hagen, at age seven, is in second grade and Koen, who's now five, is in kindergarten. Both boys are doing great, Erin reports, and "are very good at school."

Erin graduated cum laude from the University of Arkansas in 2009 with a degree in liberal arts, and then worked for eighteen months as a grants coordinator. She is now an associate for administration at a university system office and works for the vice president of administration.

Ryan graduated magna cum laude with a degree in geology in August 2011 and is now a geologist at a natural gas company in Central Arkansas.

Will Erin ever walk again? Her many friends pray that she will, but for now doctors say it's unlikely, but not impossible. Her spine was not severed; it was compressed, and she has some feeling in spots below her waist. Right now, she's a busy wife and mother with an outside job and a mission of helping others.

CHAPTER TEN

Reducing Prison Populations with Programs on Recovery

When Joe Bruton, forty-two, robbed the First Bank of Huntsville in Fayetteville, Arkansas, with a variety of drugs and alcohol coursing through his veins, he was unarmed and wore a hooded sweatshirt to conceal his identity.

The fact that he was loaded was the usual. (Drugs are implicated in 80 to 85 percent of the crimes committed.) They gave him courage but also impaired his thinking.

On that rainy March day in 2005, he walked up to one of the windows, told the teller he wanted to take out a loan, and, when advised that he would have to fill out a form, said he wasn't talking about that kind of loan. He was talking about the kind where she would give him cash and he would repay it later.

After hearing his threat to jump over the counter and grab the money in her drawer, the teller handed him two stacks of twenties adding up to about two thousand dollars, and Bruton left after giving the security camera a cursory glance. It was a costly mistake.

Bruton's intent was to use the money to get his car back from the repo man and rescue his wife and three children, who had finally been rendered homeless by the addictions that had plagued him from the time he was a teenager.

Instead, after getting his car, Bruton spent the rest of the money on drugs and, in a bizarre twist, began planning a ski vacation for himself in Colorado. It never happened. He was arrested at the Salvation Army in Fayetteville for the robbery and, later, an added charge of drug manufacturing.

Authorities took him to the Washington County Jail in northwest Arkansas, where they put him in a "rubber room" to detox. Fearing he would die getting off of the huge amounts of drugs in his system, which included fifty or more pain pills, Bruton begged to be sent to a hospital, but his request was denied. It seemed likely that if he lived through detox, he would spend the next forty years of his life in prison.

———

GOD'S PLAN

As it turned out, "God had something else in mind," as Joe put it to 118 inmates gathered on a sunny April afternoon in the gymnasium at the Arkansas Department of Correction's Tucker Unit near Pine Bluff. Joe and fifteen other inmates had successfully completed a two-year program, the late Chuck Colson's Christian-based Innerchange Freedom Initiative (IFI), which focuses on developing life skills and biblical values.

Bruton had been released six months early and had come back to speak to his classmates, whose crimes ran the gamut of writing hot checks and drug dealing to homicide, and who were in various stages of completing the program.

It is hard to believe that four years from detoxing in the Washington County Jail, Bruton, clean, sober, a responsible husband and father, and a member of the first IFI graduating class at Tucker, would be addressing his classmates as a free man.

In his address, Bruton hit the high points of his recovery, and later, in an interview with me, he supplied some of the remarkable details of what his drug-fueled life was like, what happened, and what his life is like now.

First, a quick overview of what his drug-fueled life was like. While actively abusing alcohol, Bruton had managed to become an honors student and athlete at his Houston, Texas, high school who went on to graduate from the University of Arkansas at Fayetteville with a bachelor's degree in geology and from Oklahoma State University with a master's degree in engineering. He later founded and led Environmental Technology Specialists, a fifteen-man engineering firm in Fayetteville with all the perks, including a company plane. Bruton had a house in the suburbs with his wife, Janie, and their three kids, Joe Jr., Lucas, and Samantha.

Over his lifetime of drinking and drugging, Bruton had been detoxed seven or eight times and been to rehab a dozen times or more, but the detox at the Washington County Jail, the one he thought would kill him, was perhaps his mildest. He thinks it's because he sank to his knees and finally surrendered to God and began his true recovery.

Bruton's journey to the bottom and eventual rendezvous with God at the jail had begun to pick up speed when, twenty years earlier, at age twenty-four, he began more aggressively using and selling drugs. It was also at about that time in 1988 that he married Janie and began raising a family.

————

BUSTED

In 1989, Bruton was arrested with fifty-two pounds of marijuana, and in 1990 was sentenced to two years at El Reno federal prison in Oklahoma. After completing his term and a stint in a halfway house, he began studying for his master's degree in engineering at Oklahoma State, got his degree, and joined Apogee Environmental, a first-rate firm in Tulsa.

In 1995, he got off parole from his El Reno sentence, left Apogee, and founded his own firm, Environmental Tech Specialists, with backing from individual investors and business from his old friends at Apogee. The firm grew to its fifteen employees, added a Cessna, and, for a time, prospered.

The firm was thinly financed, and when accounts receivable got slow in the bad economy, Bruton couldn't cover his payables. Instead of declaring bankruptcy and salvaging what he could, he tried to pump up his bank account with odd jobs, including telemarketing—and also manufacturing and selling meth.

The company foundered in 2000, and from then on, Bruton worked at odd jobs, sank deeper into his addiction and depression, and contemplated suicide. He began to hear voices and sometimes couldn't do the simplest task, like dialing a phone.

Deeply in debt and facing dispossession, Bruton responded with his ill-conceived bank heist. It was the only thing he could think of to do.

At his trial, under a plea agreement, Bruton was sentenced to thirty years, with fifteen years suspended. The agreement also stated that Janie was exempt from any prosecution for possible involvement in making meth in their home. Under sentencing guidelines at that time, Bruton would only have to serve four years.

He began serving his sentence at Pine Bluff's Brickey's Unit, a notoriously violent place, and quickly got into trouble with seven young inmates who were terrorizing another inmate. When Bruton attempted to intervene, the gang turned on him "like a pack of wolves" and beat him severely before the guards stepped in.

Still, while at Brickey's, Bruton continued his pursuit of God. He joined the Principles and Applications for Life (PAL) program developed by chaplain Kenneth DeWitt a decade earlier at Newport's McPherson Unit for women. PAL covers substance abuse as part of its broader, Christ-focused curriculum. Bruton was also able to attend AA meetings at Brickey's.

———

CUMMINS PRISON

Things took a turn for the better when Bruton was assigned to Cummins prison near Pine Bluff, where the warden, aware of his engineering background, put him to work building a chicken house on the prison grounds. Armed with blueprints no one else could fathom, Bruton finished the job in a few months.

In August of 2006, Bruton applied to IFI, and following an interview with Scott McLean, head of IFI in Arkansas, he was accepted and transferred to Tucker.

Inmates who want to get into the IFI program must meet certain requirements. Participants, who can opt out of the program at any time, must be within eighteen to twenty-four months of their release or parole date. They also must be healthy, have no enemies in the prison, and be functionally literate.

Those accepted into the IFI program rise early, attend morning and evening classes, have jobs at the complex, and—during the evening hours—read, write letters, and play board games. Those seeking their degrees use this time to study for their GED tests. IFI inmates watch no television and are separated from the rest of the prison population except for meals. They don't stay in cells; rather, they bunk together in a large dormitory room.

With a goal of learning to live by six core values—integrity, responsibility, productivity, affirmation, community, and restoration—those who graduate must meet four conditions after release: 1) They must have regular meetings with their mentors, who meet them at the gate upon their release; 2) They must keep a job; 3) They must attend a church or other house of faith; and 4) They are expected to be active in another social group.

Bruton also attended the Quest for Authentic Manhood class developed by Fellowship Bible Church pastor, Dr. Robert Lewis, founder of the international Men's Fraternity program. In his commencement address, Bruton said, "I never opened a Bible. I thought the only truth out there was mathematics."

His return to society, he says, was "textbook perfect" by IFI standards. For one thing, he knew he would have a place to live. When Bruton had gone to prison, Janie and the children had been left homeless and had gone to live with Janie's sister. But soon, Janie got a job with Wal-Mart's optical service and, with help, was able to buy a small house.

When Bruton was in IFI, he asked for and received forgiveness from his wife and children. So he knew that when he got out of prison, he would have a place to live. When he left Tucker, Bruton's mentor met him at the gate and led him through the reentry process.

"My guy picked me up at the gate," Bruton says, "took me around to settle unresolved misdemeanor charges—parking tickets and other minor offenses I had accumulated during my drinking and drugging—helped me get my driver's license back, and took me to check in with my parole officer. Janie didn't even have to take off from work."

JOB AT GEORGE'S

Bruton's mentor helped him get a nine-dollars-an-hour job on the night-shift line at George's chicken plant in Fayetteville. He also drove Bruton to a car dealer, where the newly released man bought himself a Dodge Neon for fifteen hundred dollars to drive to work in.

Bruton found and joined the Inside Out Church in Fayetteville, where he has received help from Pastor Jim Muse and the entire congregation. He also has a 12-Step program sponsor.

"The usual prison routine," Bruton said, "is to give the guy a hundred dollars and a bus ticket, and he's on his own." As it often turns out, this leaves a just-freed prisoner vulnerable to the nearest drug dealer, who will start him on the path back to prison. National statistics show that as many as three out of four inmates go back to prison within three years for missing parole or committing another crime.

After two years with George's, Joe joined Goodwill Industries of Arkansas, where he is building a reentry program for ex-prisoners modeled after his experience with the Prison Fellowship program.

I asked Joe to further describe what happened to him after his release. Here, in his own words, is what he said:

Since my release and with the continued help of my personal Lord and Savior, Jesus Christ, I have been a productively employed, church-going, sober, law-abiding, tax-paying husband and father who is actively engaged in his community and working in the reentry field.

In October 2010, Goodwill Industries in Northwest Arkansas hired me as a program coordinator, a reentry program for ex-offenders to rebuild their lives. I facilitate classes on character development and share my experience, strength, and hope with others that are in the reentry process.

I am also a graduate of the Prison Fellowship Centurions program, and am recognized by Washington County, Arkansas, as a jail minister, which permits me to go into the Washington County Jail and share with the inmates there.

I am also an Arkansas Department of Corrections (ADC) volunteer authorized to enter state prisons and minister. I am an IFI volunteer and mentor, frequently speak at IFI functions and am active in its Out4Life program.

I am certified by the State of Arkansas as a care coordinator. I assist clients with substance use disorders (SUDs) in obtaining proper treatment to aid them in their recovery process.

Part of my job with Goodwill is to assist Out4Life clients in getting jobs and assisting them in building their reentry networks. I also teach classes on mentoring and interview prospective mentors.

———

IFI FOR WOMEN

Several years ago, fifty women convicts, vowing to change their lives "from the inside out," moved into Arkansas' J. Aaron Hawkins Center for Women at Wrightsville prison one October and plunged into their IFI program, which was also under Scott McLean's direction at that time.

For the next eighteen months, they would follow a rigorous, dawn-to-dusk schedule focusing on life skills and biblical values with the hope of making a new beginning in their troubled lives.

Female inmates who want to get into the IFI program must meet requirements that are virtually the same as those that must be met by the men. They also keep a schedule that's similar to that of their male counterparts, rising early, attending classes, and working during the day and playing board games and studying for their GEDs in the evening. Like the men, the women are not kept in cells but rather bunk together—all fifty—in a large and immaculate dorm room. The overall décor, while muted, is pleasant. Clearly, neatness counts. They also strive to live by the same core values as the men, and they must meet the same four conditions after release as the men in order to graduate.

A December dedication luncheon at Wrightsville several years ago offered the women inmates, dressed in their attractive prison whites, a departure from the somewhat austere daily routine. Slightly giddy in the party atmosphere, they bustled about, arranging the buffet, mingling with the guests, loudly applauding the speakers, and singing hymns at the tops of their lungs during the musical portion of the program.

The spontaneous gaiety provided a touching moment, considering the wretched lives most of these women had endured and the growing possibility of redemption.

Regrettably, in September 2011, IFI discontinued its operations in Arkansas (as well as in Kansas and Missouri) "because of the challenging economic times," but McLean has stayed on to form a new ministry, Pathway to Freedom, to carry on the work of IFI.

"The curriculum and Bible-centered values will remain the same," McLean said. And, like IFI, Pathway to Freedom is seeking most of its support from churches.

THE PAL PROGRAM

At the Department of Corrections McPherson Unit for women at Newport, Arkansas, two successful programs are available: a PAL program, which, as mentioned earlier in Joe Bruton's recovery story, was founded by chaplain Kenneth DeWitt, and a newer Prison to Purpose (P2P) program founded by former inmate Stacey Smith as basically an extension of DeWitt's program.

STACEY SMITH

Smith, forty-two, had five years of training in biblical solutions to problems in prison under DeWitt. She also had the experience of being a criminal.

She was first arrested in May 1993 with five kilos of cocaine and was given a sixty-year sentence, which took her first to the county jail, then to Tucker prison near Little Rock, which was a woman's prison at the time. Four years later, she was sent to McPherson, where she finally met up with Chaplain DeWitt.

An unwed mother of two small children and a confirmed addict at the time of her arrest, Smith, by her own account, stayed high most of the time, and it didn't make much difference what drug it was. "Whatever was available," she says.

Visits to five different treatment centers had failed to sober her up, and when her trial was over and the cell doors slammed behind her, she was numb and almost relieved that the nightmare of her life on the outside was over.

Incarceration ended her addiction problem. "I detoxed in the county jail," Smith said, "and six months later I became a Christian. A woman came to my cell, we talked, and I was saved."

Smith's spiritual transformation didn't produce much of a change in her at first, and she quietly settled into the routine of prison life. The first two months she was assigned to the "field squad," she says, which meant she was part of a gang chopping grass with a hoe in the surrounding fields. She graduated after that to clerical jobs, and in 1998 was transferred to McPherson, where Chaplain Dewitt, whose principal job was to make the lives of women inmates more bearable and meaningful on the inside and to prepare them for life on the outside, was about to launch PAL with the support of warden Jackie Nowles.

With his promising curriculum, DeWitt approached Nowles about a classroom, and the warden gave him an entire barracks partly occupied by women inmates. They eventually filled the barracks with fifty-six women, including Smith, who were committed to doing the PAL program.

———

STREETWISE AND BORED

So how did this lone preacher do with a room full of streetwise women, many of them skeptical and some with an attitude?

No problem. DeWitt has the demeanor of a kindly preacher but a steely resolve when it comes to getting across his message. Besides that, the women had time on their hands. Too much time. And they were bored.

"I believed in my heart what he was teaching," Smith said, "but sometimes, because of my preconceived ideas, I couldn't get it into my head. He challenged every one of those ideas until he convinced me. And that's the way it happens with everyone. Chaplain DeWitt is driven to giving these women the truth."

And so the program grew from two hours a day for five weeks to eight hours a day for twelve weeks. And the women changed. They changed because they took the actions DeWitt demanded.

The barracks—really a two-tiered cellblock decorated with attractive murals—acquired a new name: "The God Pod."

"The PAL training barracks came to be known as the problem-solving unit of the prison," DeWitt says, "and people called on us for help."

One of the projects they took on was the commissary, where the people who were working "just couldn't get it right," DeWitt said. "We put some of our experienced program participants in there, and they resolved the problems and were a blessing to those in charge."

MARY LEE ORSINI

Mary Lee Orsini, convicted of murdering her husband, Ron, in Little Rock in 1981, became an active PAL member two years before she died in August 2003. She credited the PAL program with changing her life.

Orsini, whose trial had dominated the headlines, had never admitted her crime, but on July 17, 2003, believing it was the right thing to do, she confessed to authorities that she had indeed shot and killed her husband over money worries. It was less than a month before her death.

KIMBERLY SHARP

Kimberly Sharp, a member of the PAL program at McPherson, is also serving time for murder. On August 17, 2002, she was a nineteen-year-old babysitter for a child at a home in Otter Creek—a Little Rock subdivision. The child's parents were involved in a nasty divorce, and the father, who was not living at the home at the time, came to pick up the child.

A dispute developed, and when it escalated, Kim, who was under a doctor's care for bipolar disorder and depression, got a gun from somewhere in the house (accounts differed as to the source) and shot and killed the father.

After a two-day trial beginning October 13, 2003, Kimberly was found guilty and sentenced to forty years at McPherson, with at least twenty-eight of those years to be served. She spent her first months in the psychiatric unit and entered the PAL unit in June 2004.

At this point, she began to undergo a profound change, according to her father, Dale Sharp, who is very active in addiction and recovery circles. Kimberly's lawyers had filed an appeal on a point of law and in March 2005, the courts upheld the appeal and she was released pending a new trial.

"Because of what the Lord has done through the PAL program, I got to spend three months with our brand-new daughter," Dale says with tears in his eyes. He adds that the tragedy also brought him and his wife, Jan, "closer to the Lord."

At the new trial, Kim was convicted again, but the sentence was reduced to fifteen years—thanks in part, Sharp says, to an eloquent appeal to the jury from her mother, Jan. With the reduced sentence and credit for time served, Kim is eligible for parole in the year 2014. She will be thirty-one years old.

———

PROFOUND AND FAR-REACHING IMPACT

The PAL program has had a profound impact on the lives of hundreds of women. Bridgett Curtner, for example, said:

I was an addict and believed there was no hope for people like me. I was told I had a disease, and I would have to fight it for the rest of my life. Eventually, I gave up and accepted that I was always going to be the way I was.

Looking back, it was when I gave up that God took control. It wasn't long after this day that I was arrested for manufacturing meth and delivery of a controlled substance. I was sentenced to ten years in prison.

[Through PAL,] I was learning the truth about life, about me, and about God. I learned why God created me and that I had a purpose. I learned that all I have been through God can use and make it work for my good. I no longer have to live in the bondage of my addictions.

Just as with Curtner, Stacey Smith's life changed, too. And because of it, Gov. Mike Huckabee granted her clemency in 2003. She was released from McPherson prison in March 2004 after serving twelve years, free to pursue her ministry on the outside.

As of several years ago, DeWitt's program had reduced recidivism at McPherson from more than 50 percent to 11 percent in the previous three years, and had transformed many hardened inmates into model prisoners.

DeWitt's PAL program prepares inmates for life on the outside, but what about when they actually get there? It's not easy.

"When women get out of prison, they get a hundred dollars and the name of their parole officer," Smith says. "That's basically it. They are full of fear. They fear rejection, and they're afraid they'll mess up and end up back in prison. They fear, too, the fact that the world has changed since they went away."

———

PRISON TO PURPOSE

Smith's Prison to Purpose (P2P) program makes PAL available to felons when they are released and also to church leaders and their congregations. P2P is working now to establish a network of mentors throughout the state to encourage, support, and coordinate future training for released prisoners and their families and to equip them to grow and mature spiritually, emotionally, and physically on the outside.

Several years ago, Smith told me about a woman, recently released from Newport, who had called for help. She had cancer, was undergoing chemotherapy treatments, and was also HIV positive. Her poor health plus deteriorating relations with family members had thrown her into a panic.

Smith responded.

"As it happened," she said, "I had a family member with cancer. I understood her feelings and talked to her about how I was able to cope. Basically, she needed some emotional support. Beyond that, I just took her back to what she had already learned in prison."

KAIROS

Finally, there is Kairos, another Christian ministry that is a volunteer, lay-led, ecumenical and international program, in which "men and women volunteers bring Christ's love and forgiveness to incarcerated individuals and to their families." Its programs include a men's and women's ministry that addresses the spiritual needs of prisoners. Kairos volunteers go into prisons in teams of thirty to forty to pray, share the love and forgiveness of Jesus Christ, share meals, and fellowship with the incarcerated on a one-to-one basis.

In addition, Kairos offers an "outside program" that provides spiritual healing to families of the incarcerated, who often feel that they, too, are "doing time." Spouses, parents, and other relatives of prisoners meet with teams of Kairos volunteers to share their faith and gain strength from Christian community. Kairos also operates a torch ministry for youthful offenders.

SOBERING STATISTICS

All of these Christ-centered programs, as well as traditional 12-Step programs like Alcoholics Anonymous, Narcotics Anonymous, and Cocaine Anonymous, are proven effective, but there aren't enough of them, often because it can be difficult to penetrate prison bureaucracies. The result is reflected in some sobering statistics.

For example, three decades of growth in America's prison population has quietly nudged the nation across a sobering threshold: for the first time, more than one in every one hundred adults is now confined in an American jail or prison. According to the 2008 report issued by the PEW's Center on the States, the number of people behind bars in the United States continued to climb in 2007, "saddling cash-strapped states with soaring costs they can ill afford and failing to have a clear impact either on recidivism or overall crime."

For some groups, the incarceration numbers are especially startling. While one in thirty men between the ages of twenty and thirty-four is behind bars, for black males in that age group, the figure is one in nine, the report states.

Gender adds another dimension, the report continues. Men still are roughly ten times more likely to be in jail or prison, but the female population is growing at a far brisker pace. For black women in their mid to late thirties, the incarceration rate also has hit the one in one hundred mark.

Growing older, meanwhile, continues to have a dramatic chilling effect on criminal behavior. While one in every fifty-three people in their twenties is behind bars, the rate for those over fifty-five falls to one in 837.

Prison costs are blowing holes in state budgets, but are barely making a dent in recidivism rates, which translates into as many as three out of four released from prison end up back in prison.

In exploring options for reducing recidivism, lawmakers are learning that current prison growth is not driven primarily by a parallel increase in crime or a corresponding surge in the population at large. Rather, it flows principally from a wave of policy choices that are sending more lawbreakers to prison and keeping them there longer.

Larry Norris, head of the Arkansas Department of Corrections until the end of his term in 2010, said, relative to lowering prison populations, "If you are afraid of a prisoner, lock him up forever, but if you are just mad at him, work on rehabilitating him and letting him out." That, Norris said, would go a long way toward lowering prison populations.

———

PRISON ENTREPRENEURS

One program that responds uniquely to the need for rehabilitation is the Prison Entrepreneurial Program (PEP) launched in the Cleveland, Texas, system by Catherine Rohr in 2004.

Rohr's rigorous program takes inmates, whose skills as drug dealers and gang leaders put them behind bars, and makes successful businessmen and responsible citizens out of them. The centerpiece of its curriculum is a four-month, Harvard-style master of business administration program, and it has attracted national attention.

Regrettably, Rohr, five years into it, became improperly involved with some of the inmates in her program. She resigned and the PEP board replaced her and has built effectively on her good work.

Early studies showed that after five years, the PEP program had reduced recidivism for participants to fewer than 5 percent, way below the national average of 69 percent.

I had a chance to see Rohr in 2008 while she was still leading her program. On a cold and rainy day in early December, I joined a group of Arkansas prison officials, businessmen, and pastors for a two-day visit at the Cleveland prison and the PEP offices in Houston. Our first day began at the Cleveland unit, where Rohr was teaching her class.

Rohr is an attractive woman whose savvy, toughness, seriousness of purpose, and faith make her a formidable presence. She was born in Montreal, Canada, and moved with her family to the Bay area of Northern California at age seven. At the University of California at Berkeley, she played rugby. She also has a blue belt in Brazilian jujitsu.

After graduating from Berkeley, Rohr took her first job with Summit Partners in Palo Alto, California, a venture capital firm doing multimillion-dollar deals. Three years later, she moved to American Securities in New York, a private equity firm, where she and her lawyer husband set up housekeeping in an expensive Manhattan apartment.

It wasn't enough to satisfy their thirst for "meaningful" lives, and one day Rohr and her husband packed up their belongings in a trailer, left New York, and headed southwest to Houston. It was there that Rohr developed the rudiments of the PEP program—an intensive course that included a "business plan" competition.

She signed up MBAs from Harvard Business School to edit the inmates' proposals. Other top business schools have since been added to the mix. Rohr also sent letters to hundreds of executives around the country inviting them to come to a prison in Texas to judge business plans, and she began a fundraising effort that brought in $1.7 million for PEP in 2007.

Referring to the gang leaders and drug lords in her student population, she says, "These guys have already proven to be entrepreneurs. We're just helping them excel at something they're already good at, legally."

It's not easy getting into the program. There is a 180-page application to fill out, which takes a week to finish. Only 20 percent of those who apply make it into the program—with only 60 percent of that number graduating. Those who are accepted have demonstrated a personal commitment to change, a strong work ethic, and leadership potential.

———

THE "CHICKEN DANCE"

For those who are accepted, the first day in the program is a seventeen-hour session in which PEP begins, among other things, to attack the "prison tough-guy persona" with such ice breakers as making them hug and do the "chicken dance," which looks as silly as it sounds. They also begin doing public speaking, which they will do hundreds of times before they graduate.

While writing a business plan is the main focus of the PEP program, the curriculum involves far more than that. The authors also have to present their plans to prospects and conduct themselves in a businesslike way. As visitors to the Cleveland unit, we got a firsthand look at how effective that training is.

When we arrived, the students of the class of 2010 put on a show for us that included several presentations of business plans and meetings with us in small groups to dig a little deeper into the content of the plans.

In the cheery classroom area in the center of the prison, the inmates in blue uniforms were immaculately groomed, clean-shaven, and beaming. Their tattoos, some of them apparently full body, were the only reminder of their criminal past and in fact dramatized the transformation that had clearly taken place. The good grooming is no accident. In PEP, there is both a business curriculum and a life skills curriculum.

When it comes to the business side of the program, inmates are given an *AP Stylebook* on style, usage, and punctuation, which they memorize.

As for life skills, students learn PEP's "ten driving values," take a personal inventory, and begin looking at their behaviors and what they need to work on. Students also identify their personality type and how they display it through both healthy and unhealthy behaviors.

A sampling of PEP's exhaustive handbook on "survival rules, guidelines, ethics and more" contains the following sample entries:

- No attitude…no being a jerk, no "gangstas" thinking you're better or smarter than anyone else.

- Color doesn't matter…Black, White, Hispanic (and let's not forget the few Asian brothers we've got)—we're all created equally. Prison may be segregated by race, but we're washing the penitentiary off of you.

- Hygiene required…don't stink. Brush your teeth. Don't be a slob. No hairy faces.

- No sagging and no high waisting…PEP's not "gangsta," so pull 'em up. And don't make us look excessively nerdy by hiking them up either.

- No pimp nails—even if you're not a pimp…Hate to tell you this, but it's really gross when you explain that you keep a long pinky nail so that you can pick your nose and clean out your ear wax.

- Don't overanalyze…chill out. If we have a problem with you that you need to know about, we're gonna tell you. Learn from your mistakes, forgive yourself, keep a great attitude, and know that you're loved.

———

HIGHLY PROFESSIONAL

All of us in the Arkansas contingent met individually with small groups of PEP inmates to discuss their business plans and personal goals, and all of us were bowled over by the high level of professionalism.

One young man who presented to all of us and then got together with me later has an idea for promoting bilingualism in companies. Delivering his presentation in both English and Spanish, he made a strong case for the value of the improved communications that would result, and is seeking to raise ten thousand dollars in startup costs.

PEP encourages outside investment in the budding companies, with a share in the business being negotiable. Investors deal with PEP, not the inmate, at least in the initial negotiations.

At the end of 2007, PEP had graduated 369 inmates from eight classes at a cost of fifteen thousand dollars per student; maintained a recidivism rate of less than 5 percent; and assisted forty-six graduates in launching businesses that included a real estate investment company, a hedge fund, a T-shirt printing operation, a Bible cover producer, and an educational software company.

Graduates achieved a 98 percent employment rate within four weeks of release, with average starting rates of eleven dollars an hour.

For those who complete the prison program, there is a high-energy graduation for which family members (who are kept in the loop from the beginning) and execs fly in, graduates wear caps and gowns (many for the first time), and PEP gives awards to the top business plans and presents the class valedictorian. Graduates qualify for PEP aftercare services, which include housing, access to a network of executives, clothing, and some medical insurance. While in aftercare, graduates may elect to attend E-School, an extension of the MBA program held on Tuesday nights.

During my visit to Cleveland, I talked to or heard from a dozen inmates and former inmates or staff members at PEP, and everyone had a history of drug abuse that had been a factor in their arrest and incarceration. Most of them were not then involved in 12-Step programs, believing the success they were achieving in PEP and IFI eliminated the root cause of their addictions and the need for a recovery program.

I agree that in the PEP and IFI groups, substance abuse will probably decline without a 12-Step program, but we must remember that addiction can strike anyone at any time under the right circumstances, particularly if you have been an addict in the past. The world is full of "successful" people who have succumbed. For the "Ten Driving Values" of the PEP program. see Appendix 5.

THE LEN YATES STORY

Finally, as we contemplate the recidivism problem and the need to rehabilitate and release the inmates we are not "scared of," as Mr. Norris put it, let us consider the Len Yates case and whether his sentence is appropriate and fair.

Fifteen years ago, police arrested thirty-year-old Len Yates, owner of the Canon Grill in Little Rock, on rape and drug charges. Classified as "date rape" because of the involvement of the drug Rohypnol, the case was widely covered by the media. Ultimately, Yates was convicted on one count of rape and sentenced to thirty-five years in prison. He will not be eligible for parole until 2021. The sentence was harsher than what he might have gotten because of a change in the law in 1997 shortly before his apprehension. Under the new law, he must serve a minimum of 70 percent of the sentence with no time off for good behavior. The prior law called for a minimum of 50 percent and time off for good behavior.

But for this increase in minimum time to be served and no time for good behavior, for which he would have been qualified, Yates could be applying for release this year instead of nine years from now. This is not to minimize the feelings of the victims in this case, but to suggest that a reduced sentence would make room for one more in the prison system since Yates will be living at an Arkansas Department of Corrections-approved location out of the mainstream at his parent's home.

On an icy January morning in 2008, I interviewed Yates, now almost forty-six, in a small conference room at Arkansas's Wrightsville Unit. He spoke about his life and how it has changed. By sharing his story, he hopes to help others avoid the bad choices he made and "turn to God."

Dressed in prison whites and now clean and sober, Yates said he engaged in more than ten years of heavy drug abuse, which led up to the violent crime he ultimately committed and is now paying for. A graduate of Catholic High School for Boys in Little Rock and Southern Methodist

University in Dallas, Yates began smoking marijuana when he was twelve years old and drinking alcohol when he was fifteen.

The pot was more of a lark than an addiction, at least at first. Yates was a delivery boy for the *Arkansas Democrat* daily newspaper and a friend, who delivered the state's other daily, the *Arkansas Gazette*, suggested one day that they "smoke a bowl." Yates tried it and became an occasional user.

But it was alcohol, not pot, that gave him the comfort he sought in ticklish social situations like dating girls and being a part of the "in crowd," an association he desperately sought.

―――――

DESTIN PARTIES

At eighteen, Yates, responding to the lure of spring break partying, rented a condo in Destin, Florida, and immersed himself in the sex and drug lifestyle. Soon after, he moved to Destin and added ecstasy to a drug list topped by cocaine and alcohol.

By the time he was twenty, Yates had become a hard-core drug abuser, but there was also a side of him, he says, that wanted to live the American dream with "the kids, the house, the dog, and the picket fence," and so at age twenty-eight he got married.

It was a disaster. He briefly tried to give up drugs, but his wife, he says, had married him because he was a party guy and didn't care for the change in his demeanor. The marriage ended in divorce, and he resumed drug and alcohol use.

Three years later, on the night of March 11, 1997, Yates, wasted by his daily use of cocaine and the bottle of wine he had just chugged, fell on his knees and cried out to God, begging Him, if He was there, to stop the addictions that plagued him.

"I was a criminal, a drug addict, and an alcoholic, and I was heading toward a bad end," Yates said.

The next morning, he was arrested at the Canon Grill and taken into custody following a police investigation that had culminated in his arrest. It did indeed stop the drug use, and Yates thought to himself, "Can this be God's plan to save me?"

Yates was put in handcuffs, taken to the county jail, and chained to a bench, where he was kept on suicide watch for the next twenty-four hours. After that, he was put into a two-man cell alongside a man charged with a capital felony—a fate Yates preferred over being exposed to the violence of the jail's holding cell.

Following his trial, Yates spent a year in the nightmarish pandemonium of the county jail, then was sent to the Arkansas Department of Correction's Cummins Unit and assigned to the "hoe squad" in a place dubbed "little Saigon" by the inmates. The men, sweating all day in the field, were tormented at night by mosquitoes infiltrating the barracks through broken windows.

"It was hell on earth, and I didn't know how I could ever do my twenty-five years in such a place," Yates says.

Still, he visited the chapel as much as possible to pray and give thanks. God must have heard him, Yates says, because it was not long before the chaplain requested he be assigned to work as one of his clerks.

A little over a year later, in January 2000, Yates was transferred to Wrightsville, where he began working with the chaplain, an assignment that was interrupted for a year when he was sent to the Ouachita River Unit in Malvern to participate in a "Reduction of Sexual Victimization Program." The program deals with sexual addiction and problems associated with these addictions, including anger.

"I was a sex-addicted, drug-addicted, angry person," Yates said, adding that "rape is really not about sex; it's about anger, and you can't have anger in prison. The consequences are too serious."

———

ACCEPTANCE

By the time he returned to the Wrightsville Unit, Yates said, he had come to terms with his anger. "Part of anger resolution," he said, "is acceptance. It is also about living life one day at a time."

At Wrightsville, his circumstances changed for the better, too. Working in the chaplain's office made it easier for family visits. And Yates is particularly grateful to all the church members who come to the prisons. Through them, he says, "I have been able to live a little easier and help others who literally have no contact with the outside world."

Yates says he has worked through the many "whys" that arose in his mind the first few years of incarceration, and says that he is a better person today for what has occurred. He believes God will create something good from his situation.

He also has tried to help troubled youths and others brought into the prison by speaking to them in groups, especially while he was serving on the inmate panel in Malvern.

"Basically," he said, "I told them my story, hoping that they would see the lesson in it and avoid prison life."

In a recent letter to his mother and father, Yates wrote:

I never would have imagined the life I am now living, but I am thankful for it.... There are days that are hard, but we all have our struggles, so who am I to feel sorry for myself? I am fortunate to be healthy and have my family and the friends I do. Sure, I look forward to the day when I am released, but I am thankful to God today for my life.

These days, Yates works in the mornings with the chaplain on the prison's Principles and Applications for Life program. In the afternoons, Yates, putting his business degree and experience to work, handles administrative tasks associated principally with the kitchen operations. He has also developed a newsletter for the Inmates Council.

Because of his sex offender conviction, when he is released, Yates will be restricted in terms of where he can live, and his parents—Tommy and Yvonne Yates—have sold their house and bought a twenty-acre tract outside Pulaski County that meets the legal requirements affecting their son. They are living in their new home now and are awaiting his arrival.

Yates doesn't know if his sentence will ever be reduced—his one appeal was denied—but he has decided to rely on God for that outcome. "I'm a firm believer in miracles," he says.

CHAPTER ELEVEN

Combat Veterans Overcome Addiction and Make a Difference

Bob G. served with the U.S. Marines in Vietnam for sixteen months and for many years has been treated for Post-Traumatic Stress Disorder (PTSD) stemming from his combat service during the late sixties. During the thirty-two years after his service, overcome by his fears, anger, and addictions, he lost his family and went to prison three times—once for murder. He also attempted suicide ten times. At one point, he was given a year to live because of his numerous afflictions. There's even more bad stuff to report about his experiences, but you get the picture.

The symptoms of PTSD include: re-experiencing (e.g., relentless nightmares), unbidden waking images (flashbacks), hyper arousal (e.g., enhanced startle anxiety, sleeplessness), and phobias. Many veterans who are afflicted with PTSD try to self medicate with alcohol and illegal drugs—with predictably bad results. Bob was one of them.

But here's the good part: Today, Bob is a happy man with a family and a mission. Because of his service to others, he is loved by many who know him. And he loves them back. He is the unofficial face of Recovery Central, a new Little Rock facility for 12-Step meetings, mainly Narcotics Anonymous. He sponsors more people than he can count, and he does it by the book (See *The Narcotics Anonymous Step Working Guides* and *Working Step Four in Narcotics Anonymous* available online).

When Bob is your sponsor, you can figure you're going to spend a year working with him on the steps. And you're going to attend meetings. And you're going to take his "suggestions" about what else you need to do to recover.

As big as he is, he's no drill sergeant. No one escapes a meeting without a hug from Bob. Not if he can help it. Of course, it's kind of a one-armed hug, not a full embrace, especially with women. He hugged a young woman once at the end of a meeting, and she burst into tears. In response, he quickly backed off and said, "I'm so sorry; I didn't mean to offend you."

Smiling through her tears, the young woman said, "You didn't offend me! It's just that I've never had a hug."

Bob has been clean and sober for ten years, and he and his wife of eleven years, also a former meth addict and in recovery for the same length of time, live in North Little Rock, Arkansas. She is his second wife, and they have children and grandchildren between them. She works, and he draws full disability and devotes whatever free time he has to helping others.

Bob also suffers from diabetes, heart problems, and pain from back, neck, and knee injuries sustained in a rocket attack in Vietnam. The injuries require that he regularly attend a pain management clinic, but it was the emotional pain that nearly killed him.

After his return from Vietnam, Bob wrecked ten cars trying to kill himself, and he killed another man in a pool hall gun battle, which brought a murder charge that put him in prison for the first time. He has been in prison three times, covering a span of more than eight years.

He served thirty months at the Cummins Unit state prison in Arkansas for the murder charge, another two years at a state police facility on related charges, and then another four years at FCI Memphis, the Federal Correctional Institution's medium-security facility, on drug charges.

He received eight medals and ribbons for the sixteen months he spent in Vietnam, and when he got home at not quite twenty years old, he continued his abuse of the alcohol and drugs that had occupied him nonstop in Vietnam to help him deal with the pain. Thirty-three years later, he found a way to begin his recovery.

Here is Bob's story as he tells it:

I come from a middle-class, Protestant family. My father and the majority of my uncles served in WWII and Korea. When I graduated from high school in 1966, I felt a calling to serve.

I was introduced to alcohol at the age of thirteen and drank on and off until Vietnam, when it became daily. My father and all of my uncles and most of the aunts were alcoholics or well on their way to it. They never talked about their war experiences.

After eight months of basic training at boot camp in San Diego, where I also received infantry and truck driver training, I volunteered to go to Vietnam.

Soon, I found myself on a C-130 loaded with officers and NCOs [non-commissioned officers], and Da Nang [Vietnam's major port city on the South China Sea] was our destination. I was a private first class and the lowest-ranking passenger on the plane.

As we approached Da Nang, the senior officer told me that the planes had been taking sniper fire, and my job would be to jump off upon landing and test the waters. I didn't even have a gun at that point, and I realized how insignificant I was. I was nothing more than a decoy.

NO SNIPERS

When I jumped out into the 130-degree heat that day, there were, as it happened, no snipers. Still, I was now convinced I would never make it home alive, and I disavowed God. I also began drinking whatever I could find to kill the fear and pain.

After about six weeks, I was assigned to a truck driving detail to pick up body bags brought in by helicopters for shipment to the states in closed caskets. I would haul the remains of these young men, some grossly distorted by their wounds and the heat, to the morgue for transfer to the caskets.

I lasted about two months before being sent for R & R [rest and relaxation] in Hong Kong. I couldn't sleep, and all I could think of were the families who would never know of the devastation inflicted upon their loved ones by their wounds and the searing heat. I spent five days in Hong Kong bars and brothels.

I was at the most northern marine base in Da Nang called "Red Beach" Force Logistic Command 7th Motor Transportation Battalion. We took convoys all over hauling troops, ammunition, and supplies throughout 1967 and the Tet offensive of 1968.

Certain that I wouldn't be coming home, I volunteered for any dangerous mission, like driving trucks loaded with hair-trigger explosives. I also realized that I felt exhilarated, more alive, afterward.

With my constant drinking and reckless behavior, I got into trouble and was demoted to private. My sergeant, realizing what was happening, sent me for three more days of R & R, and then for the rest of my tour I stayed around the base camp.

I returned to the United States nine days before my twentieth birthday, got married five days after returning, and stayed more or less drunk the whole leave. I spent another year completing my three years of service requirement.

The woman I had been dating and married went to my duty station with me. One night, I came out of a blackout/nightmare choking her and thinking she was a Viet Cong. She put up with drinking and subsequent drug addiction for about thirteen years.

Within five months after discharge, I wrecked and totaled our car and got my first DWI. As time passed, I totaled another eight or nine vehicles (I was the only passenger), and nine DWIs followed. I was forced to go to driving classes and lost my license.

―――――

A GOOD DAY TO DIE

I lived each day like it was a good day to die. I hung out at the most dangerous bars and clubs fully armed. I slept with nineteen guns in and around my bed.

When I did make it home, I would get up all through the night and go in and make sure my children were breathing and would check every door and window. And I would go out into my back and front yards checking my perimeter.

After my second trip to prison, I knew I was insane and full of anger and began to look for help. When my mother picked me up at the prison gates, I knew I had a choice. I could keep living like I had been or I could commit myself to the Veteran's Administration [VA] hospital's mental ward.

At first, I didn't want to admit I was powerless over my mental problems or my disease of addiction. Fortunately, after a trip to a hospital emergency room and talking to the doctors and nurses about my abuse of drugs, I ended up going to my first drug/alcohol program and got a taste of recovery.

I learned I didn't have a moral failing or lack of self-control, but a disease. I also found over the next seven weeks that I had PTSD, and would have to go into the hospital for treatment.

I spent the next two years in and out of the program and psych wards. I learned that my alcoholism and drug addiction (which by this time was called poly substance abuse) was secondary to my PTSD, and I began going to outpatient PTSD and drug/alcohol groups at the VA and the Vet Center for treatment.

I was doing everything I had been told to do except get a sponsor and go to meetings outside the VA. At the time, I used the excuse I couldn't trust anyone. Deep inside, as psychiatrists had told me through suicide attempts (one-car crashes) and the deadly lifestyle I had led, I felt I didn't deserve to live. After all I had seen, I had survival guilt.

Not using drugs was vital to my recovery, but it was not enough. I was miserable. I wasn't doing anything to change.

I wish I could say I turned my life around then, but I didn't. It took over eight more years, another stint in prison, a heart attack and two congestive heart failures.

After one more drug bust after being told I had only six months to two years to live, I finally went to my first meetings. At first, I went to meetings to get a paper signed attesting to my attendance to keep from being held in jail.

STARTING TO FEEL HOPE

I didn't realize at the first meetings I would hear other stories like mine, and I started to feel hope. Also, I had found out that I could possibly get a heart transplant if I tested clean for a year.

Today, I know my higher power had a plan I couldn't fathom. I was put on a new drug that caused my heart to improve, and that has allowed me to continue my recovery and to develop a life worth living.

The most important lessons I've learned and try to pass on to other combat veterans is that I have to treat my PTSD through psychiatric care, medication, and talking to and working with other combat veterans from all the wars.

Working on my alcoholism and addictions is something I do with guidance from my sponsor, who helps me work and live the 12 Steps and traditions in my life and to pray to a God of my understanding.

I had eleven years clean July 19, 2011, forty-two years after returning from Vietnam. Today, I'm a husband, father, son, brother, and friend. Today, when I see a man or woman in uniform I tell them, "Thank you for serving."

A key to Bob's recovery was his decision more than ten years ago to confront his addictions by going to Alcoholics Anonymous and shortly after that, Narcotics Anonymous. These 12-Step meetings, which are available free to all who seek recovery worldwide, gave him a recipe for success and a host of new friends to share it with. Bob also makes better use of Veterans Administration treatment options—in this case, Vet Centers (described in the next section).

Twelve-Step meetings work. They are accessible, and free. So there is always a place to go, get a cup of coffee, and be with people who have similar problems. Being with people and forming relationships is a key. The biblical principles upon which AA founder Bill Wilson based his 12 Steps, are, of course, vital, but they were not meant to be copied and handed out for people to read at their leisure at home. They were meant to bring people together in common cause. Addicts tend to be loners, and this is especially true of combat veterans.

RANGER DANNY REED

Former Army Ranger Danny Ray Reed II, who was engaged with special operations, had this to say in *Faces of Combat* by Pulitzer Prize-winning author Eric Newhouse:

"When you come back," Reed said, "you're either a workaholic or an alcoholic. If I wasn't working, I was drinking. It helps for the first couple of hours but then it takes you back into that frame of mind you don't want to be in. I drank so bad I had a two-day blackout, and that's dangerous."

During that blackout, Reed got into a row with the crew of a United Airlines flight to the point where they refused to sell him more drinks, which almost landed him in jail. Instead, he ended up in treatment for both his PTSD and his alcohol addiction, which led to this interesting observation about 12-Step programs.

Step one is admitting you do have PTSD. Step two was to quit drinking and drugging. They're different in some ways, but PTSD and alcoholism are a lot alike in other ways. You have to admit you have those problems. You can't be in denial about it. And you have to realize that it's something that will not go away and can't be cured. All you can do is learn to live with it.

————

VET CENTERS

VA hospitals provide treatment for PTSD, but they are big and at times impersonal, and some vets don't want to deal with them. Recognizing where these combat veterans were coming from, the federal government, in 1979, created a kind of welcoming, storefront operation in shopping malls and other accessible locations called Vet Centers. Staffed with a counselor or two and a secretary, the Centers were at first intended to serve the Vietnam veterans but were later expanded to include all veterans who had served in a combat zone. That includes World War II, Korea, Lebanon, Grenada, Panama, Persian Gulf, Somalia, former Yugoslavia, and the global war on terror.

————

FREE SERVICES

All the services are free and available to all combat veterans except those who have been dishonorably discharged. There are two Centers in Arkansas, one in North Little Rock and the other in Fayetteville, but they do offer outreach services.

The readjustment counseling services include: individual, group, marital, and family bereavement counseling; medical referrals; employment counseling, guidance and referral; alcohol /drug assessments; information and referral to community resources; sexual trauma counseling and referral; and community education.

I interviewed Van Hall, a veteran and a readjustment counselor at the North Little Rock Vet Center—a spacious and welcoming facility with a staff of five serving hundreds of veterans—about the need for the Centers and how they operate.

"Unfortunately," Hall says, "some of our veterans, particularly the Vietnam vets, have had bad experiences with the Veterans Administration in the past, and don't want anything to do with it. The low-key, highly personal Vet Centers provide an attractive alternative to large hospitals."

Vets who are mad at the government may miss out on treatment or benefits, and Hall encourages them to come in and find out about what's available to them. Actually, he notes with a smile, wives, learning of special benefits, sometimes push their husbands to find out what they are entitled to and to get the help they need.

Hall notes that his VA Center offers a host of material helpful to veterans, including a paperback book titled, *The War Within—One More Step at a Time* by cartoonist G. B. Trudeau, creator of Doonesbury. It concerns the rehabilitation of B. D., a regular character in the strip who struggles with PTSD and a reluctance to deal with it.

An estimated four hundred thousand veterans suffer from PTSD going back to World War II, and as the fighting continues in the Middle East, the casualties are mounting and so are the cases of PTSD.

PTSD is not unique to the battlefield, many psychiatrists point out. It can be found among rape victims, those who survived the Oklahoma City bombing, or 9/11, for example. But these events aren't quite the same, some doctors contend.

Dr. Dennis Grant, who served in Vietnam, put it simply in a recent *Wall Street Journal* article when he said, "Daily life in a combat zone is different than a civilian event."

———

COCAINE ADDICTS

Norrith Ellison, sixty, is another Little Rock area Vietnam vet who has turned his addiction to a drug—cocaine—into a benefit to the community.

Cocaine addicts are a special breed, says Ellison, who has been clean and sober for almost twenty-five years and started the state's first Cocaine Anonymous (CA) meeting in Little Rock in 1989.

It took him a while to get his bearings after Vietnam. He lived on the streets, drug addled and homeless, for ten years, before he began to turn his life around.

Today, he is widely known and respected in the community for his far-ranging activities in the service of addiction recovery. He was also a candidate for state representative in 2006. He lost the first round, but will likely run again.

Ellison is modest about his role in starting a CA meeting, and when asked about it, he laughs and says, "No big deal. All you really need to start a 12-Step meeting is a resentment and a coffee pot."

Ellison adds, "Seriously, I was just the guy God decided to work through to start Cocaine Anonymous groups in Arkansas. My biggest challenge in the beginning was finding the space. Nobody would rent me a room for my meeting."

No one, that is, until Rev. William Robinson Jr., pastor of Theresa Hoover United Methodist Church in Little Rock and founder of the Hoover Treatment Center, heard of Ellison's need.

Robinson said, "I'll give you your room."

Today, thirty CA meetings are held each week in Little Rock.

———

NORRITH ELLISON'S STORY

When it comes to substance abuse, Ellison knows what he is talking about. He's been there. One of thirteen children, he was brought up in the Ives Walk project in southeast Little Rock. His father was a meat packer and his mother a "domestic." The kids, he says, were well fed "with a heavy emphasis on meat," he recalls with a smile, and while the quarters were a little limiting—each child was only allowed to bring home one guest at a time—the arrangement, despite some infractions, he recalls, worked pretty well.

At fifteen, Ellison began to dabble in drugs. He started faking it with Lipton tea rolled in cigarettes to impress his buddies, but soon graduated to the real thing—pot, codeine, and LSD.

When he was eighteen, he enlisted in the U.S. Army and after basic training in El Paso, Texas, he was shipped out to Vietnam, where he served as a medical corpsman. He was in the same division as Lt. William L. Calley, who, many will remember, was convicted of war crimes in the slaughter of civilians at My Lai.

HEROIN IN VIETNAM

Heroin was readily available in Vietnam, much of it bought from Vietnamese farmers, and Ellison used the drug daily. He functioned well enough to do his job, which included dealing with the most ghastly effects of combat, and thirteen months of service in Vietnam, he was mustered out in 1970 as an E-5 ("Sergeant," to older veterans).

For the next nine years, Ellison, overcome by his addiction, roamed the mean streets of New York's Harlem, Newark, New Jersey, and Waterbury, Connecticut. He was a daily drug user and most of the time he was homeless and eating from some of the worst Dumpsters on the planet.

When his father died in 1976, family members tracked Ellison down and sent him a plane ticket to Little Rock (refusing his request for money to buy the ticket) for the funeral. He came back, but returned to the East Coast until 1979, when he moved back to Little Rock for good. That was also the year he switched from heroin to cocaine.

Cocaine, Ellison says, is a drug of unbelievably destructive power.

"It really takes you down. I have seen a guy," he says, "go from a Lexus to a drawstring garbage bag in a week."

Ellison, still in the throes of his addiction, married in 1983. In the following years, the couple had three children.

In 1987, which Ellison describes as "the lost year," things began to really unravel, and on Christmas Eve of 1988 he put a pistol in his mouth and pulled the trigger. The gun misfired.

"After that," Ellison says, "the drugs stopped working, and I couldn't get high. One night about midnight, I called the 1-800-Cocaine hotline, and was directed to Larry Stone at the Restore program." Restore is a thirty-day, 12-Step treatment program in Little Rock.

Right away, Ellison says, he had a problem with the first step, part of which is to admit powerlessness.

"The nurse at Restore kept reminding me of my 'powerlessness,' and we argued at length about the need to admit powerlessness, which I strongly resisted—even to the point of getting mad. She became afraid, and I felt powerful.

"But that's when I got it. The irony of it was that she went home to her family and probably had a comfortable rest in her own bed. I in turn was going back to a cot in a lockup. For the first time I accepted my powerlessness."

The next hurdle was the fellowship aspect. Ellison was going to AA meetings, and he loved the 12 Steps, but he was having trouble connecting with the other people attending except for one person. That was Columbus A (see chapter 1). who became his sponsor twenty-one years ago and is still his sponsor today.

Ellison concluded that the experiences of his cocaine addiction were different than those of the alcoholic, and he needed more time with his kind of addict.

———

THE RAINBOW GROUP

Shortly after that, Reverend Robinson gave him the key to the meeting room at Hoover, and six men gathered for the first meeting of the Rainbow Group of Cocaine Anonymous.

Ellison didn't know whether the meetings would catch on, but he got powerful help from the late Joe McQuany and the late "Geno" Walter, both recovering alcoholics. He couldn't have found better mentors. McQuany, readers will recall, was a key leader in recovery efforts both locally and internationally. (His full story is told in chapter 6.)

Walter was best known for founding the Sunday morning Hour of Power meetings at the Wolfe Street Center, which drew huge crowds and transformed lives. He was a leader in the recovery community and quietly helped Ellison get his CA meetings off the ground.

Walter's basic text was the eleventh step, which states, "Sought through prayer and meditation to improve our conscious contact with God as we understood Him, praying only for knowledge of His will for us and the power to carry that out."

As Ellison's CA meetings began to catch on in Little Rock and eventually spread to Pine Bluff, a town southeast of Arkansas' capital city, he turned to other ways to help people recover from their addictions.

One of the things that especially troubled him was the large number of people in recovery who have a relapse (often called a "slip") and turn to alcohol and other drugs once again for a solution to life's problems.

"In my first year of sobriety," Ellison says, "I sponsored three guys, and they all got loaded. That's when I got interested in 'relapse prevention,' a program for living to supplement, certainly not replace, the 12-Step program."

Using as his text, *Staying Sober: A Guide for Relapse Prevention* by Terence T. Gorski and Merlene Miller, which comes with a workbook, Ellison began to conduct classes at his New Reality Center that also rents rooms for 12-Step and other meetings.

Speaking about the book in its preface, Father Joseph C. Martin, a renowned supporter of AA and other 12-Step programs, had this to say: "Relapse Prevention planning is a powerful new approach that is helping thousands to escape from what had previously been a death sentence."

To sustain these recovery-focused activities and support his family, Ellison has continued to work as a lineman for the local electric company, a job he has held for twenty-two years. He also has his own company, HuCOM training solutions, which designs training programs for companies and also offers motivational speeches given by Ellison. One of his clients is the New York/New Jersey Port Authority.

———

WOMEN VETS

With her blonde bob and a big smile, former drug addict Stephanie Drake, a thirty-four year old ex GI from Pansy, Arkansas, looks happy in her recovery.

She has been clean and sober for eight years now and lives in a small apartment with her son, nine-year-old, Skylar, while she attends the University of Arkansas at Little Rock (UALR). She has six years of college, part of it at a local technical college, and is close to getting her nursing degree.

Drake began her journey to sobriety at ArkansasCares, a University of Arkansas for Medical Science (UAMS) program conceived to treat mothers and children together in a residential setting (see chapter 13).

Accepted at its North Little Rock facility, Drake and Skylar moved in for six months. During her stay, she attended daily 12-Step programs at the facility as well as out in the community. And at Wolfe Street, the nonprofit facility that offers nearly fifty 12-Step meetings a week, she found the sponsor who works with her to this day.

Like anyone else, Drake has her bad days, but she regularly goes to five 12-Step meetings a week, sponsors six women, avoids bad company, and cultivates a growing faith in God. She credits God for her escape from childhood foster care, her auspicious beginning with ArkansasCares, and the health of her son, who escaped the potentially dire consequences of her drug abuse during pregnancy.

These events might be attributed by others to coincidence, Drake says with a smile, but to her, "'coincidence' is God's way of remaining anonymous."

Drake's early life was rough. She was born in August 1976 to a sixteen-year-old alcoholic mother and a missing father she has never seen and knows almost nothing about. Her mother, who still struggles with her addictions, put two-year-old Drake, and later her sister, in foster care. Drake ended up in four different homes and was raped by a twelve-year-old boy when she was eight.

But that same year, 1984, Drake and her young sister caught a break. They were adopted by what she describes as a very loving family. Packing all their belongings in a small paper bag, they moved into a nice home in a good neighborhood.

Drake, however, did not really appreciate it. Perversely, she says, "all I could think about was getting back to my own family (her mother and brother). I didn't give my new family a chance."

Still she stayed on, had six years of a "stable life," and participated in sports and other activities in school. But then, in October of 1993 when she was a junior in high school, she decided to join the Army. She enlisted and left for Ft. Jackson, South Carolina, for basic training.

———

BASIC TRAINING

"I did well in basic training, and was a sharp-shooter and expert in throwing grenades (a skill she learned playing softball)." After basic, the Army sent her to Fort Sam Houston in San Antonio, Texas, for Advanced Individual Training (AIT). It was, Drake says, a defining moment marking "the beginning of a seven-year struggle with alcohol and drugs."

It began when she arrived in Texas. "I was off base and drinking the first night, and I never stopped. In July of 1995, eighteen months after my enlistment, I requested and received an honorable discharge from the military."

She was still only eighteen years old.

After mustering out, Drake stayed in San Antonio for a couple of months with a friend, but didn't work and mainly drank Jim Beam bourbon and smoked pot before packing up and moving back to Arkansas.

By then she was using drugs and drinking daily, and when she got a call from a former Army buddy in Louisiana, she went, intending to stay for a week. Instead, she spent "two of the worst years of my life." During those years, she added cocaine, meth, acid, and the date-rape drug GHB to her to her list of drugs.

Drake supported herself by bartending/waitressing, cleaning, laying carpets, and a variety of other jobs. She usually paid for her drugs with sex, a common arrangement in the drug world.

Returning to Arkansas once again, she almost immediately picked up two DWI arrests, which put her in county jails for short periods, but she still managed to hang on to the jazzy Pontiac Firebird that complemented the seventeen or eighteen tattoos and piercings she had acquired.

As her drug habit increasingly gripped her, Drake had also taken to moving in with complete strangers, most of them meth cooks. One, believing she was a drug enforcement plant, put a gun to her head and threatened to kill her, but "through God's grace," she says, she talked her way out of it.

There was a brief respite when Drake found her little sister in Little Rock and moved in with her. Her sister helped her find an apartment and a job, and things began to look rosier.

———

ADDICTED PEOPLE

"Then," says Drake with a wry smile, "I noticed there were people like me living across the street—addicted people. I am addicted to addicted people, and soon, I was drinking every night, and eventually turned back to meth."

In the middle of all the chaos, she got pregnant, but it didn't slow down her use of drugs.

"I am deeply ashamed of this today," she says, "and only share it in the hope that others don't have to do what I've done. The fact is, I used drugs through my entire pregnancy."

When the birth pains came, the father of the baby dropped her off at Baptist Hospital, and she was on her own. Skylar's birth, miraculously, was uneventful, but aside from being hyperactive, he bore no signs of Drake's heavy use of drugs, which continued even after he was born.

"A few months into my son's life," she says, "we were cooking meth in the same house as the baby and doing the dirty drug dishes with his bottles."

When Skylar was about ten months old, Drake's biological mother showed up. "She moved here," Drake says, "and we used drugs together. Then I started using the needle and only stopped because I realized that my son could end up like me in foster care and doomed to a life of unhappiness. But despite this moment of clarity, I still didn't know how to break out of the hell I was in."

Then, she says, "My miracle happened. My adopted dad and mom, who had taken me out of foster care when I was eight, showed up when I was finally ready to change. They found ArkansasCares for me."

About her sponsor, Drake says, "She taught me how to be happy, joyous, and free. Those are things I never thought possible before I started working steps. Once I had worked steps, I had to start living them. I believed that others that had come before me found something that changed their lives and that was enough for me early on, but as time went on I had to believe in something more. That was God for me."

Drake and her sponsor "brought meetings into Arkansas Cares' North Little Rock campus over a two-year period ending in 2005, and it was an amazing experience," she said.

"I can't tell you how many women I have sponsored through the years and how many have stayed sober, but I can tell you that giving away what I have has kept me sober."

About four years ago, Drake found her brother. "I…talked to him about his own struggles with addictions and problems with the law, and just over a year ago I also made an amends to my little sister, who felt that I had abandoned her. It was painful but also healing for both of us. We cried together, laughed together, and grew closer together."

As to her future, Drake says, "Every day I turn my thoughts and actions over to God and pray that I may help someone on this amazing journey called life."

———

NEW COURT HELPS VETS

In addition to veterans' hospitals and Vet Centers, two other facilities are available in the Little Rock area to help veterans: drug courts and homeless facilities for vets.

In the late spring of 2011, Sixth Circuit Judge Mary S. McGowan convened Little Rock's new Veterans Treatment Court (VTC) on the third floor of the Pulaski County courthouse, the second of its kind in Arkansas and one of about forty nationwide.

The mission of the VTC program is to promote recovery and rehabilitation from substance abuse and mental health issues. When successful, which is most of the time, damaged lives and broken families are restored, and society benefits.

On the docket in Judge McGowan's court were ten honorably discharged young men and women veterans whose crimes mainly had to do with drug dealing, possession of cocaine, theft of property, and other nonviolent crimes. What happens to them in succeeding months will be up to them, but for now it is useful to see how the system works and to get a glimpse of how veterans fare in the forty-odd courts already functioning.

First, VTCs, like drug courts, are an alternative to standard courts in that they combine the structure and accountability of a court but with a strong emphasis on treatment. They provide a non-adversarial judicial process for sentencing an offender to probation, which consists of a strenuous treatment program that addresses the needs of the offender and requires regular court appearances to monitor program compliance.

VTCs are typically staffed by a team consisting of the judge and court staff, a prosecutor, a public defender or private attorney representing the offender, a probation officer, and a Veterans Treatment Court liaison—a key position.

Treatment services such as psychiatric counseling, thirty-day recovery programs, transitional housing, and other needed services are provided through local facilities. The process averages about eighteen months and when completed to the satisfaction of the judge, the offending vet's record is expunged.

In the Little Rock court, Toby Lambert is the Veteran's Treatment Court liaison. He supplies Judge McGowan with vital information about each vet and is also a licensed counselor specializing in the treatment of Post-Traumatic Stress Disorder at the Fort Roots veterans hospital in North Little Rock.

Fort Roots offers a variety of medical services to veterans, including a thirty-day residential treatment program when it is needed. The court may also refer veterans to outside providers in the community.

———

ELIGIBILITY REQUIREMENTS

Veterans seeking to participate in the VTC must meet the following eligibility requirements:

First, he or she must have a specified qualifying offense or crime, substance abuse and mental health issues, or mental health issues with co-occurring substance abuse.

Second, the veteran must have an honorable, general, or discharge status under honorable conditions and be eligible for Veterans Administration services.

Third, because the VTC is a voluntary program, veterans charged with qualifying offenses must agree in writing to enter into the program and to allow the Department of Veterans Affairs to communicate with the court about their treatment.

The goals of the VTC are to:

1. Hold participants accountable for their criminal offense.
2. Connect eligible veterans with comprehensive treatment services, benefits coordination, and support services available through the Veterans Administration.
3. Help veterans get their lives back on track after being arrested and keep them moving forward in their lives on the road to recovery and prevent recidivism.
4. Provide the care and treatment veteran participants need to best serve their individual needs, manage their care, and help them solve their problems.
5. Assist with assigning veteran participants to a court-appointed VA service officer, who will provide guidance on such things as submitting claims and related matters.
6. Reach out to veterans who have turned to drugs and alcohol, have mental health issues, and have other issues of a criminal nature so that they may develop skills to live a productive and sober life, find housing, and mend broken relationships.

7. Help veteran participants obtain and complete educational goals and gain employment.

So what does a VTC look like when in session? A recent report filed by CNN about Orange County, California, Judge Wendy Lindley shows the judge dispensing justice with tough talk and a little cheerleading directed at the former servicemen who've returned from war in Iraq or Afghanistan.

WELCOME BACK

"Mr. Baker," Lindley asks one veteran, "how long you been sober?"

"About four or five years," Baker says.

"Welcome back to the human race. It's great to have you around here," Lindley replies.

"Mr. Culpepper," the judge later addresses another offender, "the report from Veterans Affairs is excellent. I am going to continue you on probation on the same terms. Give him a hand, folks."

The gallery offers applause.

Lindley calls what her court does "therapeutic justice." The Veterans Affairs Agency calls it part of a veteran justice outreach initiative that seeks to avoid the unnecessary criminalization of mental illness and extended incarceration of veterans. The idea, all agree, is to rehabilitate offenders, not punish them.

For example, one veteran, Michael, who served in Army Special Operations in Afghanistan and lost a leg to a rocket-propelled grenade attack, was pleading guilty to making a death threat.

Instead of sentencing him to three years in jail, Lindley put him on probation and ordered eighteen months of supervision and treatment for his PTSD and problems with drugs and alcohol.

The approach seems to be working. For people participating in treatment courts, the relapse and crime recidivism rates and damage to the individual's family and community are greatly reduced while the success rates for staying sober and living a healthy, productive life are increased.

Ronald D. Castille, chief justice of the Pennsylvania Supreme court and a Vietnam veteran, agrees that VTCs are a good thing.

Justice Castille, writing in the Veterans Day edition of the *New York Times,* said, "Too many proud veterans resist assistance from the VA and allied private organizations, and as a result find themselves on the wrong side of the law, for reasons related more to their experience in service to country than to criminal intent."

As Justice Castille notes, the first such court was established through the efforts of Judge Robert T. Russell Jr. in Buffalo, New York. According to Justice Castille, Judge Russell's program had been completed by 90 percent of those who enter it without any case of recidivism.

———

CHRISTIAN BIKERS

When "Stroker" Wiggs, the "Bandido" bike rider who became a Christian minister, died in January 2011 in Little Rock, Neal Benschoff lost a dear friend and role model. Benschoff, also a former member of an outlaw biker group that terrorized the countryside was, like Stroker, a Vietnam War veteran.

Thanks to inpatient care at Fort Roots and regular attendance at 12-Step meetings, Benschoff has been clean and sober for twelve years now. He is also being treated at the VA for PTSD.

Like Stroker, Benschoff is now a member of the Christian Motorcyclists Association, and he spends a lot of Sunday mornings in saloons carrying a message of recovery. Sometimes he visits the church Stroker founded, the Church of the Word, in a community east of Little Rock.

Benschoff sponsors men who are struggling with addictions, and he gives his testimony when asked. Troubled by dyslexia since he was a child, Benschoff has not written down much of his testimony. The following is his story as he told it to me.

Benschoff, who lost his father in a shooting incident when he was eleven and was raised by an alcoholic mother who consorted with mostly bad men, including a member of the mob, was not well prepared for life. And because of his untreated dyslexia, school was a nightmare.

When he was seventeen, Benschoff and a Los Angeles high school friend stole a Chevy Impala. The friend got caught and was charged and convicted of the crime.

When Benschoff got the news, he figured his buddy would snitch on him, so he fled to the Marine recruiting office and signed up. This, he figured, would get him out of town with a decent cover.

He got away with his part of the theft, but the Vietnam experience and its aftermath of addiction and lawbreaking over the next thirty years, combined with his troubled childhood, almost did him in.

Benschoff went to Marine boot camp in San Diego that summer of 1966, and in September, he got his orders and headed west toward Vietnam on a Continental Airlines flight from Los Angeles. He was excited and happy. He had escaped the law, and he was a Marine with a paycheck and a great adventure ahead of him.

Three days later, Benschoff arrived at Da Nang, Vietnam, boarded an Air Force C-130, and landed at the demilitarized zone, a no-man's land between the North and South Vietnam forces where most of the fighting took place.

He realized then he had made a mistake.

———

BLACK PAJAMAS AND FUNNY HATS

"Our mission up there was to search and destroy," Benschoff said. "At first, we were fighting these farmers in black pajamas and funny hats, but later the NVA [North Vietnam Army] came in, and things got a lot tougher."

"There were daily mortar attacks, and we saw a lot of death," he said. "The second day I was there, a helicopter came back from the field loaded with dead and wounded and when the door opened, blood poured out."

Most of the soldiers drank alcohol daily and smoked pot or pot laced with opium. Much of it came from the farmers.

After twelve months and twenty-five days and a couple of minor shrapnel wounds, Benschoff, by then a corporal, flew home with what was left of the 130 men he had gone over with. Seventy, barely half, had survived.

"When we went over to Vietnam, everybody on the plane was jazzed," Benschoff said. "When we came home, everybody slept."

He took thirty days of leave in Los Angeles when he got home and began drinking "a quart of vodka a day and two quarts a day on weekends."

He didn't know it then, but the emotional scars he was treating with alcohol and hard drugs would persist for another three decades before he would begin to get well just short of the year 2000. Today, he says, he is as happy as he has ever been. Of his earlier life, he says, "I tried to act like normal people, but I could never bring it off."

His current life style contrasts strongly with the mayhem and violence of the thirty years preceding his recovery.

In March 1968, Benschoff mustered out of the Marines at age twenty-two, vowing that "nobody's gonna put me in that position again."

He felt, like many Vietnam War veterans, that his country had turned its back on him, and for a brief time, deeply resentful, he and some other vets took their anger out during episodes of violence against the white-robed Hare Krishna followers peddling flowers and love at airports.

Benschoff, a tough guy from the time he was a kid, was small at five feet, five inches tall, and he compensated by becoming an amateur boxer who also raced cars and motorcycles for money.

"I raced everything," Benschoff says, "and I could make a hundred dollars or more a race."

There was also the death of his father, a significant factor. Benschoff had been brought up within three miles of the ocean, and his father had owned a small company that made surfboards and other products associated with surfing and diving.

SHOT AND KILLED

When Benschoff was eleven, the company foreman had shot and killed his father at the office with a rifle. In a bizarre twist, the father's death was ruled a suicide at first. Later evidence confirmed, however, that the foreman had indeed shot his father, but before he could be brought to trial, the foreman himself committed suicide.

The death of his Benschoff's father, especially under these circumstances, and the drunken behavior of his mother, who died of an overdose of pills and alcohol at the age of fifty-three, helped push him into his wild life of drinking and drugging financed by his love of racing.

After his tour in Vietnam, Benschoff married "another drug addict" and began to work for North American Rockwell as a machinist. He also took courses and eventually became a union carpenter.

Not surprisingly, Benschoff's first marriage didn't work out. Both he and his wife were heavily into drugs, and he began riding with outlaw motorcycle gangs. He also became a major drug dealer. He made his own cocaine buys in Mexico and Columbia through a Florida connection. Later, he began manufacturing methamphetamine.

Benschoff sold most of his drugs through four notorious biker organizations, which he declines to identify.

"Outlaw bikers sell a lot of drugs," he said, "and two other products, women and guns."

Benschoff faced danger almost every day. One of the biker groups he supplied actually put out a contract on him to have him killed, but Benschoff eventually worked out the conflict with the gang leaders. He was never afraid, he says, and that gave him an advantage and made him successful.

"I was good at the drug business, because I wasn't afraid to kill people," he says. And he did it with either a gun or a baseball bat.

Benschoff wasn't afraid of *being* killed either. "I wasn't afraid to die," he says, "because it would get me out of the pain of living. I learned that in Vietnam."

Benschoff still has no fear of death. When asked about it, he says with a wink and a smile, "I'm not afraid to die now, but it's not because of the pain. It's because I know where I'm going."

Today, he owns his own home and a Harley Heritage motorcycle. He has a pretty healthy bank account, draws full disability from the VA, and stays in contact with his ex wife (a second marriage) and their two children living in Colorado.

"I try to do the right things with people," Benschoff says. "Life is good now. I follow through with things, I sponsor. I do what I say I will."

Benschoff, who sponsors a number of men, says he wanted to tell his story in the hope that it would encourage others to adopt a spiritual focus and seek recovery from their addictions.

CHAPTER TWELVE

Pat Summerall's Epiphany and Other Celebrity Stories

Pat Summerall's epiphany, that moment of truth when he knew that he was in serious trouble with alcohol, came while he was broadcasting the 1992 annual Masters Golf Tournament at Augusta, Georgia, for CBS. It was something he had done—and done impeccably—for twenty-four years.

In a radio interview in 2009 with Dennis Rainey, president of FamilyLife in Little Rock, Summerall, a former Arkansas Razorback, New York Giant, and premier broadcaster, described his ghastly confrontation with the truth.

"I was staying in Augusta in a strange house…I had a few drinks before I went to bed, and I got sick. I got up at three in the morning, and I went into the bathroom and threw up, and I looked at—this is kind of gross—but I looked at what had come out of me, and I didn't realize what it was. It was part of my stomach, and it was blood. And I thought, "What the heck? What's wrong with me?"

And when Summerall looked in the mirror above the basin, "it illuminated my pale and haggard face, my bloodshot eyes, and all the protruding veins on my face and nose."

He pulled himself together and was able to finish his coverage of the tournament, but the end of his drinking career was at hand. Later that year, an intervention conceived and led by his longtime friend, NFL colleague, and fellow broadcaster, the late Tom Brookshier, put him in the Betty Ford Center in Rancho Mirage, California, for treatment.

Intrigued by what I had heard on the radio and what I had read in his book, *Summerall: On and off the Air*, I flew to Dallas on a fall day and drove out to his home on South White Chapel in the fashionable Southlake section of Dallas to ask him about his story in person. It was several years before his death at 82 in April 2013.

AMAZING GRACE

From the gate in the towering stone fence bearing the inscription, "Amazing Grace," I could see a winding drive leading, it seemed, to infinity. Pat's wife, Cherie, welcomed me on the intercom, the gates swung open, and I drove in. When I pulled up, Pat was standing on the steps of a mansion in a blue shirt and slacks with a black lab, named Gracie (short for "Amazing Grace") at his side.

After a warm welcome, he led me inside—walking a little gingerly, the aftereffects of hip and knee surgery—and we settled into a couple of easy chairs. Gracie joined us on the couch.

I suggested that Pat tell me what his alcohol-addicted life had been like, what had happened to stir him to seek help, and what his life is like now. And that's what he did.

Summerall stayed at Betty Ford for thirty-three days—five more than the usual twenty-eight, he says, because it took him five days to get over his resentment against Brookshier and his intervention. He had also been somewhat unsettled at first by the assignment of a roommate whose nickname was "Psycho." But with the help of a *Big Book* of Alcoholics Anonymous and a Bible on his bedside table, he settled in.

Today, Summerall is very grateful for Brookshier's intervention. He talked to his friend on the phone several times a week before Brookshier's death in 2010. Since the day he left Betty Ford, Summerall has not had another drink, and he has found a deep faith in God.

So what was it that first launched him down the path of addiction and his close brush with death? Let's go back a bit.

Summerall grew up in Lake City, Florida. His parents were divorced before he was born, and he was reared mainly by his grandmother, Augusta Georgia Summerall. She loved him and was good to him, and he loved her in return.

As a youngster, Summerall had a crippled leg, and, to her everlasting credit, Augusta saw to it that he had it operated on successfully. In time, he became a gifted athlete in high school, college, and in the ranks of the pros, mostly as a kicker.

NEW YORK GIANTS

Summerall's older fans will remember that day in 1958 when he was the kicker for the New York Giants in the NFL championship game against the Baltimore Colts. Highlights are still shown in grainy black and white, and it is still considered by many to be the greatest game ever played.

On that day, the Colts, led by Johnny Unitas, prevailed by a score of 23 to 17 in overtime. Try as they might, Giant fans still cannot stop Colt's fullback Alan "The Horse" Ameche from crossing the goal line and ending the game.

The Giants' game against the Cleveland Browns a week earlier to win the division championship, some would say, was even better. The Giants held Jim Brown, among the greatest running backs of all time, in check, and Summerall, after missing a thirty-yard field goal, kicked a fifty yarder in a snowstorm. The Giants won.

Summerall had entered the pro ranks with Detroit and later joined the Chicago Cardinals before signing on with the Giants. Before joining the pro teams, he played both defensive and offensive end for the Arkansas Razorback college team. He also excelled at baseball, basketball, tennis, and golf.

In 1961, at the age of thirty-one, Summerall hung up his cleats and accepted a job with CBS in New York City. Over the next thirty years, paired with the likes of Brookshire, John Madden, Chris Schenkle, and Jack Buck, he prospered. And he drank. Prodigiously. It was vodka in the summer and bourbon in the winter.

And he had lots of company, including Howard Cosell, a broadcaster in his own right who, in Summerall's company one night, drank more than fourteen martinis with barely visible effect.

On another occasion, described in hilarious detail in Summerall's book, the two found themselves stranded in the Bronx late one night. They finally found a cab, which they agreed to share with another passenger, a Madison Avenue ad man.

"The ad man who was in the backseat with Howard," Summerall reports, "made it clear that he was not a fan. He'd listened to Howard's broadcast of the fight that night, [heavyweight Ernie Terrell had won], and he made some negative comments about it. The next thing I knew, they were swinging away, knocking the crap out of each other."

Summerall stopped the cab and separated the men, putting the ad man in the backseat and Cosell in the front.

COSELL LOSES TOUPEE

"Howard got in without protest," Summerall reported, "then slumped over in his seat. His toupee fell off, and I could see a gash in his head."

The ad man took another shot at Cosell when he got out at his home, and when Summerall delivered Cosell to his house, Cosell's wife asked what had happened. Summerall replied, "Oh nothing, just the usual trip home."

Summerall loved his work as a broadcaster. In his radio interview with Rainey, he said, "I think the happiest times, were certainly with Madden and Brookshire. Tom and I, both being ex players, became very close friends—like brothers almost. I never had a brother. But he and I became very close. He was the best man at my wedding. We still talk on a weekly basis."

He was a good provider, but Summerall is quick to acknowledge his shortcomings when it came to his late wife, Kathy, and his children Susie, Jay, and Kyle.

"I was not a very good father. My relationships with them, my three children, and my wife, deteriorated and began to fall apart. I didn't realize it. I didn't want to admit it to myself that I was not a very good father.... My life was on the road, and I became less and less of a father, less and less of a husband, and I didn't realize what was happening to me. Maybe I did realize and didn't want to admit it to myself. I think that's a better description."

During his career, Summerall was rarely confronted about his heavy drinking, but one exception was at the Kemper Open one year.

"I remember one of the wives took me aside. I'll never forget it. She said, 'Hey. You don't have to be the first guy at the dance. You don't have to be the last guy to leave the party, you don't have to drink the most, you don't have to be the life of the party every night. Why don't you slow down a little bit?'" The intervention didn't stop him. Not then, at least.

Since Summerall left Betty Ford, he has never had another drink, and he began to turn his attention to helping others, including his old friend and drinking buddy, legendary New York Yankee baseball player Mickey Mantle.

———

PAT AND MICKEY

Summerall and Mantle had been pals and drinking buddies going back to when they had adjoining lockers in Yankee stadium, where the Giants and Yankees played their home games. Shortly after Summerall got out of Betty Ford, Mantle pressed him for details on the experience.

"Are they big into religion out there?" he asked.

"Well, yeah—it's part of it," Summerall answered.

When Summerall asked Mantle about what denomination he was, Mantle had no idea what that meant. "I ain't never been to church," he explained.

"Being from Oklahoma," Summerall told Mantle, "you probably are a Baptist," to which Mantle replied, "That'll be fine. I'll take that."

In December 1993, Mantle checked in to Betty Ford and in early 1995, Summerall says, "Mickey was diagnosed with liver cancer. He was admitted to Baylor University Medical Center in late May of that year and then approved to get on a transplant list.

"Unfortunately, the transplant did not restore Mickey's health. On August 13, 1995, my dear friend died at Baylor University Medical Center in Dallas."

Summerall mourned the loss, but he says, "I was glad for one thing that happened to Mickey after he became sober. Despite his lack of experience with organized religion, Mickey found faith. The things he heard at the Betty Ford Center and from visits from his old Yankee teammate Bobby Richardson led him to God.

"He was baptized and seemed to gain fresh wisdom as well as peace," Summerall says. "In his last press conference, which he gave at Baylor, Mickey said he was no hero. 'God gave me everything, and I blew it. For the kids out there, don't be like me!'"

After more than ten years of sobriety, the physical damage Summerall had done to himself began to surface. Like Mantle, his liver, too, began to fail and brought him literally to within days, perhaps hours, of dying.

But Summerall got the liver he needed in 2004 when a young man, thirteen-year-old Adron Shelby, son of Melva and Garland Shelby of Pine Bluff, Arkansas, died. Summerall described the experience in his book:

Adron was just a student in junior high school when he collapsed while giving a speech in history class. He died three days later of a brain aneurysm. A few days after I received their precious gift, the Shelbys buried their son.

I talked to Melva from my heart, and thanked her and her family. I expressed condolences for the loss of her son, and I told her what a difference their organ-donation decision had made not only keeping me alive but making me a better person.

She hugged me again and said, "It's almost like I'm hugging a part of my child."

Summerall struggled for some time with the idea that someone— Adron—had to die for him to live. Why did this have to be? The answer, which came from his local pastor, was "because God's not through with you yet."

———

EDDIE SUTTON RECOVERS

Eddie Sutton, with a record of 804 victories and twenty-seven NCAA appearances, compiled over thirty-seven years of college coaching at five schools, is one of the top six most-winning basketball head coaches of all time. And he is among the most loved.

Many who follow the game of basketball know that Sutton has had his struggles with alcohol. They first came to light in 1987 when he was coaching at Kentucky, and, like Summerall, he ended up at the Betty Ford Center for treatment.

He publicly acknowledged his alcoholism, began following a 12-Step program of recovery, and resumed his career without incident for the next nineteen years. In Louisville, they even named an AA meeting after him: "the Phantom Group."

"They were determined to keep me sober," Sutton laughed, "even to the extent of starting a meeting especially for me, and it has grown and continues to attract people in recovery."

Six years ago, while a coach at Oklahoma State University, Sutton was involved in a drunk driving accident and again entered treatment, this time at Laureate Psychiatric Clinic and Hospital in Tulsa.

Prescription drugs, in addition to alcohol, were implicated in the episode. The drugs had been prescribed for intense back pain, and he had added a bottle to the mix because the drugs didn't seem to be reaching the pain.

Sutton was quoted as saying at the time, "It was a dumb thing to do. I got to where I was hurtin' so darn bad, I just succumbed to temptation and reached for a bottle."

Pain continues to plague Sutton, and at the time we talked several years ago, he had planned a total hip replacement that was expected to help.

Sutton has a special concern for young people and their struggles with drugs and alcohol, and in recent years he has met with fraternity and sorority pledge classes to tell them about his own struggles and what they might learn from them.

The first year, about fifteen hundred attended and the number later increased to eighteen hundred. Sutton also regularly follows up in person with students on substance-abuse-related matters. Sutton's latest dream is to build a National Sports Center for Drug-Free Youth in Tulsa with the goal being to "change young lives."

Steve Sutton, a Tulsa banker, says his father's recovery has been characterized principally by his desire to help others.

"If you played with him or coached with him," Steve said, "you became part of his family, and he kept in touch."

This played out most dramatically in the January 2001 charter plane crash that killed everyone on board, including ten Oklahoma State University basketball players heading back from their game at the University of Colorado.

Coach Sutton, who was not on the plane, insisted, Steve said, that he be the one to make the calls to the families of the victims.

"These are my kids," the grief-stricken Sutton said simply.

Sutton, seventy-seven, was born in Dodge City and raised in Bucklin, Kansas. He was an only child whose father was a combination mechanic, electrician, and farmer, and his mother was a cook for forty years at restaurants and the local school. Neither of his parents drank, he said, and they gave him a "great set of values."

"My dad," Steve said, "grew up driving tractors and thinking basketball."

———

MEET GARY STROMBERG

During the sixties and seventies, Gary Stromberg, a West Coast public relations executive and one-time movie producer, toured the world with the likes of the Rolling Stones, Pink Floyd, the Doors, Three Dog Night, and others and shared their appetite for women and dope—mostly heroin, cocaine, pot, and alcohol.

A couple of years ago, Gary came to Little Rock to promote his book, *The Harder They Fall,* telling the recovery stories of twenty celebrities he had interviewed. He himself has more than twenty-five years in recovery.

Gary and I hit it off, and I took him to a couple of 12-Step meetings. At one of them, he was the guest speaker and told his own story of recovery.

His book is a great read. His list of interviewees (some now deceased) includes Chuck Negron, lead singer of Three Dog Night; Grace Slick, lead singer of Jefferson Airplane and Jefferson Starship; Paul Williams, lyricist and composer; comedians Richard Pryor and Richard Lewis; jockey Pat Day; boxer Gerry Cooney; pitcher Dock Ellis; actors Mariette Hartley, Malcolm McDowell, and Malachy McCourt; and others.

In the front of Gary's book, Lewis Lapham, noted author and former editor of *Harper's* magazine, and Stephen Davis, a "best-selling chronicler of musical luminaries" (like Jim Morrison), provide stylish and entertaining comments on the subject at hand—addiction—and its victims.

Referring to his late friend Terry Southern (a drinker himself and writer of the screenplay for *Dr. Strangelove*), Lapham said, apropos of addiction, "I remember him saying to the assembled company at a table at

Elaine's, 'There is no power on earth that can loosen a man's grip on his own throat.'"

Davis, for his part, spoke at length of the miraculous recovery and resurrection of the entire Aerosmith band, and his comment on the stories of the celebrities is heartening.

"Saw toothed, stripped down, exposed, and gratefully alive, these people and their stories combine into one of the oldest forms of literature: the quest saga. These people have dedicated themselves to seeking new worlds—and to new ways of living in them. I hope these interviews will inspire you as they have moved and encouraged me."

Gary Stromberg himself tells a shortened version of his own story to establish his credentials as a reporter well qualified to cover the celebrity addiction beat.

———

RUMBLE IN THE JUNGLE

In 1974, for example, he handled the public relations for a music festival that preceded the historic Muhammad Ali-George Foreman African "Rumble in the Jungle" prizefight. As part of the gig, he traveled to Swaziland with Ali's corner man, Drew "Bundini" Brown, where the two stumbled on a Merck Corp. factory, which was producing pharmaceutical cocaine.

"Talk about kids in a candy store," Gary says.

Then there was his first movie. Fueled by two years of ever-increasing cocaine use, he produced a surprisingly successful picture called *Car Wash* with Richard Pryor. The money poured in.

After that came a spectacular flop, and it finally brought him down. It was a movie called *The Fish that Saved Pittsburgh* that was, in his words, "conceived and written in one rollicking night of gluttonous coke snorting."

Bankrupt in every way, he went home.

"Virtually broke," he said, "I moved back into the house I was raised in. A forty-year-old, failed big shot living with his parents."

It took a few more years, but the end finally came with a 12-Step meeting.

His wild ride, he reflects, "started out as great fun. For someone shy like me, drugs made me bigger and bolder. Eventually drugs and alcohol got the best of me. The fun became depravity.... I crashed and burned, but the will to survive took over. I was given the greatest gift I'd ever received. Sobriety. And with it came a new life."

Today, Gary heads a small public relations firm on the West Coast, and he talks about "what it was like" in front of audiences like the Wolfe Street Center in Little Rock with the hope that it will keep him clean and sober and change some lives. He's well into recovery now, thanks, he says, to a "higher power" he chooses to call "God."

But the book is mainly about his celebrity friends and their stories, and here is a sampling:

———

PAUL WILLIAMS

Remember lyricist, composer and actor Paul Williams?

Williams said, "You know you're an alcoholic when you misplace a decade." And he was one. Big time.

When you consider this Oscar, Grammy, and Golden Globe award-winning songwriter turned out "We've Only Just Begun," "Rainy Days and Mondays," "Rainbow Connection," and "Evergreen" during part of this time, you marvel.

Williams said, "The fast track to my bottom was cocaine. I was using it every day—an eight ball a day by the end of the eighties. A lot of money. But what it cost me was nothing compared to what it cost me."

Today, Williams visits prisons and serves on boards like the National Council on Alcoholism and Drug Dependence.

GRACE SLICK

Grace Slick, who fronted the Jefferson Airplane and Jefferson Starship bands, now clean and sober, is matter of fact about her recovery. "What keeps me from drinking now," she says, "is that drugs and alcohol don't work anymore. Alcohol makes me a jerk, pot makes me paranoid, and I'm already wired to the tits, so I can't use cocaine."

Slick started going to 12-Step meetings in 1976 and loved them. "I thought they were fabulous," she says, "because all the religions I'd been aware of had guys with funny outfits on, and you had to pay them a lot of money. And one person was holier than everybody else.... This reminds me of early Christianity."

RICHARD PRYOR

Then there's Richard Pryor. Pryor was too sick for taping near the end of his life, so Gary pulled together material from other sources and from his own recollections of their long friendship and sent it to him for his approval.

The result is far more profane and less satisfying than the twenty other pieces, but the last paragraph (editor's "bleeps" provided) offers a wistful message:

"I get scared when I'm out on stage sometimes. I want to run. If I had some drugs I wouldn't give a *bleep*. But then I come off stage, and I still wouldn't give a *bleep*. Then by the time you're fifty, you've had a lot of don't give a *bleeps*. You miss a big part of your life that way."

———

MOMENTS OF CLARITY

Chris Lawford

A couple of years ago, Chris Lawford, whose father was actor and rat pack member, Peter Lawford, and whose mother, Pat Kennedy, is the sister of John, Robert, and Ted Kennedy, is, of course, a celebrity himself and author of the book, *Moments of Clarity.*

When he came to Little Rock a few years ago to attend the Twenty-first American Bar Association National Conference for Lawyers Assistance Programs as one of the main speakers, we shared a diet toddy in the Peabody Lounge for background, and I heard him speak for an hour about his own moment of clarity in a major speech.

First, about the book. "The morning of February 17, 1986," he wrote in his introduction, "I woke up, as usual, with that weight in the pit of my stomach knowing that all I had in front of me was another day of dancing with the 800-pound gorilla of addiction."

And so begins Chris Lawford's "moment of clarity," as he reports it in his introduction to this great book about how people recover from addictions—in this case, forty-two well-known people, many of them celebrities.

Chris Lawford was born into a famous family, but he is also an actor and established author in his own right. He is also a lawyer, a graduate of Harvard University with a master's degree in psychology, and has served as a public advocacy consultant with Caron Treatment Centers, a provider of alcohol and drug addiction treatment.

Just to give a sample of who is in the book, there are some really well-known movie star types like Alex Baldwin, Jamie Lee Curtis, Tom Arnold, Lou Gossett Jr., Martin Sheen, Richard Dreyfuss, and Kelly McGillis (remember her in *Witness?*), for example.

Then there are famous musical performers like Judy Collins and Elaine Stritch, sports figures like boxer Gerry Cooney, authors like Susan Cheever, business commentators like Larry Kudlow, and politicians like former Republican congressman Jim Ramstad.

They all speak of that moment of clarity that preceded their decision to surrender and seek the new path described in part by psychiatrist Carl Jung in the front of Lawford's book, a name familiar to most 12-Step followers.

After he confronted his eight-hundred-pound gorilla, Lawford continues:

I got out of bed and walked over to the windows that looked out onto Commonwealth Avenue—I was living in one of those beautiful old Boston Brownstones, and it had giant picture windows floor to ceiling. I just stood there and stared out at the city.

Everything was gray, gray and bleak and freezing cold, and that matched what I was feeling inside. I thought, "This is bad. This is as bad as it can get."

I knew I could not exist anymore in that state. I had to either die or change, and I didn't have a gun to put in my mouth, so I had to change, and the only way I could change was to surrender. So I did. I said to whatever was out there, "You know what? I give up.

"I absolutely, unequivocally give up. I'm not talking about I give up so I can fight another day. Whatever you want me to do, I'll do it." And I realize now, that was it. That was the opening through which grace entered my life.

Later, Lawford got down on his knees and asked for "this thing to be removed," and within a few months it was. "That thing that I was absolutely powerless over, that had vanquished me for seventeen years, was lifted out of my life, and it hasn't come back since, in over twenty two years."

Those who are currently struggling with active addictions will find hope and encouragement in these pages and those who are already in recovery will find strong affirmation that they have done the right thing.

———

MALACHY MCCOURT

Malachy McCourt, a versatile actor and author who, as Father Clarence, dispensed advice to the citizens of Pine Valley in the daytime soap, *All My Children*, once said with a wink, "We all get clean and sober eventually, but its best to do it while we are alive. It's much more fun."

It was McCourt, too, who said in the depth of his addictions, "I'm an atheist, thank God."

In the end, he capitulated and put up a sign in his office donated by his wife Diana. It said, "Good morning. This is God. I will be handling your affairs today, and I will not need your help. Have a nice day."

———

VELVET MANGAN

Velvet Mangan, who started Safe Harbor Treatment Center, which has helped thousands of women find their way to recovery, tells of her moment of clarity in these terms:

I was lying in my room, wanting to take my life again. My little seven-year-old son comes in, and he lies down on my bed, and he starts to sob. He says, "Mama, when you believed in God you were healthy, and as soon as you stopped believing in God you got sick."

And it was like...all those clouds, everything that I was trying to convince myself was there, all that went away. I could not question the truth when it came from him.

And how do all these charming, passionate, and wonderfully human people stay sober? "Trust God, clean house, help others" pretty much sums it up.

———

SPILLED GRAVY

Emmy winner Ed Driscoll is a recovering alcoholic who does stand-up comedy, writes gags for people like Billy Crystal and Dennis Miller, and has trouble connecting with the women in his life. He's written a book, *Spilled Gravy*, and it's funny.

There is a thin story line that takes the reader from Driscoll's Catholic school high jinks under the thumb of Sister Ardeth to the final chapter, when, after a series of disastrous relationships, many of them fueled by his alcoholism, he finds the girl who just might be the one.

The acknowledgments in the front of the book offer a clue as to how things will be going, humor-wise, when he comments, "And, oh yeah, I guess I'd better mention my sisters too (Kathleen, Colleen, and Maureen) or they'll probably stiff me on my Christmas gifts."

Actually, before we are halfway through the book, Driscoll confronts his alcoholism. Here's how he sets the stage: "I knew there would come a time in our relationship as there had in every one of my relationships since college, where I'd be asked the question, 'Do you always drink this much?'"

For this question, Driscoll had some stock answers like, "No, not really. I guess I've just been unwinding lately," or "I guess I've been under a little more pressure than usual." Or sometimes he gave the lame offering, "Oh is it the booze? I thought I was so intoxicated by you."

But, Driscoll said, "The only honest answer was always lurking in the back of my mind, 'Hell, no. I drink even more when you're not around."

Shortly after that, swept up by passion, Driscoll bought a twenty-thousand-dollar diamond ring for his girlfriend, Rita, while musing that for that kind of money it should have been Joe Montana's Super Bowl ring. But the relationship came to a bad end.

"At least, it wasn't hard to get the ring back from Rita," Driscoll said. "(I had no idea she could throw that hard)."

Shortly after the breakup, Driscoll got into a 12-Step program and "reconnected with his faith in God." His career took off, but he continued to struggle with relationships to the point where he began to advertise in the personals on Yahoo. His ad and the responses are in an especially funny chapter.

The book ends at Driscoll's class reunion, where he has been asked to do a monologue and meets a woman named Laura. And then…well, you'll you just have to read the book. It's in paperback and, at 188 pages, is ideal for that short plane ride.

CHAPTER THIRTEEN

Wolfe Street Memories:
Learning the Steps and
Building Relationships

Joe McQuany, whose name you have seen in earlier chapters in this book, was perhaps best known for his hour-long, Monday night 12-Step meetings at the Wolfe Street Center. Newcomers and veterans alike would sit in rapt attention at these meetings while McQuany patiently explained with chalk and blackboard how they could get well.

McQuany, along with "Geno" Walter, both recovering alcoholics and both deceased, and Bert Jones, also deceased, formed the Wolfe Street Foundation Inc. in 1982. In the fall of that year, the newly formed Foundation leased 1210 Wolfe Street, which had served most recently as a nurse's residence for Baptist Medical Systems Inc., and before that as a funeral home. The men gave it a new life-affirming purpose, which was to provide rooms for AA and Al-Anon meetings. In effect, the facility became a monument to recovery.

They began cleaning it up under the direction of its first president, the late Gerald Cathey, and in 1985, the Foundation bought the building.

The afflicted came in ever-increasing numbers. On warm summer nights, they came together outside the house on Wolfe Street and laughed in the gathering dusk. When winter came, they found a congenial refuge from the cold in the Center's comfortable rooms. Many got better and were able to help others deal with their addictions.

McQuany and Walter were also the principal carriers of the recovery message contained in the 12 Steps of Alcoholics Anonymous (see Appendix 2). McQuany did it mainly with his step study and Walter with his unforgettable Hour of Power meetings.

"They are simple, basic tools of change," Joe would say of the steps. "And they are based on one of the oldest laws of human nature—whatever you practice, you become good at."

When the hour was up, the audience departed both enlightened and amused. Joe took his message, but never himself, seriously. I myself went through the steps four times, partly for the jokes.

Joe, who died in late October of 2007, was revered, but he never bought into the idea that he was some kind of saint. At his funeral at Little Rock's Pulaski Heights United Methodist Church, Joe's nephew, Pastor Mark Norman, recalled in his sermon a conversation with his famous uncle.

"I had just graduated from seminary and was rather full of myself," Pastor Norman said, "and I said to my uncle Joe, 'You and I are really in the same business.'"

Resisting the idea that the two shared some sort of lofty spiritual vocation, Joe took a long and reflective pull on his pipe, Norman recalled, and replied simply, "You save souls, and I save butts."

Joe saved my butt, and he also, I am convinced, helped put me on the path to saving my soul. And that process with Joe began even before Wolfe Street opened.

I came to Little Rock from Colorado, newly sober, in the late spring of 1979 and at some point shortly after, I began attending Joe's weekly lunch speaker meeting at Serenity House at 2500 Roosevelt Road. Awed by his wisdom and dignified presence, I became a disciple. So when Wolfe Street opened its doors, I began attending meetings there.

———

THE HOUR OF POWER

That's also where when I met Geno and began to attend what would soon become his famous Wolfe Street Sunday morning Hour of Power meetings.

"Geno," with Gerald and Jenny Cathey and several others, launched the meetings upstairs in the kitchen over bacon and eggs with a side of grits. Then he moved them into the adjoining big room following the hearty breakfast. Attendance at his 10 a.m. meetings quickly rose to two hundred and more, giving rise to ominous creaks in the old wooden floor.

There were times during the 1980s when Geno's Hour of Power became my church. It seemed more welcoming and relevant than the traditional churches I had experienced, and the people spoke honestly of the failings that had finally brought them to their knees. They were past caring about what they looked like or sounded like.

Geno's basic text was the 11th Step, which states, "Sought through prayer and meditation to improve our conscious contact with God as we understood Him, praying only for knowledge of His will for us and the power to carry that out."

I wrote an article about the Hour of Power for the fall 1990 issue of the *Wolfe Street Journal* under the headline: "God Goes to Work During a Spiritually Packed Meeting," and these are some of my notes about the people who shared:

- "Hazel speaks of a new intimacy with her husband and a closeness with her children, and she weeps with gratitude for God's answers to her prayers."
- "Steve says he is working on humility but with mixed success. He says his sponsor gave him a button because of his humility but then took it away because he wore it. Everybody laughs."
- "John, his voice cracking, says he has had a slip and has proven to himself and others that alcoholism is, indeed, a progressive disease. He says he is back in the program, and he thanks God for His grace. The applause is deafening."
- "Cecil says goodbye. Tough but oh so tender, Cecil, a man who found AA when he was sixty and became its most ardent servant,

is dying of cancer. Weak and laboring for breath, he says he is grateful to God for the program of Alcoholics Anonymous and the life of sobriety it gave him. There are gentle smiles and tears."

At the close of the article, I wrote:

On any given Sunday morning, some take the stairs up to the meeting room two at a time and others trudge. For some, as Geno puts it, the lights are on, and for others they are off. But virtually all leave refreshed by the love they find.

It is their church on Sunday morning—not the kind of church where the people show God how good they are, but rather the kind where the people show how good God is.

A SPIRITUAL WAY STATION

Under Geno's leadership, the Hour of Power developed into a spiritual way station on the journey through life, and those who chose to stop there found their lives enriched by the experience. Life began to become the great adventure it was intended to be.

I regularly attended meetings in their early days in the 1980s, and Geno was a mentor and friend. During that time, I wrote a second article about the Hour of Power in the *Wolfe Street Journal*, which appears below.

Welcome to the spiritually packed Hour of Power, a Sunday morning get-together at the Wolfe Street Center where upwards of 225 people assemble to let God go to work.

And go to work he does.

With the eleventh step as his text, meeting chairman Geno W. follows the Serenity Prayer, *Big Book* reading, introductions and birthdays with a five-minute commentary put together in the predawn hours on the focus for the meeting.

"The greatest gift in life may well be the knowledge of how to live that life. That is the gift of the program of Alcoholics Anonymous," says Geno to introduce a theme for one meeting.

"In the past," he continues, "we found the answers to life in people, places, material possessions, alcohol, and drugs. They failed us, and we are here today as part of a much higher calling. We seek nothing less than knowledge of how to change and the power to do it."

Geno develops his subject a little more, then begins calling on people. One after another they stand and testify to the joy of lives lived clean and sober on the spiritual plane. Rich and poor, men and women, young and old, black and white, fresh recruits and bleeding deacons, AA and Al-Anon (it's an open meeting)—there is a redemptive message in all their stories.

Whatever their background, the people come to believe. Those who never believed join with those who once believed in celebrating the discovery, not of another religion, but the beginning of a true relationship with God. It is an experience which produces megawatts of love.

Leaving a recent meeting, a woman said, "There is more love in this room than I have experienced anywhere."

It is available to all, lovable or not. Albert, a physician was not lovable. At a meeting several years ago, he took the floor to tell those who were there that they were fools and that he didn't need what they had. His power would sustain him, he said. They smiled at his arrogance and told him they loved him. Puzzled, he kept coming back to make his point and eventually gave in and got sober.

It seems fitting that the Hour of Power was born in the humble Wolfe Street kitchen where a few recovering alcoholics—Geno, Gerald and Jenny C. and several others convened on Sunday mornings for grits and fellowship.

———

SOUGHT THROUGH PRAYER AND MEDITATION

Before he died, Geno wrote a book with William G. Borchert, also a recovering alcoholic, as well as a newspaperman, author, and screenwriter, titled *Wisdom from the Sunday 11ᵗʰ Step Meetings at the Wolfe Street Center in Little Rock.*

The book of meditations is a wonderful collaboration of two gifted men, Geno and Borchert, who wrote the screenplay for the 1989 movie, *My Name Is Bill W.,* starring James Woods, James Garner, and JoBeth Williams. Borchert also wrote a screenplay based on his marvelous book, *The Lois Wilson Story: When Love Is Not Enough.*

Borchert and his wife Bernadette flew from their South Carolina home to Little Rock several years ago to kick off the book's introduction at the Wolfe Street Center where it all began.

The fifty-two chapters in Borchert's book coincide with the weeks in the year, and each chapter includes Geno's introductory remarks at the beginning of every meeting, followed by a prayer and a meditation. The following is a portion of his introduction of week fifty-two: "A Spiritual Awakening":

It seems like I've been searching all my life, searching for something I never had, searching for something more important than everything else I did have, something that would satisfy the yearning, fill the gap I felt deep inside. I didn't know what I was looking for, but I knew I needed to find it in order to have any peace, any meaning, any fulfillment inside myself.

During those terribly lonely times in my life when I felt myself sinking under the weight and torment of my addiction, I would look at other people—happy, smiling, seemingly at ease and I'd be filled with envy, jealousy and resentment. It seemed like they had found what I was still searching for, and it angered me.

There were times I even tried what others were doing—working hard, enjoying families, having good relationships, going to church, praying. It didn't work. Nothing gave me any respite except another drink or another drug. Then after a while, that stopped working too.

I began to ask myself if I was the only one who trod that path that led to total desperation. Was I the only one who kept asking, seeking, stumbling along that dark and despairing road that had no signs or guideposts? It was a road that led to the top of a cliff. I stood there looking down, fearing I might fall into the abyss. Filled with terror, I called out for help. God came and lifted me up. I was put on a new road, a road that led me to recovery through the 12-Step program of Alcoholics Anonymous.

Still seeking to fill that gap inside me, I was now given directions—the road map of the 12 Steps of recovery. I was told the Steps would help me find sobriety provided I admitted I was powerless over my addiction and turned my will and my life over to the care of a Power greater than myself.

That's when a voice deep inside told me that my search was almost over, that what I had been looking for all my life I could now find—a relationship with a loving and caring God of my understanding. I knew it as the beginning of a whole new way of life.

A NEW DECADE

I was invited to serve on the board of the Foundation in the late 1980s and when Bill Lloyd died in the summer of 1990, I took his place as president of the Wolfe Street Foundation and then was reelected in 1991.

During my tenure, the building—its roof, sloping floors, bad plumbing, and other physical ailments—seemed to occupy most of the board's time—except, that is, for the proposed ban on smoking and developing policies regarding childcare while parents were attending meetings.

Smoking was eventually banned in spite of protest from some members who threatened to secede, but I don't think anybody did, at least not for good. We also established the position of executive director to carry out the policies of the board, and Lew Block was the first one to be hired. He was succeeded by Susan Grayson and then Markey Ford.

The late Dr. Don Browning, who became president after me in 1992, had a vision for its development and management that his poor health and eventual death prevented him from fully promoting. He deserves mention as one of Wolfe Street's important contributors.

Don was responsible for establishing "The Committee for the Nineties" to help define Wolfe Street's role in the community in the coming years. His view was comprehensive and involved potential collaborations with hospitals, clinics, treatment centers, halfway houses, and other organizations focusing on recovery. It made sense then and may still make sense today.

Dr. Browning said:

What started as an idea ten years ago has grown to be a revered meeting place for those in recovery from alcoholism and drug addiction.

As the Center has grown, so too has the attitude of society toward accepting alcoholism as a disease. Society is more accepting of those people in recovery.

Now the attention of the Wolfe Street Foundation's board has to be turned to prepare for the expanding future of this wonderful legacy. As the people in recovery flood in, we need more space to accommodate them. When anyone needs help, we want to be able to respond.

Wolfe Street began then to respond to the growing need, and it retained its strong spiritual foundations. A board member at that time, Steve B. wrote:

Resurrection, renaissance, recovery—whichever or all—it began for me at the Wolfe Street Center. The building—and the disease and the concept of humanity—that I had hated with a visceral fury are gone, replaced by a love and spiritual bond that cannot be readily explained to anyone who has not tasted the agony of chemical addition and the gift of a second chance at life.

The Wolfe Street Center is to me, then, not so much a building as a concept, an attitude, an ethic, a way of life. It is a method of living, and a source of peace, at long last.

It doesn't really matter where Wolfe Street is. Thousands of visitors will still come, hoping to find a measure of peace and serenity. As in the past, many will find what they are looking for. Others, tragically, will not. Most will never be the same.

These words still apply.

WOLFE STREET MOVES

In the late fall of 2011, thirty years after its founding, the Wolfe Street Center matured and made an exciting move from its old location. The beloved but creaky old building was sold to Arkansas Children's Hospital. Now the Center occupies new quarters at 1015 Louisiana in a sturdy brick building bought from the Heifer Foundation and nearly twice the size of the old one, with more than an acre of lawn and parking spaces.

Aside from the meeting rooms, one of which holds three hundred, the building has an old-timers' coffee shop, a bookstore, a commercial kitchen, and a chapel, as well as rooms outfitted with Murphy beds to accommodate visiting speakers and other overnight guests.

There are also administrative offices for the director and assistant and some of the many volunteers.

The new Center also has a physical connection to the past. Twenty-eight twelve-foot-long wooden pews, each with a sponsor's name, which accommodated thousands of visitors who had come to hear Joe's lessons on the 12 Steps, are being put to use in a variety of ways in the new facility, along with the hundred-year-old chandeliers and the stained glass windows from the original facility.

Architect Brian Black of Benton directed all the modifications of the building pro bono.

The inspiration for the accommodation of overnight visitors at the Wolfe Street Center came to Ford after a visit to Bill Wilson's birthplace in East Dorsett, Vermont, a mile from where Bill and his wife are buried. Placed on the National Registry of Historic Places in 1995, Wilson House hosts local AA and Al-Anon meetings and a number of seminars.

Wolfe Street presents several events a year, including seminars on relationships, that draw many visitors—including some from out of state and from foreign countries. The Foundation would like to do even more, but has been limited by the lack of suitable accommodations for out-of-town visitors.

"In my conversations with the people at Wilson House," Ford says, "they said providing on-site rooms was essential and would provide additional income."

Today, Wolfe Street can offer accommodations for overnight guests.

———

JAPANESE VISITORS HOST RECOVERY "TEA PARTY" AT WOLFE STREET

Thanks in part to McQuany's book, *Recovery Dynamics,* Japan is making progress in its battle with alcoholism. At least, that's how Japanese psychiatrist, Megumi Gotoh, put it in an interview following tea at Little Rock's Wolfe Street Center a few summers ago.

The Japanese visitors had spent the day before at Serenity Park, the Little Rock treatment facility founded by McQuany over thirty-five years ago, and Wolfe Street was their last stop before going home.

On staff at Tokyo's Narimasu Kosei Hospital and a woman of considerable modesty and charm, Dr. Gotoh was one of a dozen Japanese visitors who had been touring the United States gathering information on addiction and recovery. Addiction behavior is her specialty.

Blocked in part by the inclination to "save face" and other cultural factors, the Japanese have been less inclined to confront their addictions than the Americans, but attitudes are slowly changing Dr. Gotah says. And, she says, acceptance is growing for 12-Step treatment options, especially those advocated in McQuany's *Recovery Dynamics.*

World War II, Dr. Gotah said, disrupted some of the healthier old-world Japanese values relating to service to others and sacrifice and replaced them with heightened self absorption and dwindling spiritual values.

"Today, it's all about money," Dr. Gotah said, "and a belief that 'I am God.'"

Following a combined Al-Anon and AA meeting downstairs in the room where McQuany had conducted two decades of Monday night 12-Step meetings, the Japanese hosted a tea in the main upstairs meeting room for about thirty people.

A key player in the downstairs meetings was interpreter Mihoko Knight, who was born in Japan but is now living in Arizona with her American husband. First she interpreted for Janet E., a member of Al-Anon from Little Rock, converting her English into Japanese, and then she interpreted for an AA woman from Japan, converting her Japanese into English.

Among Knight's many contributions to the cause of recovery, her translation of the *Big Book of Alcoholics Anonymous* into Japanese is among the most impressive.

The event hosted was more like an American ice cream and cake social than a ceremonial tea party, with lots of laughter and picture-taking as guests and hosts struggled happily with language difficulties.

On the key issue of prayer, the Japanese visitors had provided guests with plastic cards inscribed with the "Serenity Prayer" as well as the phrase "One day at a time" translated in both English and Japanese.

CHAPTER FOURTEEN

Hope for Addicted Mothers and Their Children

Cindy Crone, a pediatric nurse practitioner, helped found Arkansas CARES in 1992. It was her idea that in the long-term interest of restoring families, it would be a good idea to treat addicted mothers and their babies together in a safe place.

Cindy, who has the intensity, dedication, compassion, and optimism of a true believer in her cause, also has the professional qualifications to deliver the goods, which she continues to exercise in the service of recovery.

She has held faculty appointments with the University of Arkansas for Medical Sciences (UAMS) College of Medicine, Department of Psychiatry, and the UAMS College of Public Health. She is past president of the Arkansas Nurses Association and has served on the Arkansas Legislative Commission on Nursing.

In 2002, the American Psychiatric Society gave Arkansas CARES its prestigious Gold Award for its innovative program. Further recognition came in 2004 when the National Association of Public Hospitals gave the program its highest award, the Jim Wright award for vulnerable populations.

ARKANSAS CARES

Arkansas CARES' mission is to help substance-abusing pregnant women and mothers with children recover from their addictions in a residential setting where they live with their children and begin taking responsibility for raising them.

Cindy's approach was to keep mothers and children together while they go through the process of recovery, with the ultimate objective of building healthy families.

Can there be a more worthy goal?

Joseph A. Califano Jr., in his book, *High Society,* strongly emphasizes the threat of substance abuse to the family when he says:

The poisonous seeds of substance abuse and addiction produce not only crime and deadly and crippling diseases and accidents, but also a toxic legacy of broken families, spousal violence, child abuse, homelessness, lousy schools, permanent disability, teen pregnancy and vandalized public housing.

Substance abuse and addiction lurk just beyond the welcome mat in many homes, a threat to the American family as serious as any.

Methodist Family Health in Little Rock has taken over the operation of the Arkansas CARES program, but my first contact with it was in 2004 when it was under UAMS. At that time I visited the facility, interviewed Cindy Crone and published a report in my publication, *One Day at a Time.* It has relevance today, and this is how it began.

The thing that makes you want to weep in the little nursery at the corner of 20th and Grant is that while the babies in here are safe, at least for now, from the drug abuse subculture, many babies on the outside live on those mean streets and face neglect, abuse and a grim future.

Here in the nursery, a cheerful little eight-month old, obviously in good health, puts down his bottle, a bit reluctantly, to help greet a newcomer. Safe in the arms of Monica, the nursery supervisor, he grins a lot and appears to have no fear.

While this is going on, Gracie, twelve months, and Abby, ten months, are sitting in their highchairs enjoying a meal of strained apricots. Abby has a bit of an attitude and Gracie smiles warmly through her apricots. They are irresistible.

Other babies in the hushed and dimly lighted room are sleeping, getting a diaper change, or playing with blocks.

Here is the rest of my article in slightly modified form:

Arkansas CARES, I wrote in 2004, operates two residential community sites—one in Little Rock and one in North Little Rock—where pregnant women and mothers live with their children from infants to age eighteen.

The two treatment communities can house a combined twenty-seven families at a time and currently serve about 160 families a year. In the past twelve years, more than twelve hundred families have received treatment and critical services from Arkansas CARES.

The staff of ninety includes a pediatrician, family nurse practitioner, psychiatrist, nurses, social workers, psychologists, specialists in early childhood and special education, alcohol and drug abuse treatment counselors, nutritionists, physical and occupational therapists, and speech and language pathologists. Arkansas CARES gives mothers and children daily treatment and life skills training, emphasizing parenting, employment, and household maintenance.

———

COST-EFFECTIVE PROGRAM

The Arkansas CARES program is extremely cost effective, my article continued. The cost for housing and treating one mother and two children for four to five months with twelve to eighteen months of aftercare services is about $50,000, compared to four to seven times that amount for the option of putting the mother in jail and her children in foster homes with only health care.

It is a poor option when you consider that aside from the staggering cost, the odds are there will be limited or no rehabilitation for either the mother or children. The cycle of addiction will likely continue and the cost in dollars and misery will mount.

Another consideration is that helping pregnant mothers stay clean and sober will result in healthier babies. The medical bills for an underweight premature baby with drugs or alcohol in its system can add up to $150,000 and probably a lot more.

Alcohol use by pregnant women is the number-one cause of mental retardation in our country. It is completely preventable if pregnant women stop drinking, Crone says.

On average, the nation spends $2.9 million on resources for each lifetime affected by Fetal Alcohol Spectrum Disorders (FASD). That's $3.6 billion spent in the United States annually. If the nation spends $850,000 to prevent one FASD child, society saves money (more on this at the end of this chapter). The current Arkansas CARES annual operating budget is about $3.3 million. About one-third of it will come from Medicaid and the rest from government agencies, grants, and private donations.

HORRIFYING STORIES WITH A RAY OF HOPE

The stories of the women who come to Arkansas CARES are mostly horrifying and tragic, but now there is hope.

Consider Towanda's story.

Towanda, age twenty-nine, six months pregnant, and in search of a fix, walked up the steps to the front door of a frame house in a bad neighborhood, reached through the top of the screen door, which had no screen, and undid it.

The inside door was slightly ajar, and she pushed on it until it hit something. Squeezing through, she looked down and met the lifeless stare of a man with a bullet in his head.

Terror stricken, she backed out, fell off the porch, got up, and ran.

This was Towanda's life: violence, fear, degradation, shame, and despair. Her full-time job for the past ten years had become stealing and turning tricks with dealers to get the money to buy drugs—mainly cocaine—to stay high. Her main source had been a drug-dealer boyfriend, but he was gone now, convicted months earlier of murder and sentenced to forty years at Cummins.

Exhausted by the stress and pain of her hellish life, she put her future in the hands of Arkansas CARES.

Women come to the program in many ways—via the court system, child protective services, healthcare workers, jail or prison counselors, or family members. Or they can walk in on their own.

Towanda's mother brought her to Arkansas CARES following a hospital referral due to concerns about her parenting, and on a warm and radiant afternoon in late October, she sat—clean and sober—in front of the brick home she shared with seven other women with her eight-month-old son, Blake, on her lap.

Towanda's story of substance abuse is not unique. Far from it. Almost one in three Arkansas mothers with children under eighteen is in need of substance abuse treatment, according to *Psychiatric Services*, a journal of the American Psychiatric Association.

What is unique is the chance she now has to recover from her addictions, raise a healthy child, and lead a decent life.

———

A CHANCE TO STAY CLEAN

Thanks to Arkansas CARES, Towanda, who hadn't used drugs or alcohol for three months at the time when she shared her story with me, had an excellent chance of staying clean for at least a year, of saving her child from the ravages of substance abuse, and of breaking the addiction cycle for coming generations.

A recent study showed that 85 percent of Arkansas CARES graduates remain drug free for at least a year following discharge. These are great odds when it comes to recovery.

As she sat under the warming fall sun, Towanda was joined by several other young women and their children—most of them under five—who also live in her building. The women had just picked their little ones up from the nursery or daycare center and had time before supper to play with them.

The women talked about what it was like "out there," what happened that brought them to Arkansas CARES, what their lives are like now, and what their dreams are for a better life.

Most of them had been in abusive relationships with men and this, along with the other toxic aspects of their lives, had contributed to their mental problems—post-traumatic stress, depression, anxiety, bipolar disorder, and others—that they were suffering along with their addictions.

Grayson, twenty-two, and, like Towanda, also from Arkansas, said when she was eighteen and headed for college with a volleyball scholarship, her boyfriend cheated on her, which, she says, triggered a four-year methamphetamine dealing-and-using binge that ended in a Texas prison.

Fresh out of Rockwell prison on $25,000 bail with her two-year old son, Preston, sitting on her lap focused on her long, blonde braids, Grayson had been clean and sober for a month or so. It would take her more time to get used to the new life, which she figured is a lot better than jail.

———

DO-IT-YOURSELF METH

Like Towanda, Grayson's waking hours had been consumed with staying high. One of the many sinister aspects of meth is that you don't have to find a dealer; you can make the substance yourself.

And it's not difficult. Grayson could cook up a batch, she says, "in thirty-seven minutes." The ingredients include, most importantly, the drug ephedrine or pseudo ephedrine found in Sudafed and other cold medicines. Obtaining this can be the most difficult part of the process.

Pharmacies such as Walgreens are on the lookout for people buying quantities of Sudafed, and meth cooks have to spread it around. A batch may call for a couple of hundred tablets, so that's a lot of spreading around.

The rest of the ingredients can be found in your average hazardous waste dump—gasoline, battery acid, Drano, lye, paint thinner, phosphorous, and many more just as ominous—and explosions and fires in small labs are not uncommon. Even small labs in the kitchen of a house can cost as much as $2,000–$10,000 to clean up, and in some cases can cost more than $100,000.

Meth often has deadly side effects, including tremors, strokes, convulsions, cardiovascular collapse, irregular heartbeat, and acute psychiatric and psychological symptoms that may lead to suicide and murder.

Another woman, sitting on the steps across from the little house and looking appreciatively at her daughter's care center drawings, recalled her final days on the loose.

"When I drank or used [meth, cocaine, marijuana], everything went wrong," she said, and judging from her record, she spoke the truth. It included stealing, shootings, DUIs, prostitution, and numerous trips to treatment centers. Today, she said, she has the tools to make it, and she hopes and prays that she will.

———

LIFE-THREATENING SIDE EFFECTS

Twenty-two-year-old Tiffany, with her child, Monique, is a walking example of a life-threatening alcohol and drug abuse side effect. She has a million-dollar smile and appears to be pregnant, but it is her swollen liver and spleen that are distending her belly, and the pain and her apprehension about impending surgery sometimes cloud her face.

The mothers at Arkansas CARES' Eastgate facility in North Little Rock, most of them pregnant, some of them for the first time, live in individual apartments as opposed to the communal living arrangements at the Little Rock facility.

Like the women in the Little Rock facility, they are learning how to make a home for their children and how to care for them emotionally and physically. It takes time. They are graded on how well they maintain their apartments, for example, and some of them are on the messy side. Site supervisor Barbara Baldwin says with a smile, "They are used to chaos in their lives."

Gathered together for a 12-Step meeting one morning, some with babies in their arms or gently rocking carriages, they were, for the most part, bright, alert, and feisty. And when you hear some of their stories, you think, "This is a miracle!"

There is another piece to the "rebuilding families" puzzle: the father. In the long run, Cindy Crone would like to develop programs incorporating responsible and recovering husbands and fathers in the restoration process, but for now she will focus on mother and child.

———

CAREFULLY CATERED KITCHEN

Lynda is finally living her childhood dream.

Standing there in her baseball cap and apron in the midst of the pots and pans in the CAREfully Catered kitchen at Christ Episcopal Church (the operation has since moved to the Methodist Arkansas CARES campus along with the original Arkansas CARES operation, but the message is the same), she is one semester away from a degree in cooking. It was her dream as a kid—to be a chef—and she almost missed it.

Drugs had intruded, and the dream had become a nightmare defined by one word: methamphetamine. Her addiction took her close to the bottom. She lost her children and her freedom before she could turn her life around with the help of two programs.

One is CAREfully Catered, which is where she works now with other women in recovery—like Vera, a beginner gaining on-the-job experience.

The nonprofit catering service, launched in 2005, is associated with the second program, Arkansas CARES.

CAREfully Catered, which was created by a $500,000 grant from the Robert Wood Johnson Foundation, employs and trains these mothers who are successfully overcoming addictions. It provides a valuable piece often missing in the recovery cycle—a job and an income. In this instance, Arkansas CARES has also provided Lynda with an apartment.

CAREfully Catered prides itself on tasty and nutritious food that is also low on fats and sugars. It's all prepared under the direction of certified executive chef Ken Jones, who has twenty years of experience in the major hotels of Little Rock—including the Peabody and the Capitol. Jones has won numerous awards, including being named as the outstanding apprentice of the year by the Arkansas Professional Chefs and Cooks Association in 1996. While confessing to a few indiscretions in his younger days, Jones was not a drug abuser.

Jones' menu includes a variety of soups, salads, and entrees, along with a "lighter side sandwich board, party trays, and specialty breakfast breaks." Just give him twenty-four hours notice, and he and the staff will get your order ready.

Two years ago, Lynda, who has a ready smile and a firm grip, was in Southeast Arkansas Community Corrections, the women's prison in Pine Bluff, on drug-related charges. It wasn't the first time, but this time it was different. This time, Sebastian County Judge J. Michael Fitzhugh gave her an option: Either commit to staying clean and sober under the court's supervision or face a much longer prison term.

Lynda chose commitment, and this time she had a place to go— Arkansas CARES—where she could recover from her addictions with the help of 12-Step programs, counseling, and just learning how healthy people function in the world.

She also began attending the two-year culinary arts program at the Arkansas School of Apprenticeship on a scholarship, where she was recently named student of the year, an award Jones, her boss, had received earlier in his career.

———

BARBS PLACE

When she was seventeen, Shaina G., deep in depression and badly hooked on meth, made her second attempt at suicide.

On that day, Shaina took more than sixty antidepressant pills at once, chugging them down as fast as possible with glasses of water. Then she lay back and waited to die. Soon, there were "spiders" all over her body, and other hallucinations, scary beyond description, descended upon her.

In a panic, she tried to reverse the process by forcing herself to vomit, but she passed out, and when she came to, she was in the emergency room at the local hospital in Malvern, Arkansas. On the way, her heart stopped, and she had to be resuscitated.

Three years later, Shaina, six months sober, was getting proper treatment for her bipolar disorder. She also had become a mother of two, a month-old baby boy, Dylan, and an eighteen-month-old girl, Skylar. All three were living in the safety of BARBS Place (which stands for Babies, Adults, Recovery-Based Services) in Hot Springs, a treatment center housed in an attractive, one-story building where mothers and their young children can get well together.

Shaina entered BARBS in late November 2007 through the Seventh Judicial District drug court following her arrest on a meth-related charge. Judge Chris Williams gave her a choice to get into treatment and stay clean and sober for at least eighteen months or go to prison. Shaina chose recovery.

In late January of 2008, Shaina was scheduled to leave after two months at BARBS with her babies and move in with her grandparents while continuing with an outpatient program with BARBS' parent company, Quapaw House. Eventually, she hoped to get her own apartment. Shaina's parents, both drug addicts, were also in Williams' drug court program and not ready to take on any of the responsibility for their daughter and her children.

———

CHILDCARE

Equipped with a nursery and with access to the adjoining Quapaw-operated Linden Street Child Care Center, BARBS provides women and their children with private rooms while they participate in a rigorous program of recovery to prepare them for eventual independent living.

The curriculum for clients and their families includes a 12-Step program of recovery, treatment of physical and mental health issues, group problem solving, prenatal and postpartum care, parenting classes, adult education, job skills training, nutrition, and family counseling.

As for the children, BARBS conducts an assessment to guide their care, but the key is in helping the mothers and children bond in the healthiest possible way. When the mothers at BARBS are at work or doing their assignments during the day, Teri Grisham, Program director for Linden Street, is looking after their kids. Grisham, who has a degree in early childhood education and is certified by the Child Development Association, has been at Linden Street since it opened fifteen years ago.

BARBS occupies an attractive, one-story building whose distinguishing feature is an adjoining playground full of high-voltage kids tearing around, throwing balls, and playing games.

Anita R., mother of eight grown kids and eleven grandchildren, clean and sober for thirteen years and a certified counselor in substance abuse, is in charge of BARBS, and she brings a relaxed yet vigilant presence to the operation.

Anita has "been there and done that" (including two years in a Texas prison), and through "divine intervention" she has survived. Casual observation suggests that she is compassionate, happy, and flexible yet firm.

The stories of the women who come to BARBS are similar in that they are recovering drug addicts, but there are also differences.

TRACY'S STORY

Tracy H., thirty-seven, came to BARBS with her two-year-old son, Riley, because she had been abusing drugs and was afraid she would lose him. She had already given up one child to adoption and another to his father, and it was the threat of losing Riley that brought her to BARBS.

Tracy says she comes from "a good Christian family" and didn't use drugs all the way through high school. Then, after graduating and beginning a new job with a local optometrist, she began using pot, then cocaine and crystal meth.

At age twenty-nine, she had begun to take her drugs intravenously, moved in with a meth cook "way back in the woods" and built a life around making, selling, and buying drugs with a series of meth cooks. Often, the proceeds from making meth went to buying other drugs.

"I had a temper and a filthy mouth, and I lived like an animal," she says.

Over the more recent years, she had made sporadic attempts to get clean and sober through treatment centers. Finally, at Recovery Centers of Arkansas (RCA) in Little Rock, she learned "how to get sober." And at BARBS, she says, "I'm learning how to maintain sobriety."

It seems to be working. The Arlington Hotel in Hot Springs hired Tracy to cover the front desk daily from 7 a.m. to 3 p.m., and her eyes sparkle with excitement just talking about her job.

BARBS also offers a family program for residents who have or will have significant others involved in their lives when they complete the inpatient program. The program provides information to these outside family members and others on substance abuse and recovery. It also offers treatment for a variety of family dysfunctions facilitated by certified counselors.

DRINKING AND PREGNANCY: DON'T DO IT

Don't drink if you are pregnant or may become pregnant. Period. It sounds harsh, doesn't it? It may to some, but not to those who are paying the price.

Like this family as described by Cindy Crone.

Ginny's mother and father are having marital problems. And parenting problems. And school problems. It seems that all the problems have something in common: Ginny.

A slender, bubbly, energetic nine year old, Ginny is outgoing and friendly, yet she can't seem to make friends and keep them. Her kindergarten teacher recommended that she wait until age seven to start first grade so she could "grow up a little." Now she's struggling to pass to third grade.

Ginny cannot read well or remember basic math concepts. She's easily distracted in the classroom, and her constant activities and talking "bother" other students. She's impulsive, often getting out of her chair without permission, and more than once she's been caught lying to her teacher.

It's not uncommon for Ginny to blurt out words, or laugh or cry inappropriately. She gets in trouble at recess frequently, and becomes upset when the other children tease her. She doesn't respond to usual classroom management techniques, and her medication for ADHD doesn't seem to be working. Ginny's teacher doesn't know what to do with her, and is now asking that she be moved to a "behavior classroom."

At home, Ginny's mom has tried interventions she learned in parenting classes, like "time out" and taking away privileges, but nothing seems to work. Ginny just keeps doing the same things over and over again, no matter what the consequences have been. She takes "forever" to get ready for school, and they often are late.

It's also hard for her to fall asleep and stay asleep, and her mom reports, "We have no schedule—our whole family is worn out." Her mom says that Ginny's twelve-year-old sister, Kate, was nothing like this when she was nine. In fact, Ginny seems to act more like her six-year-old cousin. Kate "can't stand" her sister because she acts weird, interrupts her circle of friends, and embarrasses her.

Ginny loves to take care of her puppy, and her favorite playmate is the four-year-old who lives across the street. She loves to paint and play with Play Doh, but makes a mess, so her mom doesn't let her do that very often. She has a soft teddy bear that she likes to cuddle, and she has a baby toy that she refuses to give up.

———

FETAL ALCOHOL SPECTRUM DISORDER

Ginny's doctor recommended that she be evaluated at a developmental clinic. The preliminary thought is that Ginny has Fetal Alcohol Spectrum Disorder (FASD), a term describing a range of effects that can occur in an individual whose mother drank alcohol during pregnancy. These effects include physical, cognitive, and behavioral disabilities that can interfere with growth, learning, and socialization across the lifetime.

As noted, even a small amount of alcohol has been associated with FASD, the number-one cause of developmental delay and intellectual deficit in the United States. The injuries to the developing brain are permanent, irreversible, and often invisible.

Ginny's mom had stated that she didn't have a problem with alcohol. She did drink wine after work and with dinner while pregnant, she said, but never more than two glasses a day. Most days she didn't drink at all. Once, before she knew she was pregnant, she drank a little more at the lake one weekend...but definitely not more than she did when pregnant with Kate.

Besides, she said, Ginny didn't have any of the facial features usually associated with alcohol abuse in mothers. She was referring to Fetal Alcohol Syndrome (FAS), which is a specific diagnosis within FASD and has three major components: a characteristic pattern of facial differences (affecting the upper lip and eyes), below-average growth, and brain damage.

FAS, identified in 1973, occurs in one to two babies per thousand births, whereas, FASD, the more widespread and more recently identified condition, likely occurs in at least one per one hundred births. Unlike FAS, there are no outward physical signs of FASD.

Affected children have difficulty learning, remembering, and getting along well with others. They process information differently—and more slowly. They often have visual, sensory, language, and behavior problems, and are often oversensitive to stimuli (like a tag in a shirt or seams in socks). Persons with FASD are easily distracted (by noises, lights, or activities), and forgetful (like not remembering more than one instruction at a time or forgetting how to do a task learned on a previous day). Their behavior is often misinterpreted as purposefully mean or irritating.

WHAT'S UP?

Affected children often have problems with math and abstract thinking. They take things very literally—including common jargon. For example, if a child with FASD is greeted with the salutation, "What's up?" he or she may look toward the ceiling or sky to see "what's up."

Children living with FASD and their families and caregivers often become frustrated. Continuing frustrations then place affected children at very high risk for development of secondary disabilities, including mental health disabilities and, later, alcohol and drug disorders. Other secondary disabilities include learning, legal, social, employment, and living problems.

The good news is that secondary disabilities can be prevented. Children with FASD who are identified before age six have better long-term outcomes. Children whose brain disorder is understood can benefit from specific environmental adaptations to help them succeed at home, in school, and with their peers. These interventions can build on their strengths.

And, children with FASD have many strengths. They are friendly, curious, persistent, loyal, happy, and are often good with animals and younger children. They respond well to visual reminders, routines, and careful planning for changes.

As we build on their strengths and support affected children and their caregivers, a helpful rule of thumb is to consider the developmental age of a child with FASD to be two-thirds of their chronological age. For example, a six year old will be more like a four year old developmentally; an eighteen year old will be more like a child who's twelve.

Since there are no outward signs of FASD, most children with this disorder are not recognized as having it by family, teachers, or friends until the child does poorly in school—academically and socially. Medications usually prescribed for attention deficit hyperactivity disorder (ADHD) often don't work for children with FASD.

This lifelong and costly disorder is 100-percent preventable if pregnant women don't drink alcohol. While some pregnant women with alcohol addiction give birth to perfectly healthy babies without FASD, other women who are "social drinkers" and do not have an alcohol use problem can have a baby with the disorder.

The best way to address FASD is to prevent it. However, with information and help, early identification of FASD is helping children like Ginny and their families, teachers, friends, and others learn how to provide effective behavioral and learning supports to prevent secondary disabilities.

CHAPTER FIFTEEN

Prescription Pain Pill Abuse Soars

An attractive, well-dressed woman walks into Starbucks, orders a latte, removes her Armani sunglasses, and takes a seat. Several patrons look up from their laptops or newspapers casually speculating about who she might be and why she is there.

Maybe she's a professional woman on the way to a client meeting, a Junior Leaguer out for some shopping, or a soccer mom on a coffee break. On the other hand, maybe she's a prescription drug addict.

Bingo! Actually, she's a *recovering* drug addict. Jennifer (not her real name) is also a mother of two, a sales executive, and recently divorced.

Her mission on this day in early November is to meet with someone who will help tell her story to other women addicted to prescription pain pills—"desperate housewives," she calls them with a smile—about her experience kicking a Vicodin habit.

Her hope is that they will be encouraged and take the same path to recovery.

Vicodin is a trade name for hydrocodone, which is the most frequently prescribed opiate in the United States, with over 130 million prescriptions a year, according to www.hydrocodonehelp.com. Every age group, according to the Drug Enforcement Administration, has been affected by the easy availability of hydrocodone. Sometimes viewed as a "white collar addiction," hydrocodone abuse has increased among all ethnic and economic groups. The data suggests that the most likely hydrocodone abuser is a white female age twenty to forty years who abuses the drug because she is dependent on it or trying to commit suicide.

———

NATIONAL EPIDEMIC

Abuse of OxyContin, a relative of hydrocodone, is also rising dramatically and has been described by some local law enforcement officials "as a national epidemic in the making."

Jennifer had been taking a dozen or more Vicodin pills a day for five years, and finally, at the end of her rope, she had enrolled in a University of Arkansas for Medical Science program of recovery that is under the administrative control of the Department of Psychiatry and Behavioral Sciences.

A few days prior to the Starbucks meeting, she had completed a painful forty-eight-hour detoxing process to rid herself of the Vicodin. After that, as part of the program of recovery, she began taking a drug called Suboxone (also known as buprenorphine), which replaces the Vicodin and has many of its properties but is less addictive.

Within a period of several weeks, she began cutting back on the Suboxone, which is easier to kick, until she was totally drug free. The clinic also provided counseling services and encouraged attendance at 12-Step meetings like Narcotics Anonymous during the process.

At this point, Jennifer thinks Suboxone is an answer to her prayers. So does Kathryn (not her real name), who successfully completed the Suboxone program in September and is also drug-free today.

Like Jennifer, Kathryn is an attractive, divorced woman in business— she has a well-paying position in a legal firm—and has successfully overcome her twelve-to-fifteen-pill-a-day habit. Her message to pain pill-addicted women, like Jennifer's, is that they can overcome.

THE MIRACLE

So how did Jennifer and Kathryn find out about the clinic and the Suboxone program? Both, who were equally desperate, credited a miracle when they came across or were given an issue of the *One Day at a Time* newspaper published an ad headlined "Volunteers for Treatment Research."

The ad stated the following:

UAMS has free confidential treatment research programs to help adults (age 18 yrs and older) get off heroin, oxycontin, and other opiates. Treatment lasts approximately 22 weeks and includes buprenorphine and counseling.

When Kathryn and Jennifer, at different times, reported to the Substance Abuse Treatment Center—an unimposing, one-story, gray building across from the sprawling UAMS campus on Markham Street in Little Rock, which has since moved to the main hospital—they were met by research subject recruiter Amy Glenn.

Glenn explained to them the Suboxone program, which was approved for treatment by the Food and Drug Administration in 2002. The Center, which also offers a methadone treatment program, serves both a research function, which is free, and a treatment function, for which there is a charge, and Jennifer and Kathryn qualified for the latter.

Neither had the history of drug abuse that was required by the research project nor the time to go through the twenty-two-week program.

Suboxone, a narcotic drug that is legally prescribed, is taken under the tongue. It is slower acting and does not provide the same "rush" as other opioids. It also has a "ceiling effect," resulting in lower levels of euphoria. Basically, it allows the person taking it to function normally.

The goal of the Suboxone program is total rehabilitation of the patient, including withdrawal from all drugs—suboxone included. The cost for the twenty-eight-day program is about four hundred dollars.

The use of drugs like Suboxone and methadone to treat heroin dependency is not accepted as valid by everyone. But Glenn's answer is that this approach falls in the "least harm" category. Not everyone can sober up in a 12-Step program, she says, and you do what you can to meet people where they are.

Here's how it's supposed to work. If you have a heroin addiction, for example, you detox from that and go to methadone, which is a little less potent. Then, you further step down to Suboxen, and finally you become drug-free. This regimen is accompanied by counseling, and sometimes it takes a long time, but it can be successful.

―――――

A MAJOR PROBLEM

Dr. G. Richard Smith, chairman of the Department of Psychiatry and Behavioral Sciences program, has described addiction as "one of the major problems affecting the U.S." and his department has taken the lead in responding to the challenge.

UAMS opened a new Center for Addiction Research in the summer of 2004 and soon after installed Dr. Warren Bickel, who was recruited from the University of Vermont, as its director.

Bickel, who was also named a professor of psychiatry and behavioral sciences, as mentioned in chapter 4, has experience in examining the behavioral processes that underlie drug dependence and has conducted research that examines novel cost-effective ways to deliver treatment.

Alison Oliveto, a colleague of Bickel and a professor and vice chairman of research in psychiatry and behavioral sciences at UAMS as well as a senior scientist for the Center, is working on studies dealing with the pharmacology of drugs of abuse and how different medications can provide relief. While on the research faculty at Yale, Oliveto helped test and develop medications like Suboxone for the treatment of substance abuse.

In a recent interview, Bickel pulled the curtain back on some of the other projects the Center is working on aimed at helping more people recover from addictions at less cost. One project is "computer-based therapy," which will give participants help with their recovery wherever they are. Now in test use at the Treatment Center, computer-based therapy participants first give a urine sample, and then, based on their answers to questions about their abstinence or lack of it, the computer provides facts and words of encouragement about recovery.

Bickel reminds skeptics that "we have more needs than we have therapists, and we have to leverage counseling time."

Computers, Bickel adds, "also have the virtue of being infinitely patient," a significant benefit when treating someone in deep denial. The computer doesn't give up.

Another subject that interests Bickel is that "drug-dependent people don't think much about the future." Studies show that heroin addicts think ahead an average of nine days, he says, while the time horizon for the general population is four and one-half to seven years hence.

"If you are only thinking a day ahead," Bickel says, "it allows you to make choices that completely ignore the consequences of some of your decisions."

Studies of the brain, Bickel says, also show that the cerebral cortex, which provides the capacity to plan and think abstractly, among other things, "goes offline with addicts, and they go back to the more primitive part of the brain dealing mostly with emotions—the limbic." The findings confirm, no doubt, what the average citizen believes about the behavior of alcoholics and other drug users. It also suggests that getting the cortex back online and toning down the limbic are worthy goals in substance abuse treatment.

Dr. Bickle recently accepted a position at another hospital, but his work continues at UAMS.

———

JENNIFER'S STORY

Jennifer's journey began with a 12-Step program.

A recovering alcoholic, Jennifer went to her first AA meeting on Thanksgiving Day in 1991 and stayed sober for the next eight years. A series of family tragedies during those years—the death of her mother, father, brother, and first baby—unhinged her, and she turned once again to alcohol. And eventually she turned to prescription drugs as well.

The addiction to drugs began in 1999 when she gave birth to a baby daughter by Caesarean section, and her doctor prescribed OxyContin for the pain. She became hooked and has used opiates ever since.

"I needed to be perfect," she says, and she looked the part. An attractive, successful lawyer husband, two small kids—a boy and a girl—a good address in the fashionable "Heights" area of Little Rock.

But the pressure, much of it self-imposed, was intense. Her use of pills accelerated until she was taking twelve pills a day on the average, and sometimes as many as twenty. The pills, she said, energized her and made her daily struggle to live up to expectations doable. For a while.

But buying enough pills to keep her habit fed at the rate of a pill every waking hour took planning and money, which added more pressure. Her biggest supplier was the Internet, an amazingly accessible source, and she supplemented that with prescriptions from several local doctors who bought her story that she was suffering from carpel tunnel syndrome.

"It was my 'prop,'" she says. "Everybody's got a prop—back pain, neck pain—whatever it takes."

The Internet is a major trafficker in drugs. On a site like www.norcoworldwide.com (no longer active) she says, you pay a $120 consultation fee and then can order 120 pills every twenty-five days.

Sometimes the ladies who "use" form little cliques and "network." For example, Jennifer had three girlfriends—all prescription drug addicts—who networked by helping each other cope and maintain their supplies. Eventually, unwilling to share her stash or her time, Jennifer dropped out of the group.

About six years ago Jennifer and her husband were divorced, and shortly after that, she stopped drinking and went back to her AA meetings—but her Vicodin habit persisted and consumed most of her waking hours.

"Eventually," she said, "your habit manages you and not the other way around."

That's when she saw the UAMS ad.

In the detox phase, Jennifer chose to cut her use of Vicodin abruptly from twelve pills a day to nothing in two days instead of tapering off more gradually.

"I wanted to feel it, and I wanted to remember it," she said.

It was a tough forty-eight hours, during which she was sick with flu-like symptoms, severe headaches, crying, and suicidal thoughts. On the third day, when she was Vicodin free, she began taking the Suboxone, which she picked up every morning at the clinic. She took one dose in the morning and one in the afternoon on her first day, and, she says, "I felt normal." After that first day, she tapered off the size and frequency of her doses until she was drug free.

Her program of recovery further required that she meet with a counselor once a week, attend a group meeting twice a week at the clinic, and attend an outside meeting—AA or NA—once a week.

KATHRYN'S STORY

Kathryn's story is a little different. Her physician father, now deceased, was an abusive alcoholic, and while growing up in this type of home has impacted her and her brother, neither turned to alcohol to ease the pain.

Since her divorce, Kathryn, who tends to be a loner, has lived by herself—she has no children—and focused on her demanding job and such outside diversions as gardening and going to the theater.

Addiction struck when she had a minor back injury on top of having sciatica, and got her first prescription for hydrocodone. For the next year and a half, the drug, acquired exclusively from the Internet under the brand name "Norco" dominated her life.

"It numbs you," Kathryn says, "and all your problems seem to roll off."

She found in Norco a relief principally from her emotional pain, and the arrival of the Federal Express truck bearing her package of drugs was her principal source of joy. The downside was that she found herself increasingly depressed and losing sleep. The face she saw in the mirror was haggard and drawn, and she increasingly avoided people to the point that she was almost completely isolated from friends and family. She was also full of fear that her habit would be discovered and she would lose her job.

In the end, Kathryn's brother, a medical specialist who knew that she was abusing drugs, told her she needed to quit.

"It is no longer an option," he said.

That's when she saw the UAMS ad and began her recovery.

Jennifer and Kathryn volunteered to tell their stories hoping that those who may be addicted will take heart and choose life over lingering death.

———

A VISIT WITH BOBBY WARD

A couple of years later, I paid another visit to my friend Bobby Ward, a clinical supervisor at UAMS at that time.

I've known Ward for most of his twenty years of sobriety and have been entertained and enlightened at recovery meetings over the years by his story, which he delivers with self-deprecating humor illuminated by a megawatt smile.

Ward, who was clinical director for substance abuse treatment and directed the chemical dependence outpatient programs for both marijuana and opiate prescription drug addictions, has moved on since our visit, but our discussion remains relevant.

He is happily married with three kids, has been clean and sober for more than twenty years and brings to his position plenty of "street cred" and savvy from working at two treatment centers before joining UAMS.

Although not an academic type, Ward has all the qualifying credentials he needs hanging on the walls of his sunny office. Still, much of his education in the treatment of addictions comes from the streets.

Like many in recovery, he has been profoundly influenced by the late Joe McQuany, Basically, Ward got well by working the 12 Steps and by learning how to apply them from McQuany while sitting under the magnolia tree at Serenity Park and at Monday night meetings at the Wolfe Street Center.

Ward understands the terms that psychologists use to describe addiction and treatment like "matrix model" and 'cognitive therapy"—and in fact he does most of what they describe—but it is not a language addicts use, and he smiles at its academic flavor.

For example, the National Institute on Drug Abuse (NIDA) says the goal of the matrix model has been to provide a framework within which stimulant abusers can achieve the following: (a) cease drug use; (b) stay in treatment; (c) learn about issues critical to addiction and relapse; (d) receive direction and support from a trained therapist; (e) receive education for family members affected by the addiction; (f) become familiar with self help programs, and; (g) receive monitoring by urine testing.

TEACHER AND COACH

The model also requires that therapists use a combination of skills required "to function simultaneously as teacher and coach…to promote self esteem, dignity and self worth."'

Flashing his ready smile, Ward says this is basically what he does, but he might use different words to describe it based on his own experience as an addict and the 12-Step tools he uses for his own recovery. And he would probably say that ultimately, you get self-esteem from doing estimable things.

Cognitive therapy, according to the Academy of Cognitive Therapy, involves three primary activities: "education, skill building and problem solving. During treatment, the client actively applies strategies learned to the problems which brought him to therapy. If indicated, cognitive therapy is also compatible with the use of prescribed medication [i.e., Suboxen and methadone]."

Over the years, Ward has developed strong opinions about addiction and recovery. He favors the use of Suboxone and methadone to treat opiate and heroin addictions. He condemns the notion that marijuana addiction is relatively harmless. He believes that methamphetamine is perhaps the most evil drug and needs more attention. Finally, he believes that stopping the supply of drugs on the Mexican border can only become truly effective when we dry up the demand for drugs this side of the border.

There are those in the addiction field who disagree with UAMS and Ward on the use of drugs, which are themselves addictive, to treat drug abuse, but he defends it. With Suboxen, he says, the addict can begin to "start stopping" in his program of recovery, and as proof of the efficacy of the program, Bobby claims a 90-percent success rate for prescription drug addicts. His same reasoning applies to methadone.

WEED AND ALCOHOL

For those who think that marijuana is a mild and relatively benign drug, Ward, who oversees the marijuana clinic, begs to differ.

"Weed and alcohol are the worst drugs of all because they destroy brain cells," Bobby says. "And it takes one to five years to get marijuana and alcohol out of your system."

To those who suggest that marijuana doesn't really impair driving, Bobby says, "Marijuana is why they changed the Driving While Intoxicated (DWI) charge to Driving Under the Influence (DUI) to cover weed and other drugs."

Meth, according to Bobby, is an underestimated evil that flourishes in Arkansas' vast rural areas where meth cookers replace the moonshiners of bygone days.

"Like moonshine once was, Arkansas is the capital of meth," Bobby says, pointing out that authorities tend to shy away from shutting down the meth labs because of the high cost of cleaning up toxic waste.

"It's much less costly to go after the crack (cocaine) houses," Bobby says.

So what about the drug wars?

He shares with many the belief that we should spend more time drying up the demand for drugs, which he says is increasing. It makes sense financially, Bobby says.

"The average cost of substance abuse treatment," he says, "is about $1,583, resulting in monetary benefits of $11,487 through reduced medical expenses, reduced cost of crime and increased earnings."

Bobby has a good life now. Recalling the days when he was abusing alcohol and other drugs, he says, "My alcoholic life took me on a journey I wouldn't wish on my worst enemy. I spent time in many jails, caused many broken relationships, and I even sold my sister's home.

THE GRACE OF GOD

He continued:

I got sober only by the grace of God on October 13, 1990, and for that I am truly grateful. I sobered up in the Salvation Army because I was broke and couldn't afford treatment.

Since that time, I have made amends to family members and others, and with my help and encouragement one of my sisters got sober after years of abusing alcohol.

I have been employed ever since sobriety, and I have a wonderful wife, Sybil, and three beautiful boys who are all working and enrolled in college. Today, I have some really good friends, and I am totally committed to this program of recovery and helping others as "old timers" helped me.

I ended up working for a wonderful man, Joe McQuany, truly a gift from God, and I have been studying the AA *Big Book* ever since. Today, I enjoy the privilege of training counselors and serving on their certification board.

CHAPTER SIXTEEN

Sponsorship and Slogans

Don G., a writer who has been in recovery for more than twenty years, is a well-known speaker at AA conventions. He has also written a number of articles on recovery that have been published in One Day at a Time, as well as on our website by the same name. In addition, Don has written a book called Off the Walls featuring more than a thousand inspiring AA slogans and one-liners.

This is Don's chapter, and I have dedicated it to him. We'll begin with a reprint of the following article, which he wrote about his sponsor, Charlie. It was first published in the AA *Grapevine* eight years ago and in our print and web outlets a year later. An excerpt from *Off the Walls* appears immediately after the conclusion of that article.

At the end of my drinking, the bottom I hit was both terrifying and dramatic. The accumulated wreckage of twenty-seven years of alcoholic drinking and all the "isms" that come with it looked insurmountable and hopeless. I had been hospitalized, detoxed, and placed in a treatment program that had brought me to our program. While AA made no demands on me, the treatment facility did, telling me I had to get a sponsor.

Being an alcoholic, the first thing I did was complicate the situation. My sponsor would have to be perfect in every way. After a long period of frustrated searching, I related my dilemma to an AA acquaintance. He suggested the men's "deer camp" AA group that had been meeting continuously for over thirty years. They always started that meeting the same way. The chairman said, "At this meeting, we stress sponsorship. Is there anyone who doesn't have a sponsor and would like to get one?'

I jumped up out of my chair in front of this room full of men and said, "Yes, I'd like to interview several of you about being my sponsor after the meeting." The room erupted in laughter as I stood there feeling foolish. But when the noise subsided, the chairman said to me in the most gentle way, "Well, we don't have to make it that complicated. How about if I just appoint you a sponsor?"

Embarrassed and perplexed, I told him that would be okay. Looking around the room, the chairman settled on an old man sitting off to one side. "Charlie," he said, "will you sponsor this man?

The look Charlie gave me spoke volumes. He started to shake his head and wave me off, but suddenly he said, "Oh all right. See me after the meeting." (Later, I would learn that this is a traditional charade of these old-timers, and in time I would take to doing it myself.)

After the meeting, Charlie looked me in the eye and asked, "Are you willing to go to any lengths to get this program?" Unsure of what he intended by this, I asked what he meant. "It means," he answered, "are you willing to do whatever I ask you, with the understanding that I did it myself?" Well, if he'd done it, I could too, so I agreed to do whatever he said.

———

AN OLD-TIMER

Charlie was an old-timer—seventeen years sober when we began working the program together. He sponsored me the way he'd been sponsored. Shortly after we began, he asked if I'd be willing to garden with him. I certainly wasn't enthusiastic, but I had said I'd go to any lengths, so I agreed.

And so, this sober old man and I began a vegetable garden. Charlie liked to tell his friends that we were "farming" together. He showed me everything about how you plan, build, prepare, and plant a garden. We cleared and dug and tilled and raked. It was hard work, but we did it at Charlie's pace, and it felt good. I got my hands dirty.

As we began to put in rows of plants, Charlie got down on his knees in our newly tilled earth and indicated for me to follow him. There, on my knees in the dirt next to this gentle old man, he looked at me with a wry smile and said, "As long as we're down here, let's say the Serenity Prayer." We said it together, and that was the first time I'd ever prayed on my knees.

Vegetable gardens need a lot of daily care. Charlie said it was necessary to pull weeds and water the plants early each morning, and at day's end when they had stood up to the blistering sun, another watering for the night's rest and recovery. So I showed up at our garden every morning just after sunup, and Charlie would already be there waiting for me. As we worked together in the cool morning air, I'd ramble on and on about my expectations for the coming day while he listened patiently.

When I finally wound down, Charlie would allow me to choose only one, or at most two actions for that day, and disregard the rest. These were my "marching orders," and I would return to the garden at sundown to describe how all of it had gone. Occasionally, he'd make a comment, but mostly he let me come to my own realizations as he gently steered the course.

For days and months we did this together, as I slowly came into the sunlight of the spirit and the AA design for living. From our vegetable garden, we launched into the 12 Steps.

Seven years passed this way, and one morning as I answered the phones at our Central Office the way Charlie had taught me; he called and asked me to come see him. It was two days before Thanksgiving when he looked at me and said, "Don, I've got cancer, and it's terminal."

CHARLIE PASSES AWAY

For six months as Charlie grew weaker, he faced each day as a gift with a grateful attitude. He never spoke of himself, only of the program and the newcomer. Finally one Saturday, he asked me to meet him in his garden. He wanted me to move a few plants around for him.

The next day was Sunday, and they took him to the hospital in the afternoon. I got to see him Monday morning, and he was almost gone, but he said my name and he held my hand. Later that morning, my sponsor passed away.

I'll always know that Charlie called me back to the garden one last time to make sure I'd remember the lessons we learned there together and to pass them on to others. And to remind me that this sober life of ours is a miraculous gift, to be lived to the fullest one day at a time. And when it's over, to go with quiet dignity, grateful to have trudged the road of happy destiny.

From the very beginning, Charlie showed me many different ways to look at things. New or long-forgotten old perspectives on how to live that I'd ignored, forgotten, or refused throughout the chaos that had been my life.

One of the first, and ultimately one of the most important of these perspectives, was this... YOU ARE NOT GOING TO BE ABLE TO MAKE IT ALONE ANYMORE.

To get me started in that direction, Charlie prescribed a time-honored, almost sacred local AA tradition called "The Worksheet." The process was so simple it was almost frightening. But it was a wall I would have to get past if I wanted what Charlie had, and if I was willing to go to any lengths to get it.

For over forty years, the Worksheet Tradition had produced admirable results in our local area when it was practiced correctly. Just after my sponsor had "sized me up," he made a list of successfully sober people he knew, to whom he felt I could relate and from whom I might learn.

The result was my Worksheet List, and my assignment was to sit with each of those on the list individually and listen to their experience, strength, and hope. What an order! The list he gave me had twenty-one names and phone numbers, and it was intimidating, to say the least.

As I fearfully considered this path to which I had committed myself, I came across a printed flyer for an upcoming local AA conference. At the bottom, in the corner, in large block letters, was a phrase that would change me forever forward from that moment...YOU ARE NOT ALONE. I was so profoundly struck by the timely miracle of its message that I actually wept.

WORKSHEET TALKS BEGIN

And so I began my "Worksheet Talks." I recognized only one name from my list...someone I had known only by reputation in my drunken life...someone who had once carried on like me but had long ago disappeared from that scene. I called him and said, "I'm an alcoholic," to which he replied, "I know." I said he was on my worksheet list and I didn't know what else to say or do.

He told me to meet him for breakfast the next morning at 7:30, and I was there, so scared I was numb. Across that corner table he quietly spoke to me for an hour, and the similarities in his experiences and my own were astounding.

I did not utter a single word for that entire hour, and at the end, as he insisted that the price of breakfast was on him, all I could say as we shook hands was, "Thank you." With a wry smile he gently responded, "Oh no...I thank you." It would be a while before I understood that, but eventually I got it.

And so it went with me and my Worksheet Talks. One at a time, appointment by appointment, one-on-one, with both men and women who were chosen for me to help light my way, so that I would no longer be alone.

My years of brain-dulling drinking had disturbed my interpersonal skills so badly that I had even forgotten how to listen, let alone think rationally. Fortunately, all that this Worksheet Talk process required of me was my body sitting in a chair…my mind would follow later. So I soaked up everything these men and women had to say, and I was right where I was supposed to be.

One genteel woman on my list with nearly ten years sobriety had asked me to come to her home on Saturday morning for our talk. Months later, after my recovery was on more solid footing, she told me that after she'd hung up the phone from arranging our meeting, she exclaimed, "What have I done? I don't know this man, and I've invited him to my home!" Then she would laugh and tell me, "And here you came on Saturday morning, up my front walkway, clean and well-dressed, and with a look of wonder in your eye."

She had sat me down in her living room and brought me coffee in fine china. I felt like a real human being again for the first time in many months. And there, she told me her story, and she became my friend. She was a person with whom I would not normally have mixed, and suddenly she was my comrade in sobriety.

———

A NEW BEGINNING

I realized several things then about this Worksheet process. First, it was a matter of trust between my sponsor and the people he'd asked to talk to me. Second, it was a test of willingness from me, for them to see if I was serious about this effort to recover; if I would follow their directions. Third, and perhaps most important of all, it was the beginning of a new community in my life.

Once I sat with someone in a Worksheet Talk, my life experience would be forever changed. Whenever I would see them at meetings, events, and gatherings, an immediate bond between us would always be there because of the intimate hour of sharing we had spent together. Now I could really see what was happening to me. I WAS NO LONGER ALONE.

Then, as I moved around my town where I had been an inebriate for years, I ran into people I really knew, soberly rather than superficially, and we recognized and greeted one another in the warmth of our mutual common bond. On a busy downtown sidewalk I ran into a man from my Worksheet List, and we stood there conversing in mutual friendship and understanding as the chaotic world swirled around us. This is what it was all about, and what I had always wanted.

Another man on my list had invited me to sit with him in his backyard meditation flower garden. He was a student of all kinds of histories, and he loved the story of AA and its birth, growth, and progression. By his reckoning, we were the second generation of AA, the ones to whom the torch had been passed from the first groups and members who had risked and sacrificed so much, for us to also have an opportunity to recover. He looked at me and said, "We are standing on the shoulders of giants."

Time passed the way time always passes, one day, one hour, one moment after another. Each Worksheet Talk affected me, and I absorbed them one at a time, resisting the usual urge to hurry through them in order to be finished. Depending on my mood or circumstances, one or two talks a week were all I could manage, but as long as I was proceeding rather than "resting on my laurels," my sponsor was satisfied.

By the time I'd completed half my list, I began to open up a little, briefly describing my feelings when asked. During one talk, a sober member asked me how I felt about this whole approach to sobriety, and all I could say was, "Absolutely amazing."

From that moment on through all his succeeding sober years until he "successfully completed his program" and gently passed sway, every time he saw me he would smile, shake my hand, and say, "Absolutely amazing." Such was the kind of bond created in the Worksheet Talks.

A PROBLEM DEVELOPS

As with all of us, some months into my new sober life, the reality of my unresolved wreckage of the past returned. I faced a huge problem that would require a life-altering decision from me, and I was frozen in fear and inaction. My sponsor, who could seemingly always advise me in troublesome matters, said he could not help me with this one. It was the type of situation in which he'd had no experience. By this time, I'd finished all my Worksheet assignments, and Charlie asked if one of them had told a story of something similar to my dilemma.

On reflection, I realized that several of my Worksheet experiences had described similar circumstances, and one of them had related a story much like mine. Charlie reminded me that each of these people were now a part of my new sober community and would be willing to help or advise me as long as I was continuing to make an honest effort with this new way of living of ours. "So it follows," Charlie said, "that he is the one you need to ask about this problem."

I had a second meeting with this thirty year-long sober man and told him the details of my dilemma. In response, he told me the specifics of the same problem he had faced in his early sobriety twenty-five years earlier, and he told me of the decision he had made with the advice of others and the action he had taken. Then he looked at me and said, "That was twenty-five years ago, and I still don't know if I did the right thing or not, but you can see how my life has turned out." And yes, I could see it. He was truly happy, joyous, and free. Finally, he advised, "Now, you have to pray, meditate, and wait for an answer."

The hardest thing you can ask an alcoholic to do is to wait, but I did it. One morning some two weeks later, immediately upon awakening that morning, I intuitively knew what my decision had to be, and so I took the action. That was almost twenty years ago, "and I still don't know if I did the right thing or not." But my life has been a wonder of sobriety, and I have lived happy, joyous, and free ever since.

This may be the single greatest value of the Worksheet Talks, a community of successfully sober people who will always be there for us as long as we are trying to live our program one day at a time.

Certainly, there were some not-so-wonderful Worksheet experiences, but they too have left lasting impressions on me. One man drank again after nine years, and following a long and miserable time, he died drunk. Another on my list, the only one with whom I never actually met, was always "too busy" to see me, despite repeated attempts on my part. He too left our program after twelve years, never to return. Just like my "successful Worksheets," I remember these others vividly and the lessons they taught me.

The day I completed ten years of continuous sobriety was, of course, very special and very personal to me. I wanted to honor it for my Higher Power and myself, and I wanted to share it unobtrusively with just a few other special people. So I spent that entire day calling the people on my Worksheet List who, ten years later, were still alive and still sober. I was able to reach a perfect dozen of them and share my quiet, humble joy with them, and to once again thank them for the part they had played in it. This was a truly wonderful experience for me and for them.

One man on my list, now deceased but whom I still treasure, met up with me at another crossroads of my life back at three years of my sobriety. By then I had cleared away the wreckage of my past, gone back to school, and started a whole new life. After my graduation, I asked him, "What am I supposed to do now?" "Well," he said with a wry smile, "you're supposed to carry the message."

And so I have tried to practice and pass on what was so freely and unselfishly given to me. Today, it is a privilege and an honor to be asked to do a Worksheet Talk with a newcomer. And to help keep alive and maintain this wonderful tradition that set me on the road of happy destiny.

———

OFF THE WALLS

Most 12-Step meetings post slogans on the walls. They are also on bumper stickers, which, it has been said, might best be placed on the dashboard rather than the rear bumper for easier viewing by those most in need of inspiration.

A couple of years ago I wrote a book about slogans, more than one thousand of them, and I called it **Off the Walls.**

It is a collection of expressions begun after more than a decade of sobriety in Alcoholics Anonymous. I found myself passing to a third stage of the journey, having first experienced the miracle of recovery followed by the "sunlight of the spirit."

Initially, at the time, I was having difficulty focusing on meeting topics and discussions, becoming lost in my own thoughts and what I might say if I were asked to contribute.

Bob G., a sober member whom I had sponsored a few years previously, had experienced the same problem. I noticed that he had suddenly become quiet, either passing when asked to share or offering only a few words.

When he did speak, it was obviously spontaneous and inspired. Occasionally he would produce a small notebook from his pocket and inconspicuously jot down a note. I asked him what he had done to effect such a change. It was over his answer that he became my third sponsor, we having completely reversed the roles of our relationship.

Bob's inspiration was to listen in each meeting for something that had intense meaning to me and my experience…something strong enough to make my head nod up and down.

This would not occur in every meeting, but when it did, he wrote down his thoughts rather than trusting them to memory. I wanted what he had, so I too began carrying a small notebook.

From the very beginning, I soared into a new dimension of experience. All the meetings were good, the exceptional ones produced a note, and the outstanding ones produced multiple entries. My small notebook became a journal. My interest and concentration peaked, and my enthusiasm boiled over. I was on a new mission…one with seemingly no boundaries.

Tragically, Bob died suddenly only eleven months into my new journey. Continuously sober for years, he had just realized his ultimate dream, a return to his own pulpit in the Presbyterian church where he successfully transitioned to "the big meeting," having touched the lives of all of us who knew him.

Of the many gifts he left us is my journal, which to this day continues to grow in ever-widening circles. I, and many others, will never forget him.

This work is now lovingly dedicated to the memory of this little minister who opened his friendship and heart to me and to us all. I know he is nestled in the arms of his Higher Power, and I pray that he looks down with a smile on this effort to share his wisdom.

The book contains twelve hundred slogans from AA and AA related meetings, and they are organized in a variety of ways.

You might, for example, be struggling with acceptance, resentment, control, fear, or faith. There are plenty of slogans for each one. There are, for example, roughly one hundred slogans having to do with acceptance.

You know how when you tell your story to a 12-Step audience, for example, you begin by telling what it was like, what happened and what it's like now? You can find slogans relating to each of those three components plus a fourth one called "Wisdom for the Journey."

Here are some samples:

What We Were Like:
53.   When I first got here, I was like an insomniac with a mission.
77.   I thought my opinions were facts.
100. My definition of an alcoholic was someone who drank more than I did.
238. Hitting bottom is when conditions in your life get worse faster than you can lower your standards.
482. In the end, life was coming at me from all directions. I felt like a Dixie cup in a storm drain.
500. Drinking alcohol made me strangely insane.

What Happened:
3.   Practicing H.A.L.T—not letting myself get too hungry, angry, lonely, or tired—taught me that sometimes all I really need is a sandwich and a nap.
30.   This is the first place I ever experienced the wonder of being accepted not in spite of what I was but because of what I was.

73.   After I got past my shame and my guilt, I began to learn about myself—the good, the real good, and the real.

164.   AA was teaching me not only to live sober but to live life.

300.   My time in treatment was ending, and I said to myself, "I've got to find God by Friday or they won't let me out of here."

372.   The way I got here is a judge asked me a trick question: "Do you want to go to jail or do you want to go to treatment?"

What We Are Like Now:

60.   The miracle is not that I didn't drink today. The miracle is that I didn't want to drink today.

67.   Today, I use prayer to make it through. I used to use alcohol for that.

76.   We need to remember that untreated people don't know what they don't know.

119.   I don't really have much choice but to deal with things.

183.   I am not against anything that works.

220.   Over time I have developed a taste for this serenity thing you all talk about.

Wisdom for the Journey

969.   Sobriety is knowing the truth.

990.   If there is anybody who brings out the worst in you, remember that what they are bringing out is still you.

1042.   The dictionary says acceptance means to willingly receive, not to gladly receive.

1064.   Sobriety is the narrowing of the gap between my values and my actions.

1149.   There is really nothing new in AA. You can't teach an old dog new tricks, but you can teach an old dog old tricks.

Off the Walls is also organized so that if you are working on the steps there is a slogan that will apply and possibly help your understanding of it or motivate you to begin working it. For example, if you are working on Step 1, you will find:

92. Step 1 is the only non-spiritual step. Rather, it is just the plain truth—reality. To take it, one merely has to state the truth.

983. Step 1 is the only one that can and must be done perfectly.

Here are thirty more slogans you may find useful:

1. For people like us, there is no such thing as a legitimate resentment.
2. Apologies are nice, but an apology is not an amend. An amend is the correction of a wrong. It infers that in correcting it, I am not going to do it anymore.
3. Feelings are not facts.
4. Arrogance is covering up shame. Feeling shame is one thing. Hiding it is another.
5. Defining who you are and what you want is an important part of getting and staying sober.
6. The purpose of grieving is acceptance.
7. A definition of humility is "willingness to learn."
8. Isolation is the same thing as being "emotionally incognito."
9. We're responsible for what is possible, and God is responsible for what is impossible.
10. It's the principal point of happiness that a man is willing to be what he is.
11. In the end, everything comes down to working the steps, being with God and sharing with others.
12. One day at a time is not a suggested minimum…it is the suggested maximum.
13. It's not that drinking is an issue…it's that life is.
14. Today I just don't take that act of defiance that will kill me.
15. There is no "time-out" in life. Everything counts. Every day. Every minute.
16. If you want self-esteem, do estimable things.
17. The best way to learn how to pray is to pray.
18. It's easier to have a relationship with God than it is to have one with somebody else.
19. Spirituality is about living before you die.

20. There aren't solutions to imaginary problems.
21. Rigorous honesty is the absolute absence of the intention to deceive.
22. What we really want is some comfort in our lives. Seems to me the most comfort we can find is by helping other people.
23. This program is not rational. It's spiritual.
24. Humility. If you think you've got it, you just lost it.
25. In this program you start where you are, but you better not stay there.
26. I came in here to make a six-pack last a Sunday.
27. Everyone else appears to be normal until I get to know them.
28. I was convinced that I was better than all the people who were stepping over me.
29. One time I asked my sponsor if he was God. He said, 'Sometimes."
30. It's not what we drank that made us what we are…it's what we are that made us drink.

CHAPTER SEVENTEEN

Treatment and Shelter for the Homeless

The primary need of the nation's 3 million homeless people is treatment for their addictions and the depression, anxiety, and other mental health problems that often co-occur.

Shelter, as it turns out, is easier to come by than adequate treatment.

"Governments, private agencies and churches provide shelter and meals," Joseph Califano writes in his book, *High Society,* "but they lack the trained personnel and resources to move this population off the streets; away from needles, powders, pills, and cheap wine and liquor and into stable living environments."

Government efforts to provide shelter for the indigent, Califano reminds us, first began with the U.S. Housing Act of 1937 (HUD), and it turned into a nightmare.

"The goal," Califano writes, was to provide inexpensive, temporary shelter for the poor, but over the twentieth century, public housing became the permanent housing of last resort for our neediest citizens. "Drugs and drug dealers infested the nation's public housing complexes in the 1960s and 1970s and their destructive power reached magnum force in the 1980s."

HUD is still in the business of subsidizing and regulating housing for homeless populations, and a Little Rock facility, Our House, is a small but successful example of what an enlightened management can achieve with both private and public support.

Our House, which has space for eighty people, offers separate housing for homeless men and women as well as units where families can stay together for up to two years. Adults are required to have permanent, full-time jobs and are expected to save 75 percent of their earnings.

It is a place where homeless families and individuals can come and build new lives by dealing with their mental health and addiction problems and learning how to live in the real world. When they leave, most will have a plan for dealing with life on life's terms.

The record shows that 80 percent of those who leave Our House move up in housing, 71 percent have savings, and 63 percent have full time jobs.

As for the enlightened management, Georgia Mjarten has been the executive director of Our House since 2006. She is a thirty-one-year-old dynamo with an impressive resume, deep compassion, and a strong will who has taken Our House to new levels.

Managing a population, which some have likened to herding cats, takes love and toughness—and Mjarten has both the chops and the resume for the job. She emphasizes that Our House "is not a homeless shelter, and it's not charity. It's a community.

"What I have worked more than any one program to create, what we've all created, what our staff has created, what our volunteers have created—is a community."

And for the good of the community, you follow the rules. Those who do not choose to follow the rules, Mjartan adds, cannot stay.

Let's take a look at her background.

Mjartan has both an undergraduate degree from the University of Arkansas at Little Rock (UALR) and a graduate degree from the University of Ulster in Belfast, Ireland. She double majored in political science and English at UALR and withdrew from the Rhodes Scholar process to accept the Mitchell Scholars Program award given to twelve American students per year on the basis of their scholarship, leadership, and commitment to public and community service.

The scholarship, which Mjartan received in 2003, enables students to pursue graduate degrees in Ireland and is named in honor of Sen. George

Mitchell for his role in brokering peace in Northern Ireland. Mjartan received her master's degree in political communications from Ulster.

After college, she went to work with Ken Hubbell and Associates in Little Rock, managing a contract for a $40-million community development project with the W. K. Kellogg Foundation's Mid South Delta Initiative.

It has not been all work and no play.

One of the other students in her Donaghey Scholars class at UALR was Dominik Mjartan, who is, today, her husband and a vice president of Southern Bancorp, a rural development banking organization.

The two became a couple as freshmen, dated all though college, married in June 2002 about two weeks after graduation from UALR, and moved to Ireland as newlyweds.

Now, both work for organizations that have a focus on giving the less fortunate a leg up but with accountability. Southern Bancorp's founding directors included Hillary Rodham Clinton, Thomas F. (Mack) McClarty, Rob Walton, and others. Little Rock entrepreneur/investor Walter Smiley, founder of Systematics and president of Smiley Investment Co., is chairman and interim CEO of Southern Bancorps.

Both Georgia and Dominik are athletic. Georgia got her first job at Little Rock's Willow Springs water park as a lifeguard at age fifteen and hung out mostly with "the rough guys." She became an accomplished diver and gymnast and played soccer. Today, she plays soccer three days a week (Dominik also plays) and works out in a gym another two days.

Georgia Mjartan was recruited to serve on the board of Our House in 2003, at the age of twenty-three, by advisory board member and philanthropist Beth Coulson. Two years later, faced with financial and operational difficulties, the board fired its executive director and persuaded Mjartan to take the job.

Working with the board, Mjartan has made notable improvements. She has helped clients improve their lives by adding programs including free childcare and preschool summer- and after-school programs, access to 12-Step programs, and programs to teach job skills, job-search skills, and basic adult education.

She also brings in volunteers to help in areas such as financial literacy, parenting, and dealing with domestic violence.

Melissa F. forty-three, a drug-addicted mother now in recovery at Our House, has over a year of clean time and is a good example of how the program works. She came to Our House the summer of 2010, bringing with her two of her children, ages seven and ten. The three live together in a small but cozy bedroom with a TV set. They use a communal bathroom, and she prepares their meals in a kitchen all the mothers share.

The previous summer, Melissa and her children lived in a filthy and dangerous meth house in downtown Little Rock barely a mile away. She herself was using drugs but had a part-time job. Still she didn't dare leave her children alone in a wretched place overrun with people she describes as "animals."

Now, sitting in the kitchen after the bustle of lunch hour, she talks about a life dominated by drug abuse and its consequences, and gently wipes her eyes with a tissue in the telling of it. Her story, while somewhat different from others in the details, is otherwise all too common.

Melissa, who also has a twenty-six-year old son and a grandson, was raised, absent her addicted parents, by a grandmother who may have been well meaning but was limited in her ability to help. Melissa found alcohol at age twelve, soon graduated to stronger drugs, dropped out of school, sold drugs on the street, spent time in several jails and prison, and took up with men who abused and abandoned her and their children. Tragically, it is a familiar story.

She did get a taste of recovery along the way, first with a forty-five-day stay at Gateway House in Fort Smith, a rehab facility, and later, in 2008, with Little Rock's UAMS-sponsored Arkansas CARES program, where she stayed six months with her young children. She has been at Our House for sixteen months and is working toward an outside job, but for now she has duties at Our House.

On the cold February day of our interview in 2011, she sits in a warming hut, greeting visitors driving up for the monthly open house tour. When the parking duties are over, she goes back to the building where her apartment is for our meeting.

"You know," she says after talking about her drug abuse and multiple mistakes in life, "since I've been here, I'm beginning to learn how to go about things."

She had always had a faith in God in varying degrees, she says, but she had never really understood how the game of life is played.

"It's all about making good choices and taking responsibility," she says. "Nobody is going to mess up my life but me. What happened to me is not something somebody else did."

Part of what she wants to do is raise her children better.

"If I don't tell my son how to live," she says, "who will?"

On the way back to her job at the parking lot, she stops to pick up a cigarette butt, puts it in a nearby receptacle, then quietly turns and says with a smile and tears in her eyes, "You know, last Sunday at my church, my family filled up a whole pew."

Interestingly, Mjartan has also undergone a spiritual transformation. In January of 2006, one year into her job at Our House, Mjartan became a Christian. In this, she was encouraged by Corey F., the facilities manager at Our House, an ex drug addict and prison inmate who had dealt with his addiction and revived his own Christian faith in God while attending the Celebrate Recovery program at Fellowship Bible Church.

Our House is in the category of "subsidized permanent housing" under national Housing and Urban Development (HUD) agency regulations. It is a free, two-year program for individuals and families who are homeless, clean and sober, and willing to work. It has evolved into a successful model not just for housing people but for transforming lives.

At the other end of the homeless spectrum, the very bottom, there are the "unsheltered homeless" who live hand to mouth under the bridges. Ninety percent are substance abusers and most are mentally ill.

Our House will consider applications from this group, but will not accept anyone who is not clean and sober and willing to commit to a two-year program. Usually, the "unsheltered" are not looking for a commitment and are more likely to turn to another category of housing called "transitional" shelters such as the Salvation Army, Union Rescue Mission, and the Compassion Center, which will take them in, feed them, and help them sober up.

Those who play by the rules, develop a trade, and seek help for their addictions can stay longer and get well.

———

THE COMPASSION CENTER

For those living under the bridge who want to get a meal and a night's sleep, Pastor William Holloway will take them in, but they must work and attend meetings that deal with their addictions or they can't stay.

Holloway knows about life on the streets and addiction. After fourteen years of riotous living, which included time in the military, five years in and out of jails, and a lot of years in saloons, Holloway turned to Alcoholics Anonymous for help, and got off the streets of Minneapolis and Memphis.

Illiterate because of his lack of schooling, Holloway, despite his handicap, launched a successful contracting business, got married and raised a family, and eventually learned to read and write. At age forty-seven, he became a Christian and after that an ordained minister with a heart for the homeless.

Today, Holloway, now sixty-six, presides over the Compassion Center, which he founded eleven years ago with his wife, Rosemary, a minister herself, along with an investment of their life savings and a fervent belief "in the healing power of the Gospel."

The Center consists of two homeless shelters in Little Rock—one on Roosevelt Road and the other on Asher Avenue—with up to 250 or more men, women, and children under sixty-three thousand square feet of roof.

The Holloways bought the Asher Avenue building for $50,000. It served as the men's shelter for the first six years and became the women's shelter when the Holloways bought the former Salvation Army building for $350,000, this time with donations from local contributors.

What makes the Compassion Center especially interesting is the evangelistically focused entrepreneurial style of this one-time addict and street person who now runs the newest and possibly the biggest shelter operation in the city without assistance from government or a major charity like the United Way.

While Pastor Holloway's aggressive style is unique, he is also part of a national trend. Other Christian organizations are also stepping up to the plate in large numbers to address the problem of substance abuse within the ranks of the homeless and prison populations with new programs and refurbished old ones.

Seated behind his desk, Holloway, a man of substantial girth with a white crew cut (the only kind you can get at the shelter's free barbershop), a slightly banged-up, ruddy face, and a ready smile says he is by no means finished with his growth plans and then gets down to brass tacks about his current operation.

———

EVERYONE ADMITTED

Compassion Center admits everyone—men, women, women with children, and sometimes even a husband and wife with children—and it's free. The only requirement is that they are sober and not carrying a weapon. Some stay a night, "get three hots and a cot," and are gone. Some stay a little longer, and some choose to enter the Center's substance abuse program and may stay a year.

Holloway says that about half of those who come to the shelter need a meal and a bed. The other half "are at the end of their rope." The latter are the ones who are likely to stay and have a shot at recovery.

Holloway estimates 65 to 80 percent or more of the homeless are addicted to alcohol and other drugs. The men who choose recovery live in a special section of the building and enter a six-month program that includes working a Christ-centered, 12-Step program, attending counseling sessions, and working in jobs at the Center.

Ray Wells is the substance abuse program director at the Center. He is a recovering alcoholic who ended up as a patient in the VA hospital in

Little Rock after a career mainly with prison systems in Oklahoma and Colorado.

Brutalized by his job, he turned to alcohol hoping for relief, and it made him worse. His marriage failed, he lost his children, and he sank into deep despair. At the VA hospital, Wells said, he did manage to get "dry" but not sober, and was very unhappy.

Out for a walk one night, he passed the Compassion Center and decided to go in and spend the night. He liked it immediately and asked if he could talk to Pastor Holloway about a job.

Chuckling as he recalled his appointment with the pastor, Wells said, "I approached him with what I felt was a pretty decent resume that could lead to an administrative position of some kind. Pastor looked it over, and then he said, 'I see you're a cook.'"

Wells said, "I pointed out that there was nothing in my resume that said anything about my being a cook, but he persisted. 'Yep, you're a cook,' he said with finality.

"Turns out he was right," Wells said, smiling. "I started out as an apprentice in the kitchen the next day, became a cook, and eventually took charge of the kitchen."

It wasn't until later that he made the jump to program director.

THE CHEESE INCIDENT

One of Wells' favorite stories about his tour of duty as a cook he has labeled "the cheese incident." It seems the kitchen was well stocked with everything but cheese and hadn't received any for quite awhile.

"We all got together, and we prayed for twenty pounds of cheese," Wells says. "The next day—exactly twenty-four hours later—a truck pulls up and honks the horn. The driver says he has two hundred pounds of cheese for us. We accepted the shipment and we never ran out of cheese again."

Pastor Holloway is working on developing a substance abuse program for women but hasn't found anyone qualified to run it so far. The fact is, Holloway says, women seem to have more difficulty in the shelter environment than men. They often have children to worry about, plus, Holloway says, "Men are just better at camping out."

Kimberly Anderson is in charge of operating the women's shelter, a one-story yellow cinder block building in the heart of the crime-ridden neighborhood two blocks from the men's facility. On the job barely a month when we spoke in 2006, Kim had the difficult task of dealing with mostly transient women, many of them with small children, and many of them with drug problems and prison records.

There are rules covering the admittance of women as well as their behavior while they are in the shelter. One of the rules is that mothers with children get the bunks and single women sleep on the floor.

CLEAN AND SOBER

Only six weeks clean and sober herself, Kim, who suffered continuous abuse and neglect growing up in Iowa, landed on Compassion Center's doorstep on an early April day with her little girls, Aubrianna and Lyndsey, in tow.

Talking about her job with her well-behaved daughters at her feet, Anderson is noticeably composed, and when asked about the source of her serenity, she points to the heavens and says, "My Lord and Savior."

When the phone rings, Anderson picks it up and with aplomb answers, "Compassion Center, Kim Anderson speaking; may I help you?"

The person on the other end, judging from Kim's helpful responses, is seeking a place to stay, and the conversation ends with Kim giving her directions. "Yes, we're right across from Uncle Abe's Phillips 66. We'll see you in a little while."

In a neighborhood filled with night clubs, tattoo parlors, pawn shops, liquor stores, and body shops, Compassion Center's main building on Roosevelt—with its brick front, red awning, and neatly mowed lawn— stands out.

It is a small and virtually self-sufficient city that Pastor Holloway runs like a military base. Neatness and cleanliness definitely count and so does attitude. When people are addressed, their response is respectful and invariably includes a reference to the saving powers of Jesus Christ.

The day begins for everyone with breakfast at 5:30 a.m., which is followed by prayer, Bible study, and counseling sessions. Inmates have jobs at the Center, go to jobs on the outside, or are looking for jobs.

STAFF OF TEN

Holloway operates with a staff of ten, who earn $5.15 an hour, and he has fifteen interns who earn $35 a week. Most employees come from the ranks of the homeless and have been substance abusers.

Some work as cooks, some are in the warehouse/manufacturing operation, some are in retailing, and some are in maintenance. The place is spotless, and the workers go about their business with a calm intensity apparently on their own initiative. There are no supervisors in sight.

Compassion Center manufactures mattresses, bunk beds, and other furniture, operates a retail store fit for a mall, sells scrap to dealers, and distributes food and clothing free to the poor and to other charities for distribution.

On Sundays, there is a service in the Center's chapel. Holloway gives the sermon and also plays the guitar to accompany Rosemary, who leads the singing. There is an altar call at the end of the service for those who wish to declare or confirm their allegiance to Christ. Sometimes, after the service, William Holloway, in white shirt and tie, conducts baptisms in a small, vinyl kiddy pool in the backyard.

So what's next? Holloway says he's going to keep buying buildings and expanding to serve the men and women who need his help.

———

OXFORD HOUSES

There are more than one thousand Oxford Houses in the United States, five of them in Arkansas, which provide permanent, chem-free transition housing to those seeking recovery. The founders chose the name "Oxford House" in recognition of the Oxford Group, a religious organization that influenced the founders of AA during the early 1930s and even before.

It is an excellent option for a homeless person who is dealing with his or her addictions through AA meetings as well as mental health problems and can pay the rent.

Founded in 1975, Oxford Houses offer a community-based approach to treatment, providing an independent, supportive, and sober living environment based on three primary rules:

1.) Do not use drugs or alcohol and do not be disruptive.
2.) Run the house democratically.
3.) Pay your equal expense shared or any fines.

The equal expense shared cost is generally between $80–$100 a week and includes utilities. A certain number of AA meetings a week may be mandatory, as are weekly business meetings to discuss any issues that the house may be facing and for paying the bills.

The first Oxford House was opened in Silver Spring, Maryland, in 1975 by Paul Malloy, a former Senate committee staff member. Malloy had sought treatment for his alcoholism in a halfway house in 1975. Later that year, the halfway house closed due to financial difficulty, and Molloy and the other residents took over the lease.

These are the Oxford House traditions:

TRADITION ONE: Oxford House has as its primary goal the provision of housing and rehabilitative support for the alcoholic or drug addict who wants to stop drinking or using and stay stopped.

TRADITION TWO: All Oxford Houses are run on a democratic basis. Our officers are but trusted servants serving continuous periods of no longer than six months in any one office.

TRADITION THREE: No member of an Oxford House is ever asked to leave without cause—a dismissal vote by the membership because of drinking, drug use, or disruptive behavior.

TRADITION FOUR: Oxford House is not affiliated with Alcoholics Anonymous and Narcotics Anonymous, organizationally or financially, but Oxford House members realize that only active participation in Alcoholics Anonymous and/or Narcotics Anonymous offers assurance of continued sobriety.

TRADITION FIVE: Each Oxford House should be autonomous except in matters affecting other houses or Oxford House, Inc., as a whole.

TRADITION SIX: Each Oxford House should be financially self-supporting although financially secure houses may, with approval or encouragement of Oxford House, Inc., provide new or financially needy houses a loan for a term not to exceed one year.

TRADITION SEVEN: Oxford House should remain forever non-professional, although individual members may be encouraged to utilize outside professionals whenever such utilization is likely to enhance recovery from alcoholism.

TRADITION EIGHT: Propagation of the Oxford House, Inc. concept should always be conceived as public education rather than promotion. Principles should always be placed before personalities.

TRADITION NINE: Members who leave an Oxford House in good standing are encouraged to become associate members and offer friendship, support, and example to newer members.

Oxford House residents who are "voted out" of the House are required to leave the premises within one-half hour.

TREATMENT FOR HOMELESS VETS

"We put homeless veterans first."

That's the welcoming slogan of Little Rock's Drop-In Day Treatment Center.

Estella Morris, a diminutive manager with an easy smile and a quiet authority, presides over the Center, which offers meals, shelter, medical care, and a leg up in the world to those veterans willing to play by the rules.

Ninety percent of the fifty or more veterans who visit the facility every day (95 percent are men) have an addiction to alcohol or other drugs, which makes for a potentially unruly constituency.

So playing by the rules, Morris says, includes going to 12-Step meetings. The first one on the premises is at 7:30 a.m., and if you want breakfast—usually bacon, eggs, and biscuits—you attend it. The second meeting is at 1 p.m. and veterans are encouraged to go to meetings outside the Center at various locations around the city.

Fundamentally, Morris says in the facility's brochure, "Our goal is to provide veterans with a safe, secure and comfortable daytime environment with an opportunity to work toward mental, social, and physical stability."

Specifically, veterans can take showers at the Center, do their laundry, and avail themselves of a variety of medical and counseling services. A nurse and therapists on the premises can evaluate veterans and help them navigate short-term mental health and addiction problems. Counseling services help them develop the life skills that will lead to jobs, home ownership, and the other benefits that accrue to healthy members of society.

The Drop-In Center also collaborates with transitional housing facilities and treatment facilities in providing necessary care for veterans. Some of the veterans have been in prison, and others, who may not have been in prison, are facing legal problems. The Center is organized to work with the court system in dealing with these problems.

Many veterans (an estimated 25 percent are combat veterans) require medical treatment, and the Drop-in Center provides shuttle bus service to the Little Rock and North Little Rock VA hospitals.

The house rules, which include a ban on smoking, prescribe the following standards of conduct: "Drugs or alcohol use or possession, theft of property, buying or selling illegal drugs or prescription medications, possession of drug paraphernalia, acts of violence or possession of weapons will result in immediate expulsion from the facility."

Veterans are also asked to keep the noise down and are reminded that "intimidating, disruptive, or disrespectful behavior or profanity will not be tolerated."

The Center, Morris says with a smile, likes to reward veterans for good behavior and offers a variety of inducements such as hats and T-Shirts. That's the carrot. The stick is the law enforcement officer on the premises.

The facility staff members, for their part, are expected to be respectful, Morris says. In her policy statement, she states, "We value good customer service and expect staff to be dedicated and courteous and to recognize the worth and dignity of all 'persons served.'"

———

HOUSING FOR FORMER PRISON INMATES

In early January 2011, the first of sixty paroled inmates—both men and women—began moving into Hidden Creek, a new Little Rock transition facility owned by Under Grace Ministries, which is headed by Paul Chapman.

Licensed by the Department of Community Corrections (DCC), the faith-based facility is intended to improve on the sometimes deplorable and relatively unsupervised way many independent transitional houses have treated paroled inmates and others.

The DCC's Dr. Elizabeth Hooker, assistant director for residential treatment, was assigned the task of developing a Therapeutic Community (TC) program for residents of Hidden Creek. The TC approach for the treatment of drug abuse and addiction, according to the National Institute on Drug Abuse (NIDA), is not new.

In general, TCs are drug-free residential settings that use a hierarchical model with treatment stages that reflect increased levels of personal and social responsibility. Peer influence, mediated through a variety of group processes, is used to help individuals learn and assimilate social norms and develop more effective social skills.

Hooker had been responsible for helping develop TC programs in all of the DCC units. But extending it to "aftercare facilities" like Hidden Creek was something new.

"Aftercare is a vital key" to healing parolees and lowering recidivism rates, Hooker said.

With its aggressive focus on recovery and rehabilitation, the DCC, which operates five residential detention centers in Arkansas and places a heavy emphasis on rehabilitation, is notably different than the Arkansas Department of Corrections. The DCC takes nonviolent crime offenders with one- to two-year sentences and engages them in an aggressive program of rehabilitation involving a variety of 12-Step meetings, life skills programs, and behavior modification courses grouped under the heading, "Therapeutic Community." Hidden Creek draws its parolees solely from the DCC.

The opening of Hidden Creek came at a time when Gov. Mike Beebe had emphasized that he was not inclined to build new prisons, and the facility, with its focus on reducing recidivism, seemed to offer a solution.

After the opening of Hidden Creek, however, trouble began with the inmates almost immediately over the interpretation and implementation of the rules, and the executive director of the facility resigned. Hidden Creek remains a work in progress and a reminder that the rehabilitation of the addict/criminal demographic will not be easy. Still the reward in lives and dollars saved certainly justifies the effort.

CHAPTER EIGHTEEN

Stories Bring New Meaning to Recovery

Ron T., a recovering alcoholic, knows about addiction. He should. He spent years on the street, and he went through nine treatment centers and countless 12-Step meetings before he eventually gave in. I got to know him and have watched him grow after he got out of treatment and began going to AA meetings.

Ron surrendered nearly twenty years ago and has been clean and sober ever since. Today, he is a pilot for an international commercial airline, and he also works with other pilots who have had problems with alcohol and drugs.

Ron discovered something else. He liked to write, and he is good at it, as the two articles in this chapter demonstrate. The first describes a hair-raising night landing at Little Rock National Airport in a violent storm, and the second is about the loss of a dear surfer friend to drugs on the California coast.

If you have read chapter 4 of this book, you will have enjoyed his account of how he finally overcame his addictions and began his recovery at The BridgeWay hospital. When he sent me these stories, Ron said, "I have had my miracle. Maybe there will be more, but the main thing is that God has given me a new life, and for that I am eternally grateful."

THE STORM

On an unforgettable storm-filled October night in 1999, we were on approach into Little Rock National Airport, and it was bad.

"Go around max thrust flaps nine, positive rate gear up," I commanded as the ground proximity warning blared "too low terrain." My copilot froze while I struggled to overcome the inertia of fifty thousand pounds of airliner descending at twenty-two hundred feet per minute.

I was the captain flying this leg of a very long, five-leg day. This go-around maneuver is difficult in good weather, with both pilots doing their jobs. We had neither advantage.

"Anytime now, Chad," I barked at my new-hire first officer. When I reached over to retract the flaps myself (his job), Chad reengaged and began to assist me.

The thunderstorm was four miles off the approach end of runway 4 right, and the controller had turned us in tight, about a three-mile final approach, to avoid the storm. The turbulence was so intense that the instrument panel appeared fuzzy. We were in low, thick clouds with zero visibility and heading for the same runway and similar weather conditions as the American Airlines MD-80 crash earlier in the year.

Our original destination was San Antonio, Texas. We had left Detroit with plenty of fuel, but had encountered such strong headwinds that we had consumed more fuel than expected. To make matters worse, the weather in Texas had deteriorated. San Antonio was reporting low clouds and very low visibility.

Our situation required us to have extra fuel to reach an alternate airport in case we couldn't get into San Antonio. With the wind situation, we just barely had enough fuel to get there, and no extra fuel to reach an alternate if it was necessary.

"You have to stop in Little Rock for fuel," the company dispatcher said on the radio.

"We just flew over Little Rock, man" I replied. "There's a thunderstorm in progress very near the airport."

I was beginning to think our dispatcher was an idiot.

"Sorry, guys," he continued, "you have to stop somewhere for fuel now, and Little Rock is the only airport in range that is above landing minimums."

He was right. We did need fuel soon. Reluctantly, we turned the seventy-passenger airliner around and headed back to Little Rock. When we plugged the new destination into the flight computer, it showed there would be a very slim margin of fuel remaining to reach Little Rock.

"Any suggestions, Chad?" I asked. My copilot was a great guy and a good pilot. He was just new and overwhelmed. "Easy does it," he offered, and I said to myself, "Good Lord, he's lost it."

A MONSTER

As we approached Little Rock, I brought up the weather radar, and it looked bad. There was a level five thunderstorm just southwest of the active runway, the approach end, so we would have to deal with this monster. The storm cell had a hook shape, which indicated some really nasty, possibly tornado force, winds.

"Ask approach control for vectors to a short final approach," I said to Chad, who seemed to be shrinking right there in his seat. This was our only way to avoid the most intense part of the storm.

The turbulence was really rocking us now. Chad's voice sounded shaky, but he managed to make the request. "Little Rock Approach, Jet Star four eighty-five, we need as tight an approach as possible. This cell is looking pretty ugly."

"Turn left heading zero eight five," the controller replied. He was aware of our plight. He had weather radar, too. What he didn't know was that we were perilously low on fuel.

"That's pretty tight," I said to Chad." We're still real high. Ask for lower."

The controller read our minds. "Jet Star four eighty-five, you are two miles from Mynie. Descend and maintain two thousand feet till established, cleared ILS [instrument landing system] 4 right approach."

The controller knew we were high, so he started us down, but we were so near the runway it was going to be really close. A normal approach descends at about one thousand feet per minute. I pushed the nose over to twenty-two hundred feet per minute and turned in toward the runway.

The ground proximity warning on a modern jet airplane is very sophisticated. It is there to prevent Controlled Flight into Terrain (flying the plane into the ground). A computer looks at your altitude, descent rate, and airspeed to determine a closure rate with the ground.

It has a prerecorded voice that speaks in a very commanding tone to warn of an impending disaster. When you are in the clouds and you hear this warning, you are required to end the approach and initiate a go-around.

My steep descent rate had triggered the ground proximity warning. That is how we came to hear, "Too low terrain."

The most difficult part of being an airline captain is the decision making. The decisions have to be made fast, and they have to be right. My options were either to commence the go-around and hope we had enough fuel to try again, or to continue the approach in spite of the terrain warning.

In my living room, this would have been a pretty tough call, but we were in thick clouds with zero visibility nine hundred feet off the ground traveling one hundred and eighty knots. The flight deck was rocking so violently that we could barely focus on the instruments, and my copilot was frozen.

We practice these situations in the flight simulator. So my decision was more of a programmed response than a conscious thought. When I made the call to "go around max thrust flaps nine," we had about twenty minutes of fuel. When my copilot finally engaged, we were back up to a safe altitude with about fifteen minutes of fuel.

———

NO TURNING BACK

"What do we do now Captain?" Chad mumbled.

This was a very good question. We did not have enough fuel to fly anywhere else, and now the storm had moved near the approach end of the runway. Normally, I would have diverted or entered a holding pattern. These options were out because of the fuel situation.

Jet airplanes use up a lot of runway when they land. This is one of the reasons that they land into the wind. Your ground speed is slower, so the landing is much safer, and you don't risk going off the end of the runway. The wind was now gusting to forty-five knots right down the runway. This would have been great if we could have landed that direction, but now the storm was blocking that approach.

"Get vectors for runway 22 left, now," I demanded. This was the same runway from the other end. Chad was engaged now and went to work. I'm glad he didn't argue with me. This tailwind approach that I was demanding was not authorized in our manual. We would be test pilots.

"The wind is zero four zero at thirty knots, gusting to forty-five knots. Are you sure that's what you want to do?" the controller asked pointedly while reluctantly giving us vectors for this dangerous maneuver.

The approach was ugly. We were in thick clouds with very strong turbulence. It was all I could do to stay on the flight path dictated by the ILS.

If we were slightly left or right off course, we would miss the runway. If we were below the course, we would crash short of the runway. If we were above the course, we would land too far down the runway to safely stop the airplane on pavement.

Landing long (beyond the touchdown zone on the runway) was not advisable. With the tailwind, we would be landing fast, so we needed the entire runway. Missing the approach and going around was not an option either. We were just about out of gas.

We were going in one way or another. I could just barely see my instruments because of the violent shaking of the airplane.

They say that just before you die, your life flashes before you. My thoughts were focused on flying the airplane, but some thoughts of my past crept into my consciousness.

Had I burnt one too many brain cells? Had I taken one too many hits of acid in the seventies? Was I truly recovered from my affliction (alcoholism), or was I going to succumb to vertigo and lose control? Spatial disorientation (vertigo) is fatal on a difficult instrument landing.

Discipline and training enable a pilot to overcome this disorientation by ignoring the physical sensations of climbing, descending, or turning, and focusing on the instruments. The instruments don't lie (hopefully). They must be obeyed.

ALCOHOLIC THINKING CREEPS IN

Would I be good enough? Would I measure up? I was more afraid of screwing up than I was of dying. This was definitely alcoholic thinking, but it served me well. It kept me focused. I had learned to fly after I sobered up nearly fifteen years ago.

Some people who had known me in my former life suggested that I was too damaged ever to be a good pilot. On this dark and stormy night. I hoped that they were wrong.

At two hundred feet above the ground, if you don't see the runway you are required to end the approach and go around and try again.

"A thousand feet, on localizer one dot low on glide slope," Chad called out.

Suddenly, the airspeed dropped twenty knots. Airspeed is what keeps a plane airborne. Any further loss of airspeed would have been disastrous. I increased thrust to keep us flying, but now we were traveling much too fast to make a safe landing even if we did manage to find the runway.

"Five hundred feet, on localizer, on glide slope, Captain, but you are twenty knots fast." I pulled the thrust back slightly. Our chances of survival were much greater rolling off the end of the runway than crashing short of it.

I was encouraged by the fact that we were at least on course. With the tailwind and our increased airspeed due to the wind shear, we would hit hard and fast—but at least we would be on the pavement and near rescue crews.

"Two hundred feet. Nothing in sight," Chad whispered. He knew we had to continue anyway. We were going in. At fifty feet, Chad saw the approach lights, I learned later. My first indication that we had arrived was the violent collision of my main landing gear with the runway.

When we hit, our groundspeed was one hundred seventy knots; one hundred twenty-five is standard. The nose of the plane was still flying, and it was all I could do to keep it from trying to fly back up off of the runway.

I pushed the nose over, and with a bang and a sudden jolt, we were rolling down the center of runway 22 left extremely fast.

Two-thirds of the way down the runway, we hit the gust front of the storm. The rain and wind caused some unearthly noises in the cockpit. On the ground, you steer the airplane with your feet until it slows to a safe speed, and then you use a small steering tiller. My feet were moving wildly like I was on a Stairmaster at my athletic club.

The lights of the runway were going by in a blur, but we were still on the pavement. At the thousand-feet-remaining marker, we were still moving fast. I was in full reverse thrust now and standing on the brakes.

The brakes are monitored by an anti-skid computer, and they automatically release when the plane begins to skid. The brakes were cycling in and out. All I could do was hang on and try to keep it in the center of the runway and hope the brakes engaged in time to stop us safely.

———

STOPPED AT LAST

As we finally came to a stop, I could see the runway end identifier lights just a few feet ahead in the pouring rain. A warning bell was sounding, the fuel quantity indicators were flashing, and a low-fuel warning was flashing.

The storm was on the runway now, and the rain was extremely heavy. Had we done a go-around, we would have launched right into the heart of this monster thunderstorm. I had not even considered it.

One way or another, with or without my copilot, we were landing. There had been no other options. We taxied off the runway in the driving rain. Chad was visibly shaken. So was I. We had about five minutes of fuel left.

"Easy does it?" I blurted out. "What the hell does that mean? We are about to fuel-starve a fifty-thousand-pound airplane in a severe thunderstorm, and that's all you can come up with? That sounds like some kind of AA slogan. Please do not tell me that you are in the program."

"Sixteen years" he said with pride. I wanted to say, "You'll never make seventeen if you don't improve your flying skills." I didn't.

"I knew it. You put two drunks together and you see what happens," I said sarcastically.

"Yeah, I see what happens," he said; "a miracle." He was right. "How many years do you have?"

"Ten, and if I had known you were in the program, I would have really been frightened," I said as we both laughed that boisterous laugh you only hear in AA meetings.

I had always maintained my anonymity at work. I didn't want to scare anyone. The FAA and the company knew, but I told no one else in the airline that I was a recovering alcoholic.

My worst fear was this slip of the tongue. "Good morning, ladies and gentlemen, from the flight deck. Welcome aboard. My name is Ron and I am an alcoholic." It hasn't happened yet.

Chad and I had an instant spiritual connection. We had just cheated death together. We also shared an escape from addiction, which forges an even greater spiritual union.

Chad told me about the program we have at the airline for pilots with alcohol and drug problems. They always needed volunteers he said.

I knew we had some kind of program at the airline, but I didn't know much about it. Flying and working with alcoholics are two of my three favorite activities. This would be a way for me to do both.

Alcoholics are very stubborn and hard-headed, but in recovery we try to open up a little. I occasionally see God's little messages. This level-five thunderstorm must have been a memo from the Big Guy. Chad's presence was also providential.

Little Rock is where I live and sobered up, and this unplanned diversion there must have been 'the plan' after all. Who am I to ignore such a thing? I have become an active volunteer in the company's alcohol rehab program as a direct result of the diversion to Little Rock.

———

REQUIEM FOR A SURFER

Hamilton lived just a few miles from Rincon, a favorite surfing area or "surf break" among aficionados—a place where there are "rides that can run 150 to 200 yards on a good swell."

Surfing was spiritual for him, and the Santa Barbara Coast was his cathedral. He was at peace in the sea, like nowhere else. His demons, it seems, could not swim.

Hamilton could swim like a fish. His six-and-a-half-foot frame was slender, with long, taut muscles that were ideal for paddling. He once made friends with a sea lion at Rincon. It would appear off the front of his board regularly for a year or so. He thought this was his higher power smiling at him.

He was more comfortable with aquatic mammals than with the other humans on the beautiful surf break. He called them "buoys": inferior surfers who never caught waves. They just bobbed around in the California surf like buoys.

Hamilton had left his beloved Pacific Coast in the early nineties to wage a heroic battle. He had long been hopelessly addicted to alcohol and heroin. He thought the isolation of Arkansas and a secure place to stay, with Grandma, a good idea. It was. For the next five years he flourished.

He sobered up and became an inspiration to many people. Many of them were women. It seems Hamilton, a tall, good-looking California boy, was absolutely irresistible to Arkansas women. He was a man's man, too.

People were drawn to him because of his laid-back, charismatic charm. He could bring people together like no other. His recovery from the darkness of addiction made everyone around him want to do better.

By the mid nineties, the call of the surf and the Blue Pacific became too strong to resist. He returned to the sea.

The darkness is always there, waiting: patient, cunning, baffling, and powerful. It returned to Hamilton slowly. It was the pain in his lower back that deceived him. An addict is capable of actually producing symptoms that require the drug that he seeks.

His drugs of choice, opiate narcotics, were the natural choice for back pain. As the light faded from his sparkling eyes, no one will ever know just how much of the pain was real and how much was the rapacious darkness returning for its victim.

Hamilton fought the good fight. He hooked up with a new AA sponsor and attempted to submerge himself in the recovery community. But alas, the only peace he could find was in the bosom of Rincon.

He did not feel the weight of his burden in the water. They could not swim, these demons of darkness. He was lifted into the light by this right-breaking vortex. On the wave, his back was strong and his spirit soared. But humans, not even Hamilton, can stay on a wave forever. The wave must break and so did Hamilton.

It was a beautiful California morning on the Pacific Coast Highway. Hamilton's brother knew this stretch intimately. Just south of Santa Barbara near a small town called Carpenteria, the Rincon surf was breaking like never before. The spray spiraled upward in a spiritual mist.

Earlier that morning his mom had called. She was frantic. No one had seen Hamilton for a week, and they feared the worst. His brother had closed his dive shop in Malibu to make the drive to Santa Barbara to find Hamilton.

Just past the sparkling view of Rincon, he saw it: a tall, shirtless figure walking alongside the highway with a surfboard. He could recognize his brother's silhouette anywhere. He immediately turned his car around and returned to the spot. Nothing!

As he continued up the road, he saw it again. This time, he was sure it was Hamilton. Never had his brother looked so carefree and happy. In his mirror, he could see Hamilton descending the path to Rincon. Parking the car quickly, he ran down the path. No Hamilton. Stunned by his vision, His brother continued his journey to Santa Barbara.

Hamilton's back door was locked. He never locked it. The back window was cracked open slightly for the cat. It looked like the cat had not eaten in a week. Immediately his brother knew. Hamilton had lost the battle.

He looked peaceful lying there, lifeless in his bed. But this is not the image that his brother will carry. It is the image of Hamilton with his board and a broad smile on the path to Rincon that will live forever in his mind. Did the darkness win? Maybe not. Maybe Rincon will keep Hamilton up in the light forever.

CHAPTER NINETEEN

Beginning Your New Life

When you think about it, we really don't have much choice in life than to deal with things. There is no time out in life. Everything counts. Every day. Every minute.

We cannot afford to waste it.

On the advice of a friend, who was kind enough to read a first draft of this book, I recently read Thornton Wilder's Pulitzer Prize winning play, Our Town, which opened on Broadway in 1936. I read it for the first time in an American Lit class at Hamilton College many years ago and later saw the play at the Paper Mill Playhouse in Milburn, N.J. It is a classic.

A major theme of Our Town is that we too often waste much of our brief lives on things that at best don't matter. It is a perspective given to the audience by the characters, citizens of Grover's Corners, New Hampshire, who have died and are allowed to come back for a day if they choose. Those who make the choice are grief stricken by the loss of precious time they behold.

I myself spent precious years during my thirties and forties refusing to deal with things without what I perceived to be the benefit of drinks and tranquilizers. At age 49, I finally faced up to it and after the next 34 years with God at the center of my life and a spiritually based program of recovery, I am the happiest I have ever been.

Joe McQuany put it this way, "I believe the happiest an individual is going to be is when he is in this pattern of living, relying on God and other people."

Many years ago, Dr. Robert Lewis, a pastor at Little Rock's Fellowship Bible Church and founder of the international Men's Fraternity program, spoke in a sermon once about the fruitful life of the prophet Abraham and about his death at a very old but still active age. Dr. Lewis, who helped me a lot with my recovery and the restoration of our family, said with some passion that when Abraham died he was "satisfied."

At the time, I underestimated the power of the message, but now as I approach the age of Abraham I get it. Death without misgivings is, indeed, a worthy goal and I have redoubled my efforts in that direction.

In Pathways to Serenity, you have read the testimonies of those who have overcome their addictions one day at a time. And you know where to look for help. As an example, chances are if you are living in a civilized country, you can find a 12 Step meeting and be attending it within no more than a couple of hours. And if you need psychiatric help as well, it is available (but may take some digging for those who can't afford to pay for it).

Those who seek recovery will encounter obstacles, of course, many of them self-inflicted. Our denial hampers the identification of an addiction, and an unwillingness to deal with the problem and blaming others prevents recovery.

But it's really not that complicated. Little Rock's Wolfe Street Center used to have a caretaker (we called him Dr. Bob) who had boiled down his program of recovery to a simple phrase, "just don't drink." Too simple? Perhaps, but also basic.

For those who seek more particulars, here are five principles that have worked well for me. They are based mainly on the biblically based 12 Steps.

1. Trust God

In the first of their 12 Steps the founders of Alcoholics Anonymous call upon us to surrender to a power greater than ourselves. In this it differs from many programs which, instead, begin with seeking power. The first step rejects the notion that we are capable of doing life on our own but gives us considerable latitude in naming that power. I chose God, supreme ruler of the universe, as I believe most do, and later named Jesus Christ as my Lord and Savior.

2. Clean House

Among mankind's addictive behaviors, drug addictions, including alcoholism, have been particularly destructive and require special diligence when it comes to cleaning up. This includes stopping the behavior, admitting our mistakes and making amends to those we have harmed.

3. Help others

Helping others through sponsorship, and other activities, is an essential requirement of AA and most other 12 Step programs. Rightly so. I didn't warm to the idea at first but did what my sponsor and others told me and registered with the AA central office in Little Rock. I listed myself as someone willing to offer help, no matter what the hour.

The hour turned out to be midnight.

His name was Wardell, and he lived out by the airport. He was young, he was big, he was black and he was very drunk. I was old (about 50), medium build, white and newly and excruciatingly sober. Wardell seemed grateful that I had come when we shook hands on his front steps. We talked a little. I gave him a Big Book, told him to not drink and to meet me at the Wolfe Street Center the next morning to begin work on his program of recovery.

Darned if he didn't show up. Wardell got sober, I stayed sober, and the world became a better place. After a couple of years, Wardell, still clean and sober, moved away, and we lost track. I pray that he is safe and well.

4. Reject resentments

Resentments will damage your serenity and ultimately shorten your life. There is a popular AA saying, "Harboring a resentment against someone is like drinking poison and hoping the other person dies."

5. Live one day at a time (tops)

Taking life one day at a time is a concept well known to people in recovery from alcohol and other addictions. Newcomers to 12-Step programs are told by old-timers to make no more than a daily commitment to sobriety—maximum--lest they be overwhelmed by contemplating a lifetime loss of their alcohol, pills and powders.

McQuany said, "I look at the battles that go on in life, and I look at the resentments and fears, guilt and remorse, and how things block us from God and shackle us to the self. Then I look at love, tolerance, patience, courage and wisdom. These qualities have come from God and they are always with us. In our outer and inner conflicts, we can see the powers of self contending with the powers of God."

On a closing note, I do not find that self-esteem, especially when it is unearned, is of much help in building character. As my friend at the Thanksgiving retreat in Georgia many years ago said about flattery in Chapter 1, "It's okay if you don't inhale it."

I began the book with the short version of the Serenity Prayer which is recited at the beginning of most if not all of every 12 Step meeting I have attended. I would like to end with the longer version. It begins:

God grant me the serenity to accept the things I cannot change; courage to change the things I can; and wisdom to know the difference.

And it ends with:

Living one day at a time; enjoying one moment at a time; accepting hardships as the pathway to peace; taking, as He did, this sinful world as it is, not as I would have it; trusting that He will make all things right if I surrender to His will; that I may be reasonably happy in this life and supremely happy with Him forever in the next.

Amen.

APPENDIX 1

David Palmer's Recovery Story

Sherman Billingsley's Stork Club was perhaps the most famous nightclub in New York, attracting showgirls, celebrities and writers (Hemingway among them), and gossip columnist Walter Winchell tattled on all of them. It opened in 1929 during prohibition and closed in 1965. The Club's cigarette girl took this picture of Joan and David in 1950. They were married two years later.

My name is David Palmer, and I'm a grateful recovering alcoholic.

Through God's grace, I haven't found it necessary to take a drink of alcohol since April 9, 1979.

Alcohol, as the *Big Book* of Alcoholics Anonymous tells us, was not my problem. It was my solution. My problem was my defects of character—my anxieties, fears, and resentments and my unwillingness to face them. Alcohol eased the pain of these unpleasant realities—at least at first.

In the end, I still had the character defects as well as a crippling alcohol problem. During twenty years of alcoholic drinking, I consumed a quart of bourbon a day during much of that time, along with wine and assorted cocktails. At age forty-nine, my mind and body were beginning to break down.

I was born in Orange, New Jersey, on February 22, 1929, about six months before the stock market crash and the beginning of the Great Depression—both of which my family survived without disruption. My father never lost a job and my mother was a model homemaker.

My mother and father were loving and conscientious parents. My dad was a writer and publishing executive. My mother, when she married, gave up her job as a magazine editor and became a full-time homemaker. She was a marvelous cook and decorator and an accomplished pianist.

When I was eight, there was a big change. I learned that I no longer would be an only child.

My dad took me aside one day to tell me that my mother was going to have a baby, and that they thought it would be best if I went to camp for the summer in New Hampshire rather than go with them to Canada as I usually did.

I accepted this change in plans, assuming that if that's what they wanted me to do, it must be the right thing.

When I arrived at camp, I completely broke down with grief and homesickness. I cried for a week, and then I stopped. I felt abandoned, and at some point I said to myself, "Okay, if this is the way it is, I'll run my life myself. I will become self-sufficient."

I had written home about my grief and my mother immediately dispatched my father to come and get me. But after he drove all night to get me, I snubbed him and stayed at camp for two months.

My sister was born shortly after I returned home from camp. She was a beautiful baby, and I was getting homelier by the day. She had definitely taken over the limelight and, it seemed to me, the principal affections of my parents.

I didn't know what to do with my growing and unacknowledged resentments, and started to tease her and get into fights in school. I became increasingly estranged from my parents.

———

THE ALIENATED LONER

When I was thirteen, I began smoking cigarettes, hanging out with a bad crowd, and cultivating an image of the alienated loner to compensate for the insecurities I had developed with emerging acne and other perceived physical deformities.

When I was sixteen, my parents, upset with the friends I had and my falling grades, sent me to an all-boys boarding school—the Hill School in Pennsylvania—for my junior and senior years.

The first year I floundered and hated every minute of it. I flunked algebra, ended up in summer school for six weeks, and missed most of my vacation at our cottage in Canada. I deeply resented it, and that strengthened my resolve to become completely self-sufficient.

I passed the algebra exam, and in my senior year at Hill, I separated my shoulder playing football but lettered in track and graduated in the top 10 percent of my class. During that time, I also discovered the solution

I mentioned earlier to the anxieties that began to mount as I worked diligently on my image: Alcohol.

At a high-society wedding in Garden City, Long Island, when I was sixteen, I got drunk for the first time—on champagne. After the reception, I found myself driving sixty miles an hour down a country road in my parents' car with an attractive girl at my side and a backseat full of revelers.

With alcohol, I become witty, anxiety-free, and charming. Alcohol, I discovered, could do for me what I could not do for myself. I had a new friend I would not forget when times got tough or I needed a boost.

After boarding school, I was accepted at Hamilton College in upstate New York. As a freshman, my role models were the returning World War II veterans. They drank hard and played hard and were emotionally unavailable. I wanted to be just like them.

I binge drank heavily at weekend fraternity parties, but not during the week. My anxieties grew, and I began to experience mild phobias. Still, I was captain of the track team for two years, played hockey, and made Phi Beta Kappa, a scholastic honor society. My quest for self-sufficiency through achievement was on track.

In the summer of my junior year at Hamilton, I met a girl in Canada, and we began a courtship that ultimately led to marriage. Joan was not only the prettiest girl in Kingston, Ontario; she was the nicest.

Joan was four years younger than I and was attracted to my manufactured bad-boy persona and pseudo sophistication. I, in turn, was attracted to the role of wholesome goddess I had created for her.

A ROMANTIC COURTSHIP

Nevertheless, our courtship was very romantic, and in my senior year, we did all the "in" nightclubs and restaurants in New York City. That included Eddy Condon's and Nick's in Greenwich Village and the Stork Club and the Plaza's Oak Room uptown.

I was accepted at the Harvard Business School that year despite the fact that I was drunk during my key interview. On one level I felt bulletproof. On another, I felt completely inadequate.

My anxieties increased at Harvard—I was virtually paralyzed in class, fearing I would be called on—but I kept my drinking to weekends. Even so, my fears began to limit me, and my grades suffered.

While I was in my first year at Harvard, Joan went to McGill University in Montreal. I made the round trip from Cambridge to Montreal twice a month in a courtship highlighted by drinks in the fanciest bars. There were Singapore Slings at the Mount Royal and dinner with wine at Ruby Foo's.

When we married, Joan quit McGill, joined me in a fourth-floor walk-up with a fire escape in Brighton, Massachusetts, while I finished Harvard. We both wanted children, and she immediately got pregnant.

Because of the Korean War, I enlisted in the Navy after graduation from Harvard and went to Officer Candidate School in Newport, Rhode Island. I was commissioned as an ensign in the fall, and in 1954 we were sent, with a ten-month-old baby boy we completely adored, to NATO headquarters in Izmir, Turkey.

When I got my orders to Izmir, I had to run to the world atlas to find out where it was, learning in the process that this large city on the Aegean Sea had substantial biblical significance. It was originally called Smyrna, I learned, home of one of the seven churches named in Revelation, and had I looked closer I would have seen the sites of two other nearby historic churches—Ephesus to the south and Pergamum to the north.

Joan and I had both come from homes where Sunday church going was encouraged, but not regarded as particularly relevant in our daily lives, and we had no appreciation of the spiritual treasure that was available to us.

In Turkey, we had another baby boy, adored our life in our apartment on the Aegean Sea across from a mosque, and partied a lot, but I rarely got drunk.

I did well with my job and even acted in a play put on for NATO by the American contingent. I played Tom the alcoholic brother in *The Glass Menagerie*, a classic by Tennessee Williams, also an alcoholic.

———

MUSTERING OUT

After my tour, I resigned from active duty, and on a glorious spring morning in 1956, I stood on the steps of 90 Church Street in New York with a big check from the Navy in my pocket, a cute little house in the suburbs, a Plymouth with huge fins in the driveway, and a job at the world's largest advertising agency on Madison Avenue. I drank, but drinking had not been a problem for three years.

I had prevailed and my future was bright. My own resources, with a little help from alcohol, were sufficient. I didn't need anyone. To the extent that I ever thought about Him, God was irrelevant. The world was my oyster.

How wrong I was.

Twenty years later, in 1976, I was living behind the Silver Spur Lounge in Raton, New Mexico, in a broken-down single-wide. I was drinking a quart of Jim Beam a day. I had divorced my wife. I was out of touch with my three sons, who were in trouble and needed me desperately. I had spent a night in jail. And I was in debt.

The shocking thing was that while I knew I couldn't stop drinking, I thought I was managing quite well. In fact, I regarded myself as a sort of alienated yet heroic figure, my favorite role.

So what happened to bring me to this sorry state?

At the Madison Avenue advertising agency I joined when I got out of the Navy, I found myself on a very fast track. If you have seen *Mad Men* on TV, you know what I am talking about: intense competition among bright people steeped in booze.

I felt I was losing control. And when I wasn't in control, I felt anxious. And when I was anxious, I would marinate my feelings with alcohol. Up to a point, it worked, but as time wore on it interfered more and more with my job. I began to find it difficult to regulate my doses, and I would get drunk when I didn't mean to.

I quit my first Madison Avenue job and joined my dad in buying a small newspaper in New Jersey so I could spend more time with my family, and it worked to a point. But my drinking increased, and eventually we sold the paper. I went back to New York agency life with its two- and three-martini lunches and cocktail hours.

At this point, I began losing jobs. I lost two advertising executive jobs in New York. I lost another as publisher of a chain of newspapers in northern Virginia. After that, I took a job in El Dorado, Arkansas, as publisher of the *News Times*, the daily paper. With me were a very angry wife and my youngest son. That was in 1972.

———

A FULL-BLOWN ALCOHOLIC

By this time, I was a full-blown alcoholic and definitely on the down slope.

After I committed a series of awful publishing blunders, the owner fired me two weeks before Christmas and gave me a month's pay. Shortly after that, an ice storm hit and the power went out. My kids and my wife went to stay with friends, and I sat cold and alone in the empty house with my bottle.

Knowing no one would ever hire me and still seeking control, I decided to buy my own job. I persuaded my dad to help me buy two newspapers in 1974—the *Raton Daily Range* in New Mexico and the *Lamar Daily Democrat* in Missouri. He couldn't afford it, but he did it anyway without complaint.

I could barely work five hours a day on my papers and was losing financial ground when God intervened in my life in a most unusual way.

In the spring of 1978, a man appeared at the *Range*. He said he owned a chain of newspapers based in Tuscaloosa, Alabama, and asked if I would like to sell my papers. I quickly agreed and was astonished when he offered me well over a million dollars, more than twenty times what I paid for them.

After paying off the debt and settling my affairs in Raton, I headed for Boulder, Colorado, thinking that I would retire wealthy and live the rest of my life skiing, drinking, and chasing women. Numbed by my addiction, I gave no thought to my children and their mother whom I had, to my shame, divorced a year earlier.

I arrived in Boulder barely able to walk, ditched my rental car, and bought a brand-new Mercedes off the showroom floor. Next, I bought a condominium and had a fashionable downtown store furnish it. I thought I had it made, but I was wrong. Instead of being my solution, alcohol had now become my master.

One late afternoon in October, six months after moving to Boulder, I found myself at a deserted outdoor restaurant with only the bartender for company. In the lengthening shadows of the Rocky Mountains, chilled by the wind, I stood with drink in hand overcome by a sense of loneliness and isolation.

I watched the lights wink on in the little houses on the side of the slope and wished that I was living in one of them doing what normal people did—like mowing the lawn and cleaning the garage.

By November, episodes of anxiety and panic increased to the point that I could not leave my condominium. Once I called a church and asked if they could send someone over. Someone came, but his well-meaning offer of a potluck supper fell on deaf ears.

———

MY FIRST AA MEETING

I had been seeing a psychiatrist twice a week, but he couldn't fix me either, and told me to go to Alcoholics Anonymous. I was at the point that I knew I couldn't *quit* drinking by myself and I couldn't *keep* drinking.

AA appeared to be my only chance, and I attended my first meeting on December 2, 1978, at a Pearl Street storefront in Boulder.

It was snowing, and when I walked in, the people seemed to be enjoying themselves. There was no president, no board, no dues to pay, and I said to myself, "I think this is what God had in mind."

I went in looking for a fix, not a religion, and what I ultimately found in my journey was a personal relationship with Jesus Christ.

I wish I could say my recovery was all clear sailing. Far from it. So let me give you some snapshots of my early imperfections:

- I went to one hundred meetings in one hundred days, and on the one hundred-first day made myself a Tom Collins to celebrate. I went into a two-week blackout, about which I still remember absolutely nothing. After my slip (which ended at 3 a.m. on April 9, 1979, with a glass of warm vodka and Tab), I returned to AA, got a sponsor, and started working the steps.

- Despite cautions from my friends in AA about waiting for at least a year before making any big decisions, I set about trying to fix everything I had broken during years of drinking, including remarrying my wife, Joan, whose reservations I ignored.

As a result, we ran into some very rough seas, but during the process we began to develop a strong faith in God which has ultimately sustained us, healed most of our wounds, and kept us together.

David and Joan on a family vacation at Canada's Sandbanks
Beach Resort at Picton, Ontario. It's not all smooth sailing, but
the rewards of recovery are becoming increasingly evident.

Joan and I began attending Fellowship Bible Church in Little Rock
in 1981, and I became a Christian in 1986 when a friend, John Neeves,
a member of the church and a recovering alcoholic who had formed a
ministry called Born Free, brought me to my knees. A decade later, Bill
Parkinson baptized me in the Arkansas River.

Joan and I have been married almost sixty years now, if you count the
year and a half we were divorced, so we've got a shot, thanks to our faith
and a growing love for each other. You should see the Valentine's Day
cards we exchanged this year!

All three of our sons struggled briefly with their own addictions
to substances during the last days of my drinking, but when I began to
recover, so did they. They married, became successful, and are wonderful
fathers for our seven grandchildren.

I haven't lost any jobs for a while. In the past thirty years, I have worked first as a business editor with the *Arkansas Gazette* and then as a senior consultant with Cranford Johnson Robinson Woods, an advertising and public relations agency in Little Rock.

Seven years ago, I left the agency job and started a nonprofit company called One Day at a Time. Our mission is to reduce substance abuse by providing information through a publication and website about the devastating effects of abuse and by offering hope and encouragement and the possibility of redemption to those who seek recovery.

A HORRIBLE ACCIDENT

This decision to launch One Day at a Time was not a new idea for me, but it was a horrible accident involving a grandson, that propelled me into it. I am convinced that God intervened that night in a dramatic way to save his life...and to get my attention. Here's the story:

In the early morning hours of January 11, 2004, fifteen-year old Rees Palmer, my grandson, lost control of his father's speeding Jeep on an icy county road in Bucks County, Pennsylvania, and hit a telephone pole broadside.

At that moment five miles away, Rory Huff, sleeping in the back of his van, says he got "a wake-up call from God" that sent him hurtling into the black, sub-freezing winter night on what he took to be a divine mission.

"All I remember," Huff says, "is that I woke up and the next thing I knew I was speeding down Taylorsville Road at seventy miles per hour in a T-shirt, pants, and bare feet."

Within moments, Huff said, his headlights illuminated the scene of a terrible accident.

"There was a girl standing by her car at the side of the road screaming her head off," Huff said. "I stopped, grabbed a flashlight [purchased that afternoon, still in the box and, strangely, with batteries already in place] and got out of the van."

Huff called 9-1-1, dropped his cell phone, and found Rees lying half naked in the 7-degree temperature under the guardrail.

It was not a pretty sight. Rees had not been wearing a seatbelt, and the impact had thrown him thirty-five feet into the air. It would have been twice that far, police estimated, had he not caught his right leg in the steering wheel, shattering the femur and pulling off his trousers. He also suffered severe head trauma and cracked vertebrae.

Huff raced back to the van, found his overcoat, covered Rees with it, held him in his arms, and prayed.

When the police came, they wrapped Rees in a foil blanket and Huff got up to leave, stubbing his toe on the cell phone he had dropped. He picked it up, noting that he had been there for thirty-seven minutes and didn't feel cold in the least.

Rees, who had been taking ecstasy washed down with a fifth of banana liquor, survived the accident. He was in a coma for four days, had a titanium rod put in his leg, and suffered brain damage.

Over the next two years Rees continued to struggle with substance abuse and had another near-fatal accident when he fell through the skylight of a warehouse and dropped four stories to the floor, again suffering severe head trauma.

Following weeks in the hospital, to everyone's complete surprise, he began going to church and responded to an altar call "to accept Christ as his Lord and Savior."

Rees has been seriously wounded physically and emotionally and continues to struggle with his addictions. At age twenty-three, he still lives at home and has held a number of jobs, but none for very long. Yet there is hope. He goes to church without fail every Sunday and also to Celebrate Recovery.

And he remains in our prayers.

The Palmers enjoy a summer day in their boat near their Thousand Islands cottage on the Canadian side of the St. Lawrence River. Some of the seven grandchildren are at the nearby beach. From left are Christopher, Michael and David Palmer with parents Joan and David.

APPENDIX 2

How It Works and the 12 Steps
From the Big Book of Alcoholics Anonymous

CHAPTER 5

Rarely have we seen a person fail who has thoroughly followed our path. Those who do not recover are people who cannot or will not completely give themselves to this simple program, usually men and women who are constitutionally incapable of being honest with themselves.

There are such unfortunates. They are not at fault; they seem to have been born that way. They are naturally incapable of grasping and developing a manner of living which demands rigorous honesty. Their chances are less than average.

There are those, too, who suffer from grave emotional and mental disorders, but many of them do recover if they have the capacity to be honest.

Our stories disclose in a general way what we used to be like, what happened, and what we are like now. If you have decided you want what we have and are willing to go to any length to get it—then you are ready to take certain steps.

At some of these we balked. We thought we could find an easier, softer way. But we could not. With all the earnestness at our command, we beg of you to be fearless and thorough from the very start. Some of us have tried to hold on to our old ideas and the result was nil until we let go absolutely.

Remember that we deal with alcohol—cunning, baffling, powerful! Without help it is too much for us. But there is One who has all power— that One is God. May you find Him now!

Half measures availed us nothing. We stood at the turning point. We asked His protection and care with complete abandon. Here are the steps we took, which are suggested as a program of recovery:

———

THE 12 STEPS OF AA

1. We admitted we were powerless over alcohol—that our lives had become unmanageable.
2. Came to believe that a Power greater than ourselves could restore us to sanity.
3. Made a decision to turn our will and our lives over to the care of God as we understood Him.
4. Made a searching and fearless moral inventory of ourselves.
5. Admitted to God, to ourselves, and to another human being the exact nature of our wrongs.
6. Were entirely ready to have God remove all these defects of character.
7. Humbly asked Him to remove our shortcomings.
8. Made a list of all persons we had harmed, and became willing to make amends to them all.
9. Made direct amends to such people wherever possible, except when to do so would injure them or others.
10. Continued to take personal inventory and when we were wrong promptly admitted it.
11. Sought through prayer and meditation to improve our conscious contact with God as we understood Him, praying only for knowledge of His will for us and the power to carry that out.

12. Having had a spiritual awakening as the result of these steps, we tried to carry this message to alcoholics, and to practice these principles in all our affairs.

Many of us exclaimed, "What an order! I can't go through with it." Do not be discouraged. No one among us has been able to maintain anything like perfect adherence to these principles. We are not saints. The point is, that we are willing to grow along spiritual lines.

The principles we have set down are guides to progress. We claim spiritual progress rather than spiritual perfection. Our description of the alcoholic, the chapter to the agnostic, and our personal adventures before and after make clear three pertinent ideas:

(a) That we were alcoholic and could not manage our own lives.
(b) That probably no human power could have relieved our alcoholism.
(c) That God could and would if He were sought.

APPENDIX 3

Celebrate Recovery

These are the Christ-centered 12 Steps of the Celebrate Recovery program. They are almost identical to the biblically based 12 Steps of Alcoholics Anonymous, which refer to an unspecified "God":

1. We admitted we were powerless over our addictions and compulsive behaviors, that our lives had become unmanageable.
   "I know that nothing good lives in me, that is, in my sinful nature For I have the desire to do what is good, but I cannot carry it out" (Romans 7:18).

2. We came to believe that a Power greater than ourselves could restore us to sanity.
   "For it is God who works in you to will and act according to His good purpose" (Philippians 2:13).

3. We made a decision to turn our will and our lives over to the care of God as we understood Him.
   "Therefore I urge you brothers in view of God's mercy to offer your bodies as living sacrifices holy and pleasing to God—this is your spiritual act of worship" (Romans 12:1).

4. We made a searching and fearless moral inventory of ourselves.
   "Let us examine our ways and test them, and let us return to the LORD" (Lamentations 3:40).

5. We admitted to God, to ourselves, and to another human being the exact nature of our wrongs.
    "Therefore confess your sins to each other and pray for each other so that you may be healed" (James 5:16).

6. We were entirely ready to have God remove all these defects of character.
    "Humble yourselves before the Lord, and he will lift you up" (James 4:10).

7. We humbly asked Him to remove our shortcomings.
    "If we confess our sins, he is faithful and will forgive us our sins and purify us from all unrighteousness" (1 John 1:19).

8. We made a list of all persons we had harmed, and became willing to make amends to them all.
    "Do to others as you would have them do to you" (Luke 6:31).

9. We made direct amends to such people wherever possible, except when to do so would injure them or others.
    "Therefore if you are offering your gift at the altar and there remember that your brother has something against you, leave your gift there in front of the alter. First go and be reconciled to your brother, then come and offer your gift" (Matthew 5:23–24).

10. We continued to take personal inventory and when we were wrong promptly admitted it.
    "So if you think you stand firm, be careful that you don't fall!" (1 Corinthians 10:12).

11. We sought through prayer and meditation to improve our conscious contact with God as we understood Him, praying only for knowledge of His will for us and the power to carry that out.
    "Let the word of Christ dwell in you richly" (Colossians 3:16).

12. Having had a spiritual awakening as the result of these steps, we tried to carry this message to alcoholics, and to practice these principles in all our affairs.
    "Brothers if someone is caught in a sin, you who are spiritual should restore him gently. But watch yourself or you also may be tempted" (Galatians 6:1).

APPENDIX 4

Am I an Alanon?

1. Do you worry about how much someone drinks?
2. Do you have money problems because of someone else's drinking?
3. Do you tell lies to cover up for someone else's drinking?
4. Do you feel that if the drinker cared about you, he or she would stop drinking to please you?
5. Do you blame the drinker's behavior on his or her companions?
6. Are plans frequently upset or canceled or meals delayed because of the drinker?
7. Do you make threats, such as, "If you don't stop drinking, I'll leave you"?
8. Do you secretly try to smell the drinker's breath?
9. Are you afraid to upset someone for fear it will set off a drinking bout?
10. Have you been hurt or embarrassed by a drinker's behavior?
11. Are holidays and gatherings spoiled because of drinking?
12. Have you considered calling the police for help in fear of abuse?
13. Do you search for hidden alcohol?
14. Do you ever ride in a car with a driver who has been drinking?
15. Have you refused social invitations out of fear or anxiety?
16. Do you feel like a failure because you can't control the drinking?
17. Do you think that if the drinker stopped drinking, your other problems would be solved?

18. Do you ever threaten to hurt yourself to scare the drinker?
19. Do you feel angry, confused, or depressed most of the time?
20. Do you feel there is no one who understands your problems?

If you have answered "yes" to any of these questions, you may be a candidate for Al-Anon or Alateen.

APPENDIX 5

Prison MBA's

1. **"Fresh Start" Outlook-**PEP believes that every inmate is a human being in need of a true second chance (which for many may actually be a legitimate first chance). We will treat every inmate with respect, regardless of background or personal history. We strive to equip human beings to achieve their full potential. We believe that people can change, dignity can be restored, and as a result society will reap bountifully.

2. **Servant-Leader Mentality-**PEP believes that with leadership comes the overriding responsibility to be of service to others. We believe the contributions we make in the lives of others are far more important than our own accomplishments. We will lead by example with humility at the sacrifice of personal glory. PEP exists because of our desire to serve all those with whom we come in contact, especially our participants, executives, partners, donors, prison staff and the community at large.

3. **Love-**We are committed to service in love. PEP staff and leaders will be patient and kind, never envious or boastful or rude. We will not seek our own way nor be easily provoked; rather, we will bear all things and endure all things. We will rejoice in the truth and always seek out the best in others.

4. **Innovation-**We embrace a pioneering spirit and are constantly in the pursuit of innovation and improvement in our efforts to help

others. We expect dramatic change. We are committed to seeing beyond the current perception, and even the current reality, to break stereotypes and shape new futures.

5. **Accountability**-We believe that without accountability, neither our participants nor the executives with whom we work will be changed by the program. We will do everything in our power to help the participants succeed in life, but we provide only opportunities and tools; participants must want to change. Consequently, PEP only commits time and resources to those who demonstrate a desire to help themselves. PEP enforces a "no wiggle room" accountability program with participants. PEP volunteers and employees will likewise be held to a high standard of accountability, being required to take ownership of their initiatives and follow through with their commitments.

6. **Integrity**-We model and require complete honesty and integrity in all our relationships and endeavors. Integrity means more than simply the absence of deception; it means we are completely forthright in all our dealings. We say what needs to be said, not simply what people want to hear. We are truthful with ourselves, listening attentively to feedback from others as they speak into our lives, correct us and reveal to us our blind spots.

7. **Execution**-We place an emphasis on execution—the ability to get things done. We expect to deliver outstanding and timely results. Big thoughts don't matter if they are not turned into action. Self-discipline is a core element of our organization's culture. We sweat the small stuff. We hire people with a strong track record of successful execution.

8. **Fun**-Work is an important part of life and it should be fun and rewarding. We seek to create a work environment that encourages laughter, imagination, fellowship, and creativity. We regularly celebrate positive results and recognize those involved in the success.

9. **Excellence**-We are dedicated to pursuing excellence in every area, despite the difficulties which arise from setting high standards. We seek to work with and learn from the best of the best. We are

dedicated to developing excellence in leadership throughout our organization—leadership of projects, ideas and the promotion of our 10 Driving Values. PEP is committed to working with people and organizations who share our values and mission.

10. **Wise Stewardship-**We are committed to the mentality of a steward: someone entrusted with another's wealth or property and charged with the responsibility of managing it in the owner's best interest. We will apply donors' funds as promised. We are committed to being a lean organization, and as a staff, we are also committed to modest salary and expense levels. We use funds intelligently, efficiently, and strategically to achieve maximum benefit for all whom we serve.

ENDNOTES

[1]Dr. Kitty S. Harris is the associate dean of outreach and engagement in the College of Human Sciences and holds the George C. Miller Regent's Professorship in the Department of Applied and Professional Studies at Texas Tech University. This column appeared in the March 2011 issue of *One Day at a Time* and several other publications. Harris and her program at Texas Tech have also been the subject of articles in the *Wall Street Journal,* including the August 10, 2011, issue.

[2]David Brooks, "Bill Wilson's Gospel," New York Times, June 28, 2010, http://www.nytimes.com/2010/06/29/opinion/29brooks.html.

[3]Claremont.org/publications/crh/id.1793/article_detail.asp.

[4]As provided by SAMHSA and others as indicated.

[5]SAMHSA, *2008 National Survey on Drug Use and Health.*

[6]Partnership for a Drug-Free America and MetLife Foundation, *2008 Parents Attitude Tracking Study*, May 2009.

[7]Partnership for a Drug-Free America, 2009.

[8]Partnership for a Drug-Free America, *Partnership Tracking Attitude Study,* August 2008.

[9]National Center on Addiction and Substance Abuse at Columbia University (CASA), *The Importance of Family Dinners*, September 2009.

[10]Statistics based on information gathered in 2008.

ABOUT THE AUTHOR

David Palmer, Chairman and President,
One Day at a Time

David Palmer, chairman of the board, president, and founder of One Day at a Time in 2004, has been involved in newspaper publishing and public relations and advertising for his entire career.

Before joining the Little Rock, Arkansas, firm of Cranford Johnson Robinson Woods as a senior consultant in 1986, David was business and financial writer for the *Arkansas Gazette* and a correspondent for the *Wall Street Journal*.

Prior to that, David published a chain of weekly newspapers in northern Virginia and later served as publisher of the *News-Times* in El Dorado, Arkansas. He has also owned, published and edited newspapers in Raton, New Mexico; Lamar, Missouri; and Denville, New Jersey.

David's first job was with Young & Rubicam Advertising in New York City. He also worked for Burson Marsteller and for Earl Newsom & Company in New York.

David has been active in recovery circles for more than thirty years. He has been a member of the Wolfe Street Foundation, which provides 12-Step meeting rooms for those in recovery, since 1985 and served as president in 1990 and 1991.

David is a Phi Beta Kappa graduate of Hamilton College in Clinton, New York, and the Harvard Graduate School of Business Administration in Boston. Following graduation, he served three years in the U.S. Navy.

David and his wife, Joan, have three sons and seven grandchildren.